'Funny and poignant, part memoir, part me [...]
of India *charts one woman's tentative mid-life exploration of her*
mixed-race background. Her mother, a young artist and journalist
from Bombay, married a British army officer during the War and
later found herself in the conservative world of 1950s Melbourne.
Further back, there is a shadowy grandmother, an Indian orphan
who married into the then British Raj.

Above all there is India: alluring, electrifying and unfathomable.
Valerie Britton-Wilson has a sharp and nuanced eye for it all.
Starting a business between India and Australia, disassembling the
past and assembling the present, she finds herself more touched by
India than she had ever imagined.'

— **Helen Elliott,** literary critic

'Valerie Britton-Wilson's perceptions of contemporary India, paired
with those of her Anglo-Indian mother before and during the
Second World War, will be an education for newcomers to India
and for old hands. Both women show an understanding of the
social complexities of India and of its cruelty and kindness. Their
comments on the place of Anglo-Indians — both in British India
and now — are fascinating. A chapter on the attraction of India
to Western women broke new ground for me, as it will for others.'

— **John McCarthy AO,**
former Australian High Commissioner to India

'Engaging and beautifully written. At the heart of this wide-ranging
and thoughtful book is the author's search for her mother whose
Anglo-Indian identity is a source of pride and puzzlement.'

— **Brenda Niall,** biographer

i

A TOUCH OF
INDIA

A TOUCH OF
INDIA

Chutney Mary, Charming Irregularities
and an Unlikely Romance

Valerie Britton-Wilson

First published by Bloomings Books Pty Ltd in 2021
Distributed in conjunction with Thames & Hudson, Australia

Bloomings Books Pty Ltd
Melbourne, Australia
Phone +61 (0)438 182 801
warwick@bloomings.com.au

A catalogue record for this work is available from the National Library of Australia

A catalogue record for this book is available from the National Library of Australia

ISBN: 978 0 6450 7058 3 (paperback)

Cover Designer: Luke Harris, Chameleon Press
Editor: Dr Euan Mitchell
Publisher: Warwick Forge
Printed and bound in Australia by PrintStrategyManagement.

Contents

Preface

I saw what looked like a large bundle of clothes fall out of the second-floor of an adjoining flat. Suddenly people were collecting around the 'bundle' on the pavement and there was great commotion. We knew, as an acquaintance, the bachelor who lived in that flat and I realised it was he who was the 'bundle' on the pavement.

This is what nine-year-old Pearl Creed, my mother, witnessed from the balcony of her Bombay apartment in 1930.

This is her story ...

(And a touch of mine.)

1. The Search Begins

Day two in Mumbai and we were sitting in a car with possibly the most unhelpful guide in India. Probably the only unhelpful guide in India. We were in the back seat of an old Ambassador hire car. Our guide was in the front seat, sulking.

I had been here before, almost half a century ago, when this was Bombay and I was only six. Then, my sister and I ran down the gangplank of a P&O liner into the arms of welcoming grandparents. Now I was back and trying to find a house that featured in our family stories.

My mother, Pearl Creed, was proudly one-quarter Indian. She had an aristocratic French great-grandmother and a penniless Indian orphan grandmother. An intriguing combination. And although it was never a secret, the foundling who contributed our touch of Indian blood remained mysterious.

At junior school in whitely-homogeneous 1950s Australia, I used to say proudly: 'I've got English, Irish, Scottish, French, Italian and Indian blood.' My young friends would look suitably impressed, assuming I meant the Indians of the American cowboy-and-Indian shows we watched on TV. It never occurred to them to think of subcontinental India. And, to be honest, I didn't give it much thought either.

In 1999 my friend Sue persuaded me it was time to visit

1

India again. Preparing for the trip, I knew I should delve into a battered tin trunk at the back of a shed at my parents' house. It had travelled with us from England to Australia in 1954, holding precious possessions. Now it was the storehouse of family papers and old photographs. But in the flurry of getting away, it had seemed Pandora's boxish.

The current obsession with ancestry-tracing has largely bypassed me: I get easily lost in the foliage of family trees and find listening to genealogical stuff a bit tedious, even when it's my own. As a social researcher by profession, I was interested in exploring contemporary India but not especially keen to forage in my historical links.

I knew a few of the basics: our earliest link to India was a mid-18th century British MP, Sir James Creed. He became a Director of the East India Company in 1758.[1] Down his line emerged my half-Indian grandfather, Edward StClair Creed. Of Edward's three children, my mother Pearl was the eldest, born in 1921. They were raised in then-Bombay with India still under British rule.

Growing up at the tail end of the Raj, a woman of mixed European-Indian blood, my mother would have been scorned by many Britishers as a 'Chutney Mary'. But this didn't dampen her enthusiasms, nor hamper her talents. She worked as a writer and illustrator for the Times of India and, when the Second World War came, she was employed by the British Censor office in Bombay. At some time during the War, she met my British father, then a Chindit, fighting off the Japanese in the jungles of Burma.

Interesting though this was, I had been far more captivated

---

1 William Dalrymple reveals that it was common for Members of Parliament to be Directors of the EIC. It was mutually beneficial. *The Anarchy: The Relentless Rise of the East India Company* (Bloomsbury, UK, 2019)

by my mother's colourful stories — some spoken, some written — stories that had colonised my mind over the decades. A tale about a visit to the tailor with her own mother had grabbed my imagination as a teenager. My mother recounted:

> I liked to dress in the latest fashions, copied from English Vogue magazines that I pored over in the library opposite where we lived. One day my mother took me to the tailor below our apartment to order a new dress for a dance. My mother insisted that the cut of the neckline should be suitable for a demure young lady in 1930s Bombay. Wishing it could plunge a bit more daringly, I went home, up to my bedroom, and wrote a note to the tailor asking him to make the neckline an inch lower. I tied the note to a string and lowered it from my bedroom window down to his tiny shop below …

I had often pictured this mild bit of teenage rebellion and its particularly Indian form: the paper note dropped down on a string, a Rapunzelled precursor to today's text message. It had seemed an almost fairy-tale image…

Now, here I was in Mumbai, almost 50 years since my last visit. We had decided to spend the first day sight-seeing and recovering from jetlag, the second to finding the building that featured in the story of the descending neckline. We had arrived from Australia at 2 am expecting to be waking a sleepy hotel desk clerk. Instead, the lobby was teeming with people, alive with noisy chatter and bustling activity.

At the reception desk next morning, we approached two elegant, silk-sari draped women resembling colourful caryatids. One, named Dimple, listened to our requests. We wanted a car and driver for some sightseeing today, but the following day we would need a car, driver and English-speaking guide. We told her we'd be looking for a particular building in the Mumbai suburb of Parel.

On day two, we were ushered into a slightly battered hire car and introduced to our guide, Neelam. She was a slim, middle-aged woman, who greeted us politely then immediately began spouting a standard Mumbai tourist spiel. With some difficulty, we interrupted the stream of words to explain our mission. The fetchingly-named Dimple had forgotten to brief her.

So we set out with the guide in the front looking sullen and put-out. Her attitude made me apprehensive. What if we couldn't find the house my mother had lived in? What if it was awful? Why would that matter? I hadn't done enough homework, I should have investigated the papers in that tin trunk.

Our reluctant guide snapped instructions at the driver, a bright-eyed, eager-faced lad who spoke little English. He launched us into the Mumbai traffic madness with Neelam complaining that it would take ages to get there. I had given her a street address and knew the apartment block was called Willingdon House. I thought it was about 13 kilometres away, perhaps 30 minutes or so. But she was right. It wasn't that simple.

The car had poor visibility out of grimy windows. But watching my heritage pass by became even harder after Neelam said she was getting a rash from the air conditioning. She ordered the driver to stop while she moved into the back seat on my side, squashing me into the centre. The broken springs in the seat had been so bulked up with layers of sponge rubber that my head touched the roof. Now I couldn't see anything.

Was she punishing us for not doing the expected tour? In early chit-chat I had proffered my Indian heritage as a possible talking point. In Australia I was accustomed to my drop of Indianness being a matter of curiosity, at least amongst Australians of my generation. But Neelam wasn't interested, and my (perhaps narcissistic) expectation of commonality was rebuffed. Even after two decades of subsequent annual trips to India, this lack of interest still intrigues the social researcher in me. Perhaps it was something else to explore.

The turbulent traffic, and a sulking guide, made finding the house difficult. The street-naming and house-numbering systems often defied logic and we've learnt over the years to ask passers-by, that maps are no help, and that addresses seem to be in flux or in code! But we were innocents on this first trip.

As we floundered around busy roads and unlikely back lanes, Neelam offered no suggestions and made little effort. We got out of the car ourselves to ask directions, often with difficulty, though everyone tried hard to be obliging. I felt that the whole exercise was an imposition on Sue and on our short time in Mumbai. Our guide made it clear it was definitely an imposition on her.

Despite the language barrier, the driver was helpful and plainly embarrassed by the guide's attitude. She lived nearby, so we dropped her off and proceeded with our now very eager driver who tirelessly tried to make amends. His English blossomed after Neelam's departure. He described her as 'very proudy', a charitable description. Sue and I had other adjectives in mind.

After several wrong-turns, he eventually delivered us to a decrepit-looking colonial building. When my mother's family lived there in the 1930s, Willingdon House would have been newish and relatively pristine. But, by the time we arrived, its better days were long gone. We were relieved Neelam wasn't there to look down her nose at it.

2. Another Inauspicious Start

My first visit to India in 1954 didn't get off to a smooth start either. There was an unexpected impediment: our touch of Indian blood. We were living in the quiet and beautiful city of Winchester where my father taught music and Spanish at Winchester College. He was offered a new position in Australia as Director of Music at a prestigious private boys' school in Melbourne. It was an exciting prospect, including the long sea trip to the other side of the world. We would break journey in Bombay so that my mother could see her family again after a nine-year absence. My sister and I, aged three and six, respectively, would meet our grandparents for the first time.

In India and Burma during World War Two, my father had met Australian soldiers who, like him, were helping defend the British Empire from the invading Japanese. My mother had experienced unruly Aussie soldiers on Bombay streets, enjoying leave from various battlefronts. My sister and I knew about koalas and kangaroos, but we'd never met an actual Australian.

Not anticipating any problems, my father took the train to Australia House in London to complete migration application forms. He was English born and raised, and my sister and I were both born in England. In the space for 'wife's place of birth' he wrote 'Bombay'.

The official at the desk looked perturbed and said, 'Does she actually have Indian blood?'

'Yes,' said my father.

A pause. 'How much Indian blood?' he asked.

Dad replied, 'Well, her father is half-Indian, so she would be one-quarter Indian.'

Silence.

He had stumbled into the White Australia Policy. The Immigration Restriction Act of 1901 was the very first Act of Parliament of the newly federated nation of Australia. The freshly hatched country was determined to ignore its darker-skinned original inhabitants and filter out threatening (coloured) mixtures from other places. In fact the White Australia Policy was not officially off the books until the 1970s.

In 1954, some fifty years after the original legislation, my mother's blood spectrum required official investigation to see if she would qualify for a Government-assisted sea passage to Australia. This was the era of the 'Ten-Pound Pom', a scheme designed to build up Australia's population by offering cheap ten-pound fares to like-skinned folk from the United Kingdom.

We were told that someone from Australia House in London was coming to our house in Winchester to meet us. We greeted the official in our super-posh English accents, bred in a twee primary school, where having a tummy-ache involved sitting politely in the headmistress's office sipping milk of magnesia from a crystal sherry glass. We ushered him into the sitting room, my father making small talk while mother served tea. My parents were puzzled about the reason for the visit, but presumed it must be part of normal application procedures.

It was flattering that the Australian government showed such personal interest in prospective new arrivals.

Imagine their surprise and horror when they realised that my mother was being assessed — literally, physically scrutinised — by a very junior official, to make sure she was not too dark-skinned. And my sister and I were being inspected, presumably to ensure we were not throwbacks. By some mysterious process (did our visitor have a skin-colour chart up his sleeve? or clandestine leeches?) it was later determined that my mother was not a mere one-quarter Indian but more than one-third Indian — and hence ineligible. How or why they settled upon this curious one-third remained a mystery.

The upshot was that we two girls passed the duskiness test, but our mother, Pearl, did not. She wondered if a summer holiday in France, some weeks before the inspection, had darkened her skin a bit. If so, it was a costly suntan. My father and his two one-eighth Indian girls — newly diagnosed by Australia House bureaucracy as one-sixth Indian — only the three of us qualified as bargain-basement immigrants. Mother would be allowed into Australia but her fare must be paid in full. This treatment was a distressing start to what was to be a lifetime spent happily in Australia.

3. Life — and Death — Seen From a Bombay Balcony

Marooned with Sue on a Mumbai footpath, amidst a swirling mass of vehicles and people, at last we were close to where my mother had grown up. This maelstrom was what she was used to, and probably missed in Australia. In her old age in Melbourne, Pearl told us she didn't want to be in an old folks' home gazing at trees, no matter how beautiful. She'd prefer to be near a busy intersection. And now I know why.

The building we were looking at was a decrepit three-storey late Victorian apartment block, with balconies around the top two floors. And — yes! — there were small shops below. Was this the site of the tailor and the demure neckline? I was pretty sure it was the right place. But as I looked at Willingdon House, amidst the confusing bedlam of modern India, I struggled for a point of view — my mother's in the delight she had found in her life there, or my own now in modern Mumbai. Was it my mother as a young girl peering over the balcony at life on the streets below? Or was it my mother transported here now to see this forlorn building, with peeling paintwork and pock-marked concrete? Or should it be just me in the present with fresh eyes, unconstrained by how it once was? I wished I could just stand and gaze and think. An impossibility in this busy Mumbai street.

My mother, Pearl, had attended a well-known art school, the JJ School of Art, located in the heart of Bombay. At the age of 20, she had her own regular pages in the Illustrated Weekly of India, a publication of The Times of India, one of the largest circulation papers in the world. This was unusual for a young woman in an era of restricted opportunities. Also it was end-of-Empire India, with the Quit India independence movement stirring, the Second World War approaching, and thus a complex time to be of mixed European-Indian blood.

As we grew up, first in England, mostly in Australia, colourful stories of Pearl's Indian upbringing had emerged. Many years before her death, I had retrieved a foolscap notebook from that tin trunk in which I found the following vivid evocation of life — and death — seen from the balcony of their Willingdon House apartment:

"There is more apparent cheerfulness on any street in India than you will see in the sombre-peopled streets of the Western world. From 1924 when I was three to 1935 when I was fourteen I enjoyed a front-row seat from which to view the whole panorama of street life. I remember with enormous pleasure leaning over the terrace wall and 'just looking'. Opposite, across the main road, were the playing fields of the huge 'railway Colony', home to large numbers of Anglo-Indians employed by the railways. If I leant further over the wall I could watch everything that happened on the pavement beneath and, since all blocks of flats in India had ground floors given over to shops, I could see who went to the *dhurzi's* (tailor's) shop; who went to the *moochi* (shoe-maker); and who went to the *bowree* shop. This was the equivalent of a mini-supermarket today and had an enormous clientele.

I doubt that many children or adults would have witnessed what I once saw from my vantage point on the terrace. My parents had people to dinner, my baby brother was probably asleep but I had been allowed to 'stay up'. I was in my usual position, leaning over the terrace wall, watching the night-sights and enjoying the night-smells (always more exciting than their day equivalents), when I saw what looked like a large bundle of clothes fall out of the second-floor of an adjoining flat. Suddenly people were collecting around the 'bundle' on the pavement and there was great commotion. We knew, as an acquaintance, the bachelor who lived in that flat and I realised it was he who was the 'bundle' on the pavement. I rushed to tell my mother Mr ? had fallen off his balcony. She, in the midst of a good meal with guests, said, 'Ssh — don't interrupt.' I persisted but by that time an ambulance had arrived …

Before I had reached twenty I had seen people killed on the roads, people drown, and I once saw a man fall to his death from a train. Far from hardening me to the inevitability of death, it has made me over-fearful about losing those nearest to me.

My vantage point from the terrace brought me never-ending fascination. Night-viewing was the most exciting. The street lights, and the shadows, cast a sort of glamour over the shabbiness and the poverty of the day. The workers would eat their main meal at night and then stroll out onto the streets, often with their families, and that is when the women would buy the small garlands of marigolds, or frangipani or jasmine that they wore in the coils of their hair. The night-hawkers of food had small flares on their baskets or hand-carts and what they sold seemed infinitely more exciting than by day. There were always the sellers of roasted chenna (dried peas) and choori (crumbled toasted flatbread).

The four most delectable-looking things, which had me drooling from my view on the terrace, were the *puri* sellers; the *kulfi* man; the *ice-gola* maker; and the man who sold pink toffee wrapped around a greased pole. Puris were a puffed-up pastry bread, round in shape, and the puri man would break the puff with his thumb and scoop into it what looked like a mash of potato, onion and coriander in lemon. I never saw this magical process close-up, but the relish with which it was eaten will never match the eating of puris today as I see them in Indian restaurants around the world.

The kulfi man always <u>ran</u> through the streets, the flare on the basket on his head spluttering as he ran. Kulfi is icecream so it was understandable that he should run (no sophisticated freezing containers then!), stopping only when some lucky children were allowed to have a kulfi. Ice-golas were primitive icy poles. Big chunks of ice were shaved and the ice-gola man would mould the crushed ice round a stick and then pour red or yellow syrup over the ball of crushed ice.

But the children's favourite was the pink-toffee man. He carried a long greased pole over his shoulder that had a thick snake of malleable pink toffee wound around it. He would fashion bits of it into whatever shape the children requested! Little girls usually asked for necklaces.

All these delicacies required much handling so it was understandable that I was never allowed to sample them! As vindication for my mother's policing of our health (she was a fanatic about cleanliness), I was lucky to escape dysentery, typhoid, cholera, malaria, jaundice and there can be few people who spent the first 25 years of their life in India who escaped these illnesses. But oh how I longed to taste the gourmet delights of the streets!

Then there was the life in the courtyards. Snake-charmers and monkey-men and singers would perform in the courtyards and we would throw coins down to them from the balconies. Vendors would call out their wares and be invited up to the flats if we needed fruit, or anything else, from a hairpin to silk kimonos. Chinese vendors brought the latter, plus beautifully embroidered table-cloths and underwear.

What I remember most about the flats was that the floors were a mosaic of small pieces, irregularly-shaped, of white china set in concrete. They were obviously broken crockery and I would lie in bed trying to decipher small sections of words on them '-ade in Eng' or 'Staff-'. It was obviously English china and one wonders now from whence all these thousands of pieces came! Were they rejects from factories in England sent out to be further broken, or did young English brides unpack their wedding presents when they arrived in Bombay and, finding them in pieces, throw them out in disgust, only to have wily Indian servants sell them to a local mosaic factory? ... Was there a Hindustani equivalent that also fed the factory? Whatever the source, I remember the deliciously cool feel of the floors under my feet as I got out of bed ..."

Mumbai

The Gateway of India (completed 1924) in foreground, Taj Mahal Hotel (1903) behind on left. In 1973 an additional multi storey wing was added behind the original hotel. Ferry boats ply the coast and take visitors to nearby Elephanta Caves.

Victoria Terminus, Bombay. This dramatic main railway station was completed in 1888. It was designed by a British architect in high Gothic style to commemorate the Golden Jubilee of Queen Victoria, then Empress of India. Re-named The Chhatrapati Shivaji Terminus, in honour of the great 17th century Indian warrior chief who founded the Maratha Empire

David Sassoon Library and Reading Room was completed in 1870, in similar style to other public buildings in this part of Mumbai, and named for a well-known Jewish philanthropist. A statue of Sir David Sassoon stands inside, created by sculptor Thomas Woolner, friend of the then Governor of Bombay, Sir Bartle Frere. Woolner was a pre-eminent sculptor of his day, creating iconic works in several British Empire countries, including statues of James Cook in Sydney and Sir Stamford Raffles in Singapore

Marine Drive, sometimes referred to as the Queen's Necklace, due to its encircling lights at night, runs along the shoreline of the Arabian Sea in central Mumbai. On its built side are many decrepit Art Deco buildings that have fortunately now been protected from demolition

4. Lost in a Family Tree

Sue McFall is an architect and we became friends when our children met in primary school. She was puzzled that I hadn't been to India since I was a child. She envied my slightly exotic heritage, compared with her straightforward Anglo-Celtic background, and kept urging me to join her on a trip. She didn't understand my reluctance, given her fascination with my mother and her stories.

Although Pearl was a good storyteller, I remained fairly detached from what sounded like another world, remote and complex. Which it was. A trip to India had just seemed too daunting. At a writers' festival I heard the noted travel writer, Pico Iyer, comment that despite his own Indian heritage, and extensive authorship of books on other places, India felt somehow too difficult.

On our first family visit in 1954, when I was six, we had stopped off in India en route to taking our tinted (tainted?) blood to the other side of the world in Melbourne, Australia. We visited India again when I was ten, living with our grandparents for six months in the hill-station to which they had retired. But in the intervening 40 years, I had stayed away. Now here I was in Mumbai-not-Bombay in 1999, aged 50-ish, and thinking I might explore some of the evocative images implanted in my head.

The prospect of a trip had made me wonder about my Indian great-grandmother. How did an Englishman, Louis Creed, come to marry an Indian woman? I knew that his father, grandson of the aforementioned Sir James, had married the Vicomtesse Cecilia Aurelia de Bourbel de Montpincon, whose family had fled to England ahead of the coming French Revolution of 1789. They met in England through close family connections.

Bravely — and I don't know what prompted them — Henry Creed and his French wife, Cecilia, with their then-trio of children, moved to India, to a tea plantation in the Nilgiri Hills, a beautiful area in south-west India. There they produced, apart from the tea, seven more children.

According to the family tree (written in French), most of their offspring married into respectable European families. The marital names are carefully positioned on the relevant tree branches. But I knew that one son, my direct ancestor Louis Creed, married a local Indian woman. She is not mentioned at all. What could be the story here? I had heard the word 'disgraced' applied to him, and assumed it was because he lost all his money and had to be bailed out by a sister who lived in France. Now I realise it was more likely the act of marrying 'a native' that invited this disgrace. And his wife was not even from an eminent Indian family. My great-grandfather had married an orphan, picked up from the street by the neighboring tea-planting family.

To have plunged from the top echelons of one social spectrum to the very bottom of another, in one generation, was surely fodder for further investigation?

5. On the Threshold

When I finally stood on the doorstep of Willingdon House, the temperature was in the high thirties and it had been a two-hour search to find it. We were tired and dishevelled. There were scrappy-looking shops at street level. I remembered the story of my teenaged mother in the *dhurzi* shop …

I see her standing in what I had imagined to be a charming little shop.

I picture the tailor, with measuring tape around his neck, defining a demure neckline.

I picture her mother's expression, probably alternating between pride and disapproval, as they negotiate the dress details.

… But now what did I see? One shop had a hoarding saying 'Megamart Factory Outlet', another 'Lee Jeans'. But there was an arched entrance way tucked between, and we tentatively made our way through.

We entered a courtyard, electric cables dangling, and a couple of dilapidated cars parked. Dusty bluestone cobbles with paan stains and puddles of unknown liquids. We had to watch our feet. There were stairs leading up to the residential floors. I knew my mother's family had occupied the whole first floor, two apartments linked by a long corridor. I'd been told there were two balconies, two courtyards, two terraces overlooking the small shops beneath, then out over the main road and across to an oval and the large railway community buildings beyond.

We trudged up gloomy wooden stairs, brown stain worn off, edges thick with dust. On the first-floor landing there was a dark brown door with a doorbell beside, set in grubby plaster. Now that I'd found myself literally on the threshold of my mother's life, I felt oddly paralysed. Sue the Intrepid urged me to press the doorbell. I hesitated. She did it for me and a middle-aged Indian woman opened the door. Sue explained why we were there. The driver translated. The woman looked indifferent but gestured that we could come inside.

Standing awkwardly in a murky entrance area, we were hemmed in by tall, dark furniture. The occupier had kindly allowed complete strangers, with a garbled story, into her home. It felt presumptuous and intrusive. That was my excuse to myself. But I think I couldn't grasp the past nor have a casual look at the present, gaping at it through someone else's life. Perhaps I was scared it would be disappointing, too unlike the mental picture I had? What I had already glimpsed was disheartening. Nothing here was what I had imagined from my mother's stories.

There were too many layers to unpack. I wasn't up to it. I had a quick peep in, thanked the woman profusely and went back down the stairs. I think Sue was disappointed in me. And rightly so. I was disappointed in myself. After all the trouble of finding Willingdon House, I was fleeing.

As if the day hadn't been challenging enough already, our driver with his new-found confidence and liberation from the guide, reached terrifying speeds along the famous Marine Drive en route to our hotel and dinner. Dubbed 'The Queen's

Necklace' in tourist brochures, because of its long curve of night-time streetlights, Marine Drive was home to an astonishing number of Art Deco apartment buildings, mostly occupied, we were told, by fixed-rent sitting tenants who wouldn't leave until death removed them. Consequently, neither penny nor rupee had been spent over the decades since they were built.

As well as some superb public buildings, most in Gothic Revival style, Mumbai has a rich trove of domestic, residential Victorian-era buildings, not surprising given its colonial history, but noteworthy nonetheless. This unique heritage may not last much longer in a city with a booming economy and bursting population. In Mumbai, real estate per square-inch is amongst the most expensive in the world. Developers inevitably cast their eyes upwards, envisaging more and higher tower blocks. Of the old private buildings that remain, most were as decrepit as Willingdon House.[2]

---

2   I was pleased to learn that some Victorian Gothic and Art Deco areas in Mumbai have since been included on a World Heritage List.

6. Blundering Into Bollywood

Our first day in Mumbai had been allocated to visiting major landmarks, getting our bearings, and recovering from jetlag. Several of the main tourist sights had featured in my mother's stories of living and working here from the 1920s up to the end of the War. So, after only a few hours sleep, we had emerged from our air-conditioned hotel to be bludgeoned by a wall of heat. And to the extraordinary disjunction between life in a five-star hotel and life outside.

Almost immediately, probably lying in wait, beggars swooped like aggressive magpies and touched our feet. It was unexpected and shocking. We felt invaded and had to stop ourselves reflexively kicking out. It seemed such a repellent act and desperately servile. No doubt they were well aware of the disconcerting effect this has on hapless tourists.

We later learned that a glancing touch of hand to foot is an act of respect by younger people to their elders, or someone of lesser status to a superior. There is something innocent and charming when a young man quickly genuflects to touch the foot of an elderly relative or respected elder. But even this, through modern Western eyes, looks uncomfortable (literally as well, since we lack the flexibility to accomplish such a deft move).

Geographically, Mumbai is a contrivance, a compilation of seven islands linked by reclaimed swampy land. I am surprised at how tidal it is. Years later, staying in a different hotel, I had a tiny glimpse of water from my hotel window. There were little boats, there were people washing themselves and laundry was being bashed clean on concrete steps. But when I glanced out later in the day, there was no water to be seen.

Buddhist, then Hindu, then Muslim kingdoms and sultanates pre-dated the Portuguese takeover of Bombay in the early 16th century. The British East India Company had meanwhile established a trading base further north up the coast at Surat. But when Charles II of England married the Portuguese Catherine of Braganza in 1661, the entire city of Bombay became part of her dowry: Portugal gave Bombay to the British as part of the marriage settlement!

A few years later, King Charles rented Bombay to the East India Company for 10 pounds a year. About two hundred years later, in 1858, the British Government officially took over Bombay from the East India Company, entrenching India as the jewel in its imperial crown. For two centuries Bombay remained primarily a trading hub, a British governor declaring it would be a centre of racial and religious tolerance. It remains a melting pot, attracting migration from all over the country, and, while the Indian capital now is in New Delhi, Mumbai is still the financial centre of India. And much else besides.

Our first stop was to see The Gateway of India, situated on the waterfront. I knew my father had arrived here by sea from England in 1941. His regiment passed through Bombay en route to Burma, as part of the famous 'Chindit' campaigns,[3] aiming to hold back a Japanese invasion of India. Now aged 96, living in a care home in Melbourne, he said he would like his ashes scattered here, near The Gateway.

Close to The Gateway is the Taj Mahal Hotel, where my parents had their wedding reception, after a tension-filled wartime courtship. More of which later. But, on our first day in India, after the heat and crowd of The Gateway area, we happily sank into the cool contrast of this famous hotel. First opened in 1903, it is said that Jamshetji Tata (of a well-known Parsee family), was prompted to build it because Indians were not permitted to enter the best British hotel of its day, Watson's Hotel, then located nearby.

Whether that story is true or not, it is a nice irony that for decades 'The Taj' has been the hotel of choice for well-heeled British visitors. Also nicely ironic is that the same Tata Company is currently the biggest employer in the British steel industry, owns British Jaguar and Land Rover car companies — and owns what seems the most British of brands: Tetley Tea!

And a diversion to explain that Parsees or Parsis, meaning Persians, are followers of the Zoroastrian religion, one of the world's earliest monotheistic religions. Their emigration to India started in the eighth century, to avoid persecution in Persia/Iran after a Muslim takeover. There is a nice legend about their arrival on the coast of what is now Gujarat. It is said that the local Hindu ruler sent them a cup of milk, brimming over, to show that there was no room in his kingdom for more people. The Persians responded by adding a spoonful of sugar

---

3   See Chapter 15 for more details.

to the cup. The sugar disappeared, sweetening but not spilling the milk. An allegory for assimilation and enrichment. Such subtle diplomacy.

Zoroastrian beliefs can be summed up as good thoughts, good words, good deeds. Educated, literate, tall and fairer skinned, they are still supposed to marry within their own community. However, with declining numbers overall, many remain childless, including the current elderly patriarch of the Tata company, Ratan Tata. They are highly influential and successful in many fields: industrial, commercial, military and philanthropic. But now only about 25,000 remain in India.

Back at the Tata family's Taj Hotel, we made our way up a richly carpeted, curving stairway to the Sea Lounge on the first floor, overlooking the Arabian Sea. My mother told us tales of social life at the Taj during the War. There was much drinking of cocktails, gin-and-tonics, plenty of the best Scotch whisky. They attended chamber orchestra concerts, with Zubin Mehta's father, Mehli, conducting. There were regular tea dances and she recalled being on the dance floor when a stiff-backed English Colonel waltzed sedately past and she caught this snippet of clipped-upper-class conversation: 'You just take two eggs ...' Rivettingly romantic small talk!

Replenished by a cool *nimbu pani*,[4] Sue and I set off to see more sights, starting with the extraordinary Victoria Terminus. Now officially re-named Chhatrapati Shivaji Terminus, after a great Hindu warrior rather than a past Queen of England, it is an extraordinary cathedral-like railway station. Of Indo-Saracenic Gothic design, it's described in our guidebook as 'a

---

4   Freshly squeezed lime juice, with chilled water, lots of ice, served with a tiny jug of sugar syrup to sweeten to one's taste. Or salt added, as Indians often prefer.

highly embellished riot of buttresses, pinnacles, domes, towers and spires'. My mother's workplace, The Times of India, is situated nearby. It was a long bus ride from the family home to the office, so she would book a room at Victoria Terminus to shower and change before going out in the evenings.

At nearby Crawford Market we saw eunuchs, or *hijra*, slightly menacing men/women in garish dress and makeup. They roam in packs, demanding money — often from wedding parties — casting threats of inauspicious happenings if they are not paid off. But we also spied a pair of sallow-skinned elderly women in tweed skirts and thin jumpers. They were Anglo-Indian. Their clothing looked literally moth-eaten, holes held together roughly with safety pins. Could they not afford repairs? Would this be my mother had she stayed? It was a glancing encounter and we moved on.

Next stop was The Prince of Wales Museum, renamed The Chhatrapati Shivaji Maharaj Vastu Sangrahalaya (abbrev CSMVS, thank goodness!) Hot, stuffy and rather gloomy, it was hard to appreciate the wonderful collection of Indian miniatures as intermittent power failures turned off lights and fans. (It has since been renovated and much improved.) We ducked into the coolth of the nearby David Sassoon Library where the attendant was fast asleep in a huge planter's chair. Walking straight past, we could have helped ourselves to anything on the dusty shelves. Some years later, on another visit, the same attendant was fast asleep in the same chair.

We had time for one more place that day. On a list of places to visit in the Colaba area was the colonial church of St John the Evangelist, built in 1847, dedicated to soldiers who died in both the Sindh campaign and the First Afghan War of 1839-42.

When my children were younger, we visited Westminster Abbey where one of my Creed ancestors is commemorated, killed in action in India, and connected with the Afghan Wars.

At home I have a publication called The Gordon Creeds in Afghanistan, containing the field notes of Henry Creed who fought in the First Afghan War in 1838-9, and of his son Richard who fought in the Second Afghan War forty years later. It is an account of their experiences, father and son, both defending the Empire's interests. The notes are illustrated with Richard's charming ink and watercolour drawings, and carefully describe local customs, food, landscape and horticulture.

Afghanistan was the unfortunate 'playground' for what was known as 'The Great Game', the tussle for territory, power and influence between Britain and Russia that went on for over a century. The British always feared that an expansionary Russia would push its way from Afghanistan into India, the most prized, and lucrative, part of their Empire. There was nothing playful about this so-called game: the 1839 War was a disaster for the British, who were routed, with massive casualties. In the final British retreat of 16,000 people — soldiers and support staff — only one man made it out to tell the tale.

Forty years later, the 1878 War was shorter and less disastrous. It was triggered when the Afghan ruler welcomed a Russian envoy while rebuffing a British envoy. The British responded by invading with 50,000, mostly Indian, troops. After a couple of years, they managed to install an amenable ruler and peace returned for a time. But there was a Third Afghan War in 1919 and, as we all know, fierce rivalries and never-ending tragedy continue to blight the poor Afghani people to this day.

Clearly my two soldier ancestors survived to tell their stories.

When I first saw their memoir in my youth, Afghanistan seemed an almost imaginary place on the remote periphery of consciousness. Now, sadly, it's a regular part of our daily news. In these globally-connected, well-travelled days it's hard to imagine just how exotic were places like India and Afghanistan. The following excerpt illustrates the extraordinary scenes this young Englishman, Richard Creed, witnessed. I love his description of 'gaudy' Persian carpets and the 'promiscuity' of eating with one's fingers:

Pesh Bolak is considered [to be] a place of great sanctity, and is visited in February by numerous pilgrims ... I was hospitably entertained inside the fortified enclosure by the Chief of Pesh Bolak, and after the usual meal of kedgeree, which was eaten by dipping the fingers in a promiscuous way into the dish, and drinking strong tea without milk, and very much sweetened with sugar, I had the pleasure of seeing the Chief say good morning to various members of his Family.

He conducted us into a large room with only one large decorated chair in it, which was placed at the furthest end. The floor was covered with gaudy Persian Carpets. The Chief at once sat down on the chair and clapped his hands, on which his eldest son, who was a tall young man, dressed in white with a green puggerie, entered at the far end of the apartment, advanced to his Father, made a humble salaam, and knelt before him. The Chief then placed both his hands on the top of his son's puggerie, and the latter made another salaam, this one being made when [still] on his knees. [He then] rose and left the room. Three other sons entered in turn, performed the same ceremony, and retired. The Chief would not see them again until the following day, unless he required them.

We set out for the church, expecting a slightly depressing experience of colonial abandonment and neglect. Arriving at the outer wall that rings the church, we were confronted by rows of trousered bottoms sitting atop the edges of the wall. Their owners, mostly boys and young men, were peering into the church grounds. There was buzzing excitement in the air.

At the gate we were sternly turned away by an implacable security guard: 'Sorry, no entry.'

'But we have come all the way from Australia to see this church.' Not persuasive enough. 'But my ancestors are buried here.' Even this exaggeration (untruth) didn't sway him. What could be happening to close a mostly unused church to the public?

The answer was Bollywood. The church had been taken over as a film location. The caravanserai filled the grounds with trucks, cables, lights. We hailed someone who was walking in past the guard. 'We're from Australia visiting this church, we only have today, could we please come in?' He asked us to wait. After a consultation inside, he beckoned us in, overruling the security guard — who flashed murderous looks.

The church pews were packed with glamorous young men and women wearing fashionable tee-shirts and jeans, laughing and chatting noisily. We had no idea what the film was, and certainly no chance of imbibing the vibes of my ancestors — though I felt I'd slightly misused them by claiming they were buried there. While standing discreetly at the rear doors, a loudhailer complained we were 'in screen' and must move. We had gate-crashed a Bollywood movie on our first day. People in other parts of India like to tell us that Mumbai is a 'very racy' city. We had a very racy start.

7: A Watchful Woman: Finding Her Place

Starting from her Bombay balcony, my mother remained an inveterate people-watcher all her life. My sister and I used to nudge her in the ribs on bus trips because we thought she stared too obviously. But a fascination with the small details of everyday life was evident in all her creative work. Her Australian oil paintings showed fractious children being pulled reluctantly from the beach at the end of a hot summer day; or shoppers hovering over vegetables in the local greengrocery store; or schoolchildren chatting animatedly on bus stops.

As a newspaper columnist in India, or later interviewing new migrants for the Australian Government, her perceptive insights into the daily detail of people's lives continued. She wrote poems for friends at key life moments. In the 1950s and 60s she was commissioned to write radio advertisements, the dialogues always realistic, witty and finely-tuned. She even scripted a few episodes of a long-running Australian TV favourite, *Prisoner*.

Perhaps a people-watcher who is essentially sympathetic and interested, not judgmental, is different from a watcher whose stance is critical. Now we are older, my sister and I both think there's a difference between being observant and blatant staring. But our children, in turn, find us embarrassing. I also hope it's evident that, like my mother, despite criticisms and lamentations about the India I encounter over two decades, my love for the place shines through.

A salient point about Pearl is that she was Anglo-Indian, of mixed blood in British India, not fully accepted by either Indians or British. The derogatory term for women like her was 'Chutney Mary'. She had to find a place, and careful observation is part of an outsider's armoury. This is true for mixed blood people everywhere. And it's often the small things that count when trying to fit in: the nuances of behaviour, mannerisms, pronunciation, intonation and so on. I think a painterly and watchful eye would have helped Pearl fit in anywhere. But imagine trying to locate oneself in the intersection of an Indian caste system and a British class system? It can't have been easy. It helped that she was fair-ish skinned and attractive: tall, slim, with brown eyes, dark, wavy hair and a generous warm smile.

Back in Melbourne, I decided to delve properly into that tin trunk. When we were young, my sister and I used to sit on it and imagine exotic contents. Or balance carefully along the heavy timber palings in which it was encased. I asked my parents where it was. What a let-down: it's gone to the tip. The repository of Creed family history is now a more manageable, but very unappealing, blue vinyl suitcase with rusty-looking zips and broken flap buckles. Not at all romantic.

The documents inside the suitcase confirm the aforementioned Sir James Creed of Blackheath, Member for Canterbury in the British Parliament, Fellow of the Royal Society, a Director of The East India Company in the middle of the 18th century. One of his twin grandsons, Richard Creed, who is commemorated in Westminster Abbey, was killed in action in India. Richard's twin brother, Henry, and Henry's son Richard were the father and son whose Afghan Wars field notes are sitting in my bookshelves.

These are interesting but fairly conventional British Indian antecedents. The East India Company (EIC) was a trading behemoth. Founded in about 1600, at one stage it was said to be involved in half the world's trade, including cotton, silk, salt, indigo, opium and tea. It was the world's first joint-stock company and wealthy merchants and aristocrats owned the shares. Directors were often also Members of Parliament, just like Sir James, a helpful nexus for the EIC, its interests well represented, and protected, at the highest levels of government and society.

Although it started ostensibly as a trading entity, it was a story of plunder and competing national interests from the outset: on the maiden EIC voyage their ship captured a Portuguese vessel. So the EIC immediately butted up against other nations' trading ambitions in India, including Dutch and Portuguese traders, but it was especially the French against whom major territorial battles ensued. Importantly, The Company, as it was known, also grabbed influence and territory from a declining Mughal Empire. It developed an enormous army, over a quarter of a million men, far larger than the British Army. It issued its own currency. Over its 250-year history on the subcontinent, the EIC effectively ruled, directly or indirectly, almost all of India. But, in 1858, the British Crown took over and the British Raj was born.

In the suitcase I discovered a photo of a headstone in a cemetery in Bangalore, in south central India. The headstone reads:

To the memory of Louis James StClair Creed, son of the late

Lt Col Henry Creed, Bombay Horse Artillery (East India Co) and of Cecilia Aurelia Creed, eldest daughter of the Marquis de Bourbel de Montpincon. Born at St Albans Herts England. Died March 1917 in Bangalore in his 64th year.

Intriguing. In a cardboard postal tube I found the family tree, translated from French, showing that this son, Louis, was the third of ten children born to Henry and Cecilia Creed. Again I see that each of his siblings married well, the girls especially, and mostly to foreigners — a titled Belgian, a well-to-do French man, and one to a Greek man. But Louis? Again I find no details of a wife, neither in the records and photographs from this Bangalore cemetery, nor in the family tree. Yet I knew he had a wife and four children.

This is what I had heard about our corner of the family history: my mother, Pearl Creed, born in Bombay in 1921, was the first of three children of a part-Italian/British mother called Hope Grainger, and a half-Indian/British father, Edward StClair Creed. This Edward was the eldest of the four children of Louis Creed who is commemorated on the headstone in Bangalore. And it is Louis who had an Indian wife, Edward's mother. This blood-mix made the offspring and their descendants officially Anglo-Indian, part of a then-recognised sub-set of Indian society. But ... a big but ... never fully accepted into the British (far less the Indian) social systems.

At various times during British rule in India, inter-racial marriages had been encouraged. Indeed, in the 18th century, almost one in three British men took Indian wives or mistresses. This was thought to contribute to stability and order in society. Men satisfied their sexual and dynastic needs by marrying, settling down, fathering children. The most flamboyant example was Sir David Ochterlony, British Resident (Governor) in Delhi in the early 19th century, who lived and dressed Mughal style and had thirteen wives who he took every evening on a promenade around the Red Fort, each on her own elephant.

More generally — and less dramatically — colonial administrators in the 18th and early 19th centuries thought intermarriage with Indian women would bring into existence a cohort of people who could be a mainstay of the British administration. The mixed race offspring of these unions would form a capable, loyal, willing workforce able to act as a buffer between the British and the vast native population.

And this is exactly what happened. Most Anglo-Indians worked in administration, many for the railways. They lived in their own residential communities, often clustered around the rail nodules of the major Indian cities. These residential areas had libraries, community halls and clubs, providing lively and self-sufficient social lives as part of yet another group in Indian caste-based life. They identified with the British, rather than with the Indians: they spoke English, attended Christian schools and churches, dressed like the British, and developed a distinctive fusion cuisine.

My mother's family was a bit different because her father, Edward Creed, didn't work for the railways, nor for the British, but was an electrical engineer with the Tata Company. When the Creed family was living in Willingdon House, my grandfather was supervising the electrification of Bombay, his headquarters then at Dharavi, amidst greenery and space. In fact, it was Lord Willingdon, then-Viceroy of India, who officially opened this new electricity station. These days Dharavi is probably India's best known and largest slum area.

After some primary schooling at The Cathedral School in Mumbai (then-Bombay), my mother was sent to boarding school in the hills, thought to be better for the health than living in a big city. It was St Mary's Girls School Poona (now Pune), run by the British Wantage Sisters, high Church of England with nuns in wimples imposing strict, but mostly not cruel, discipline. The other students were a mix of white offspring of the colonial masters, well-to-do Anglo-Indians and a sprinkling of Indian girls. Though stricken with homesickness early on, Pearl seemed to fit in without too much difficulty, and eventually became head girl.

At St Mary's, the students took exams that were set and marked in Cambridge. Their results came by sea and took three months to arrive. Their British curriculum was replete with robin redbreasts, daffodils and hedgerows. Pearl learnt French and Latin. She did well, especially at art and literature. Having won art prizes, when she finished school she decided to enrol at the Sir JJ School of Art in Bombay, a quite daring and unusual choice for a young woman at the time.

Sir Jamshedey Jeejeebhoy — what an exotic name — was another wealthy Parsee businessman and philanthropist. The School trained many of India's best-known graphic artists, painters, designers, ceramicists. It is still a vibrant institution, located opposite Crawford Market in central Mumbai. It comprises several large Victorian buildings set in lush gardens. It had been home to Rudyard Kipling, whose father was one of the school's first Principals.

On our first day in Mumbai, Sue and I had walked around the Sir JJ School of Art, explored its mix of buildings, admired its handsome trees and observed its young men and women looking like art students anywhere — though less wildly alternative in dress than in other countries.

I imagined mother here, perhaps shy, perhaps unused to a co-educational environment. In fact it opened her eyes to a whole new world.

8: A Very Bohemian Adventure

Pearl had entered a vastly different environment from the circumscribed discipline of a high-church girls' boarding school. Now amongst mainly Indian students, one of very few females and the only Anglo-Indian, she chose to study Commercial Art thinking it would be a way into the dashing new world of advertising illustration. But she was disappointed to find a focus on lettering and letterheads, subjects she found mechanistic and boring.

So, in the long vacation between terms, she set out to find work as an unpaid apprentice in one of the advertising agencies that had just sprung up in Bombay in the late 1930s. This led her into what she describes as a 'very bohemian adventure':

My parents, probably aware that I was disappointed with my chosen course, supported me to the extent that my dear father acted as chauffeur and drove me from one advertising agency to another. I had my portfolio of drawings and cartoons (I rather fancied myself as a cartoonist!), a pathetically childish collection to present at my first choice, the most prominent agency at the time, J. Walter Thompson. My father waited downstairs in the car while I waited nervously to meet the Head of the Art

Department. I was finally shown in to the office of a smartly-dressed but coldly handsome English woman. Very few words were spoken: she held out her hand for my portfolio, staring at my face while she turned the pages, never once glancing down at them, and handed the portfolio back to me saying, 'We don't take on apprentices.' I was prepared for rebuffs, but I have never forgotten the turning of the pages without looking at them ...

Cheered on by my father, we drove on to the next agency on our list. Small and privately-owned, it was called 'Protos'. This was less impressive. It occupied about four rooms of a new, but rather shabby (everything becomes quickly shabby in India) office-block in the city centre. Any confidence I might have felt had already been crushed by the aptly-named Mrs Wood of J. Walter Thompson! I was only just 18.

Imagine my joy to be received by the courteous and smiling, if rather sinister-looking, boss and told I could start at once. Protos obviously had nothing to lose: I was only asking for an unpaid job and since I was probably the only young, local girl asking for such work in the whole of Bombay, he might have been rather intrigued to employ me. [My mother modestly doesn't mention that she was also quite pretty!] He was a Frenchman, Jean Theop, and his assistant, Louis Dunne, was French-Irish. There was a rather pompous man whose name escapes me who made up the trio of 'management'.

I couldn't wait to rush down to tell my waiting father that I had a holiday job and that I had discovered that Mr Theop lived not far from us in our quiet beach suburb of Mahim. (We had moved from Parel then.) My father's pleasure I could see was tempered by worry. After a little more questioning it was established that Mr Theop lived in THAT house down the beach from ours. People talked about it being 'strange': bells hanging from the verandah and PARTIES! Looking back from now I realise that it was probably a comfortable ménage-a-trois — homosexual — and that the house was 'artistic' rather than decadent. That is my guess. I was certainly never asked to it, nor to any of the parties. Once when I was ill, my father visited it to tell Mr Theop I would not be at work the next day. Curiosity, or the wish to let Theop know that I had a protective family? Probably a bit of both ...

The Art Department of Protos consisted of four artists, three of whom had Irish names — O'Neill, Flanagan and Callaghan. All four were Anglo-Indian, probably more Anglo than Indian. I never asked nor discovered how they came to be in the comparatively new field of advertising in India. Most Anglo-Indians, apart from those who became teachers, went into government jobs: the Customs, the Telegraph, the Police, the Railways...

All four were kind and welcoming to me, which must have been a strain, since it would have put constraints on their conversation to have a young girl in their midst. They ranged in age from about twenty-eight to thirty-five. As an eighteen-year-old they all seemed old to me! Harry Flanagan who had a reputation as a rake in the Anglo-Indian community (in spite of having a very beautiful wife) — another worry for my parents — wore the most beautiful and impeccable shirts in dark colours. I had never before seen shirt-sleeves that converted from long to short. He would arrive in a long-sleeved shirt, sit at his desk, ceremoniously unbutton the press studs which kept the halves together, and presto! He had a practical short-sleeved shirt to work in. He was the least friendly to me of the four.

Flanagan and Ralph O'Neill were the senior artists, and O'Neill was brilliant at his work. I have never seen anyone with such facility with pencil, pen, brush and camera. He was a natural artist, probably untrained and certainly un-sung. He had a devil-may-care, happy-go-lucky attitude that matched his Irish name. He was ugly — a large mouth filled with large teeth (one of which flashed gold!), a Ronald Coleman moustache, and a rather pitted skin. But he entered the office with a high-shouldered brisk walk, breathing goodwill, and made a sort of clicking sound out of the corner of his mouth by way of greeting each of us. If I could, I would have 'clicked' back, but I was still too unsure!

On the Saturday (we worked a half day on a Saturday) of my first week, he said, 'Everyone come home to lunch with me.' Only Flanagan couldn't and I rang my parents to tell them where I was going. So the two bachelors and I accompanied Ralph back to his flat in Colaba (which is a nice inner suburb bordering on the Taj Mahal Hotel), where the other two had obviously been before. I didn't know then that the O'Neills kept a sort of open house. There was very little money, but that didn't matter. They loved people around them and were completely unaffected about anything lacking in their lifestyle that would have deterred others, more pretentious, from entertaining. Mrs O'Neill (I am sad that I cannot remember her name) was tall and plump and had a beautiful calm face and a smooth pale-golden skin. Nothing ruffled her. They were a perfect match, and he was lucky to have a wife who happily endured a precarious lifestyle.

In India one could judge the financial state of a household not just by the number of servants, but the way the servants

38

were dressed. A 'good' mistress saw to it that her servants had sufficient clothes to always look clean, and the table servant usually wore a long white jacket when serving at the table — certainly at dinner. When we sat down to lunch at the O'Neill's, I noticed that their table servant looked scruffy and as though he did all the jobs of the household. He was probably the only servant. As the female guest, the large tureen was brought first to me. In the bottom of it was enough stew for a modest serve each for two people. There were five of us, remember, and I had to do some quick thinking to take one-fifth of what was there, which amounted to half a potato and a little gravy! I spread this as widely as I could across my plate. But I needn't have worried. The O'Neills seemed completely unaware that there was a scarcity of food (or perhaps they were more used to starving than I who had a very healthy appetite!) and lunch proceeded with lots of laughter and happy talk. They set an example in not embarrassing one's guests by apologising for something that cannot be helped. I have tried to remember that.

Their rented flat had three large rooms and very little furniture. I imagine they were people who had had to move often — probably because of unpaid rent! There were two children who I cannot recall meeting. Lunch over, I was amazed to hear Ralph say cheerfully, 'Time for a nap, everyone get on the bed!' Certainly the afternoon siesta is a feature of life in the East, but I hadn't quite expected that end to lunch! I must explain here that the rather imperative and lascivious-sounding phrase 'get on the bed' seems to be used only in the East (though I have once heard South Africans use it) because that is what one literally did for an afternoon rest; lie on top of the bed clothes not get 'into' the bed clothes. My mother (ever concerned about my father's well-being) would say after he had had his lunch, 'Ted, go and get-on-the-bed for half an hour before you go back to the Office.' My father would loosen his tie as his only concession to getting undressed, and get-on-the-bed.

Having declared we must all 'get on the bed', we were shown into the bedroom, which at first appeared to have one very large iron bedstead but in fact was three iron beds pushed together to make one large bed. Completely naturally (except for me!) everyone climbed on top of this large bed — Ralph and his wife side-by-side and me between the two bachelors! As a small child I had got-on-the-bed with my parents, and with visiting cousins for an afternoon nap, but, since then, the boarding school to which I went had raised strange doubts about bed-sharing. At St Mary's girls slept in 'cubicles' and going into another girl's cubicle would have brought on the wrath of the Matron, plus a black mark, so what getting-on-the-bed with another girl would have earned in punishment one hates to think! There were always dark rumours ...

So here was I, only eighteen months out of St Mary's, lying on a bed with three-quarters of the male Art Department of Protos, plus one wife (all fully clothed!). I was so aware of how it would look to my parents, if they could see me, that I can remember exactly what I was wearing. A yellow cotton dress with a vee-neck and cap sleeves, a flared skirt and a rather dashing multi-coloured striped cummerbund! I hope I had at least taken off my shoes. Everyone seemed to doze off quite easily, except me!

Delhi

Mughal Emperor Humayun's tomb in Delhi, commissioned by his wife in 1558, a grand garden mausoleum, often regarded as a precursor to the Taj Mahal in Agra

Busy streets in Old Delhi

The Lodi Gardens in New Delhi comprise about 90 acres of lushly treed parkland as well as several Mughal tombs. Pathways are dotted with earnest joggers and leisurely amblers while shady corners enable amorous trysts

An elegant and expansive corridor in The Imperial Hotel, New Delhi. The scent of massed tuber-roses in huge vases pervades the air in the grand reception area

9: My Re-incarnation as
a Business Person in Delhi

*The British 'wanted to rule as princes! So in the rule of King-
Emperor George V they added another to the seven successive capital
cities which had, at one time or another, waxed and waned upon
the bitter plains of Delhi, beside the Jumna River.*[5]

The trip to India with Sue left me completely hooked on this
vast fascinating country. Friends speculated that this was due
to my dash of Indian blood. Maybe there was some deep-seated
connection within my DNA. But Sue felt the same, and she is pure
Anglo-Celtic Australian. We discovered we were each separately
ruminating on how to justify regular trips. We needed a reason, a
purpose, and began to discuss what pretext we could find. Could
I belatedly invoke some of my mother's adventurous spirit?

Like most female tourists, we had bought items of clothing
made from Indian cotton, much of it handwoven. The garments
felt good to wear because the fabric itself was so nice. But when
we got back, we realised they didn't look right in our brighter

---

5   Jan Morris, *Stones of Empire*, OUP 1983, Penguin edition 1994, pp. 179-83.

Australian light, nor on our paler skin, nor on our differing Western body shapes. The colours and cuts didn't suit us and they were not always made well. We wore them in summer around the house, feeling like ageing hippies.

We wondered if we could access handwoven fabric and then design clothing in styles that did suit us. Surely, if we liked the feel of it others would too? At that time it was quite hard to find pure cotton clothing and even pure cotton by the metre was rarely available in the small number of fabric shops that still exist in Western cities. We also knew it was hard to find clothing for our age group that is interesting without being over-designed. There was very little in either local or imported brands that appealed to us. We assumed other women might feel the same way.

So, in a nutshell, could we design clothes for our age group, to our design taste, and fabricated from Indian handwoven cottons? As an architect, Sue was used to the design/production process. As a social researcher, mine was not an obvious career link. But I had often made my own clothes and enjoyed devising interesting touches. Could we create a business that would justify more trips to India? At ages 52 and 56, approximately, we took the plunge. We each put in some money and sought advice from experienced India hands in Melbourne. We registered a business name, made flight and hotel bookings. We were eager and excited.

Our first business trip to India had to be in May, which was hot and humid. But we wanted our first 'collection' to be ready for sale by the upcoming Australian summer. Our travel agent, an Indian from Bangalore, was immensely helpful, introducing us to his family who would later take us on searches for silk-cotton fabrics in his home city.

By chance most of our contacts were in Delhi, not Mumbai,

so we moved away from my mother's city and began an interesting relationship with India's capital.

Delhi took over from Calcutta as India's capital city in 1911. As Jan Morris describes: the British 'wanted somewhere elevated, central and allegorical, somewhere in the line of Indian history, where they could be seen as true successors to earlier dynasts.'

Historically-recorded dynasties in the Delhi area date back to the 10th century and crumbling remnants are still dotted around Delhi today. But myths and legends allude to even earlier dynastic incarnations, each one overtaken by another, each somehow doomed to fail and be replaced. Nehru described Delhi as 'the grave of Empires and the nursery of a republic'.

The last great Mughal Emperor had inhabited the 17th century Red Fort in what is now called Old Delhi. In the early 1900s, the British began to construct their new capital on Raisina Hill. This New Delhi consisted of a suite of grandiose buildings, designed by Edwin Lutyens and Herbert Baker, set in long, broad ceremonial roadways — Kingsway and Queensway (now Rajpath and Janpath). At its peak was a palace suitable for the Viceroy, plus enormous Secretariat and Legislature buildings. The buildings loom in their vast pinkish stone blocks, neo-classical in form but with Mughal, Buddhist and Hindu touches.

The new capital city plan included a grand archway, a shopping area (Connaught Place), miles of surrounding roadways, parklands, vast numbers of trees, lesser palaces for lesser beings such as the Commander-in-Chief, and the Governors or Chiefs of States. Then there were multiple mansions and villas (bungalows), suitably graded in size, according to one's importance in the hierarchy of British rule. As described by Jan Morris, the ladder of official precedence had 61 rungs

— demonstrating just how synchronous were the Hindu caste system and the British class system.

Arriving in still lavishly-treed New Delhi (a city dismissed by Mumbaikers as rather hick), our plan was to contact the well-known Fabindia company where several of our initial clothing purchases had been made. Fabindia was founded in 1960 by an American, John Bissell, to produce and sell handcrafted garments and homewares. His aim was to support the myriad small artisans in villages all over India. Later, under son William, the range extended to jewellery, organic food products and skin care. Fabindia now has over 200 stores in India and overseas, and supports more than 90,000 artisans. Along with Anokhi, it is probably one of the stores most visited by overseas tourists. And, because it sells classic saris and *salwar kameez* (long *kurta* and pants outfits) for women, plus traditional *kurtas* and waistcoats for men, all in handwoven fabrics, it is said to clothe Indian politicians and intellectuals.

We arranged to meet the manager of their main retail store in Delhi, who kindly facilitated our path to the wonderland of handloom fabric in the Fabindia 'go-down' or warehouse. We were free to fossick and buy. What a treat! The warehouse was walled floor to ceiling — and I mean floor to ceiling, literally — with vividly-coloured folded bolts of fabric strewn across the floor and in piles up the walls to ceiling height. All this was ours for the choosing.

But once the initial thrill was over, we realised that the preponderance of oranges, yellows, turquoise, greens and pinks would not suit our needs. This was the problem with the clothes we had bought on our initial trip: colours that didn't suit us, or prints that were too youthful, or too 'ethnic-looking'.

Clothes we couldn't wear. Like many Melburnians we wear mostly black. However, this treasure was impossible to resist. We chose several bright 'shot' colours (one colour in the warp threads, another in the weft) and, from then on, black cotton jackets with colourful linings were to become our stock-in-trade, a staple of all future collections.

We contacted an agency, sensibly thinking that we would need help at first. FC Wacziarg was a buying agency for large fashion retailers around the globe. Somehow we got an entrée and one of their staff helped us put together part of our first range. They also introduced us to a young designer who agreed to do a small quantity of meticulously hand-detailed Indian-style garments for us. This was Puja Nayyar.

In the ensuing years, Puja became very well known in Indian fashion and has remained a young friend to us. We went together on an adventure into Old Delhi, precariously balanced in single-file bicycle rickshaws, searching for interesting braids. Sadly, many beautiful rolls of old braids, intricately hand-made using fine silk and metal threads, are now burned at high temperature to extract the gold or silver from the threads. We understand the economic need, but it is such a travesty. We bought a few rolls, not knowing whether we would use them, but feeling we had saved them from a fiery euthanased demise.

At the time we were launching into this new, for us, rag trade world, a Frenchman, Francis Wacziarg, had embarked with Indian partner, Aman Nath, on a brilliant new venture. They were converting forts, palaces and other interesting heritage buildings, into charming, authentic-feeling hotels, rescuing crumbling edifices and using local crafts to decorate them. We booked in for two nights at their first such venture — the

Neemrana Fort — only partially renovated at the time and located about two hours by road from Delhi.

Staying in this 15th century fort, built over 10 levels on a horseshoe-shaped plateau, was an utterly memorable experience. At the time, the prices were low and we decided we could afford a room each — a welcome respite from sharing hotel rooms. Sue was shown first to a large room with a four-poster double bed, an expansive sitting area and a balcony overlooking the valley below. Wonderful. Then I was ushered up, and up, and up, via increasingly disintegrated steps, until finally reaching an eyrie perched right at the top of the fort, having skirted workmen all the way up.

The room itself was smallish but with a spectacular view. When night fell it was pitch dark. No lights to guide me up these perilous, uneven steps, low walls over which to stumble to one's death thousands of feet below. Fabulous but terrifying. Plus vulnerable to the curious eyes of those pretending not to watch as a middle-aged woman on her own made her tentative way past the rubble of desultory renovation work.

At dinner, on a candle-lit lower balcony, under a dark starry sky, we enjoyed delicious food. There were only a few other guests in this enormous fort, so we had the undivided attention of the staff. But we asked if we could please share a room! Inadvertently, we discovered that this was a very good ploy for being shown all the rooms that had been renovated. We gasped appreciatively at every turn, then settled on a vast room: two giant beds, marble floors, large bathroom cleverly integrated so as not to add a jarring Western hotel-bathroom look, a delightful sitting area, cushions covered in simple hand-block prints, unpretentious, allowing the setting to be itself without overdoing the gloss. And our own *jharokha,* a carved marble balcony jutting from the outside wall, hundreds of metres up.

In the morning, a knock on the door introduced us to the notion of 'bed tea' — tea or coffee brought to your room (and here it came in silver pots on silver tray) before rising for breakfast proper. Silver service on our marble balcony in a 500-year-old fort perched high on a hilltop! It was like living in an Indian miniature painting, overlooking spidery kikar trees that splay horizontally, nothing but birds and forest noises in the stirrings of morning.

Sadly, from our point of view, Neemrana Fort Hotel has been a victim of its own success: expanded into conference facilities, rooms ranging from pokey and dark to vast majestic suites (and everything in between), all carefully graded and priced accordingly. It has become a popular venue for large noisy weddings and Delhi weekend getaways. It's still a very good place to stay, but nothing like the wonder we experienced on that first visit.

Somehow, through all of this, the MOTI Clothing Company, Melbourne, Australia was born. *Moti* is the Hindi word for Pearl, my mother's name. A tribute to her, to the origin of my connection to India. And a nice short graphic for labels. Only later did we discover that, pronounced slightly differently, moti also means fat lady — causing some merriment to our husbands and to Indians we met over the following decades, especially when ordering size XXXL for some of our more generously-sized customers.

10: Being a Chutney Mary

William Dalrymple pointed out in *City of Djinns*,[6] that the British have really disappeared as a people as far as Indians are concerned, even though, when he wrote it in 1993, it was only 50-odd years since they officially left India. Monuments remain. Language remains. And, as is constantly pointed out, there is a legacy of parliamentary democracy, the legal system, railways and cricket. Oh, and bureaucracy, to which Indians have taken with extraordinary enthusiasm! But in general, Indians seem uninterested in the British. Dismissive actually. Any reference to British rule is almost entirely negative.

And, of course, there are very good reasons for Indians to dislike the British intensely. Imperial colonial powers are almost always predatory, greedy, sometimes cruel, and mostly neglectful or indifferent to the fate of native peoples. The Brits were no exception, albeit sometimes well-meaning, in the patronising way of rulers. British rule was born out of trade, as they took over The East India Company, and motivated by trade, as evidenced repeatedly by fierce rivalry with the French and Portuguese for territory and trade.

---

6   Harper Collins, 1993.

Throughout British rule there were horrific examples of callous and cruel policies and behaviours. Indians experienced (and remember) the horrors, for example, of the Bengal famine, when, as thousands lay dying from hunger on the streets of Calcutta, Churchill decided to redirect ships of grain to England. When British officers in Calcutta remonstrated, pointing out the extent of the starvation, the great man replied that there were 'far too many Indians anyway'.

There are so many other examples of brutal, brutish behaviour, most notably the Amritsar Massacre in Jallianwala Bagh in 1919 when unarmed women and children, gathered to celebrate the Sikh New Year, were massacred as they picnicked in a park. This horrifying episode became a marker of colonial violence and oppression and was the beginning of the end of British colonial rule in India. Even Churchill denounced it as 'monstrous'. Meanwhile, the great Independence leaders like Gandhi and Nehru were regularly incarcerated by the Brits. Then finally, the British departure from India culminated in the Partition of the country, during which millions died.[7] All of this has left justifiably angry, bitter memories.

However, my mother's childhood in the 1920s and '30s was classically Empire, modelled on British manners, clothing, education. The British royal family, the frolics and foibles of British aristocracy, all were grist to this Anglo-Indian imagination. The young girl, watching from her balcony, saw an extraordinary parade of India's classes and castes going about their daily lives. But, across the road in the Anglo-Indian

---

7   See also Chapters 13, 14 and 23 for more.

community library, she pored over British comics and magazines. She called it her 'Tatler-education': admiring blonde British debutantes, while absorbing all the nuances of British social hierarchy, particularly its horsey county sub-set.

This was probably not as 'foreign' to someone growing up in India as it might have been to colonials in the Antipodes where equality is taken more seriously. Like the British social system, a finely-tuned awareness of one's place is still central to Indian society. In his book, *Being Indian*,[8] Parvan Varma describes 'the coordinates of status': the ways in which Indians 'read' another person's caste and social position, calculated from myriad cues including surname, occupation, religion, diction, degree of English spoken, qualifications, parents, clothing, jewellery and skin colour. In their acceptance of hierarchy and class/caste, the British and the Indian systems were very compatible.

Today, outside India, Anglo-Indians have settled successfully, adapted and mostly flourished. Lists of well-known Anglo-Indian singers and actors always include Cliff Richard, Engelbert Humperdinck, Ben Kingsley, Merle Oberon. The Indian diaspora is huge — and in some countries very influential. As they have progressively inter-married, many people worldwide will have a touch of India in their blood. It sometimes pops up quite unexpectedly. It is said that Rupert Penry-Jones, the blonde, blue-eyed, quintessentially British-looking actor, has a touch. British actress Olivia Colman, who played Queen Elizabeth in The Crown, has a bit too. When she won an Oscar in 2018, for her performance as another English queen in *The Favourite*,

---

8   Viking, Penguin, 2004.

Indian newspapers greedily latched onto her Indian antecedence (she is about one-sixteenth Indian). And I fancy you can see it in the very dark brown of her eyes.

But some Anglo-Indians left in India seem sad. Once numbering about 800,000, there are now only about 100,000 remaining, and many are old, having refused or been unable to leave India even as their children departed. Of those that remained, their children and grandchildren have married Indians and been assimilated into the mainstream. Presumably, the remaining Anglo-Indians will gradually disappear as a distinct grouping. I visited several Anglo-Indian families in Bangalore where I sensed a weight of unfulfilled longing: a longing to be an accepted part, to be central, not peripheral, to be not left behind.

The Indian Constitution actually mandated two reserved seats for Anglo-Indians in the Indian Federal Parliament and similarly in some State Parliaments.[9] Several Anglo-Indians have risen to great heights in the Indian military, in the arts, sport and music. There are vibrant Anglo-Indian communities, especially in Kolkata, Mumbai, Chennai and Delhi. An Indian acquaintance, who had attended boarding school in Pune about a decade after my mother, said that the Anglo-Indians always won the prizes in sport and music. He described them as gregarious, fun to be with, happy-go-lucky, and less earnest than their Indian counterparts.

I can't help wondering if Pearl's skin colour was why the aptly-named Mrs Wood at J. Walter Thompson so disdained her portfolio. And one wonders too about the continuing

---

9 These seats were recently abolished by the Modi Government (2019/20).

obsession with pale skin in India (and other Asian countries) today. The marital columns in Indian daily newspapers list fair skin, usually now described as 'wheaten', amongst the most highly valued attributes.

On which topic, I have discovered something disturbing about my ancestor Sir James Creed. Not only was Sir James one of those (possibly) venal EIC Directors, as described by William Dalrymple, but he also peddled a dodgy product. He made his fortune from taking out a patent on white lead. This was an important ingredient in artists' paints (think Flake White), later found to be carcinogenic. And worse still, white lead was used, mixed with vinegar, as a face-whitener (think white-faced Elizabethan aristocrats), often with lethal consequences. One assumes he wouldn't have known then what we know now about the dangers of lead poisoning, but nonetheless Sir James's previously lilywhite image in my mind is now tarnished. (And how sad that there is still demand for skin whitening products to this day.)

In my mother's case, being young and attractive probably helped to circumvent the snobberies and slights she might otherwise have suffered. I realise now that her job as a regular columnist and illustrator for the The Weekly Times of India was quite something. She was only 20. Most educated Indian women did not work. Most Anglo-Indian women were stenographers. Pearl must have been spirited and determined, and her parents unusually encouraging.

I have recently found some of her columns. They were tucked into a brown file at the bottom of that blue suitcase. More wickedly, I discovered that she also wrote film reviews, under a pseudonym, for an industry magazine called FilmIndia.

This was the decade in which notable Art Deco cinemas were built, especially in her home city, Bombay. I learnt that her parents, tolerant though they were, would not have approved of her going to films, much less writing about them in a film magazine bought by the general public.

The 1930s and 40s were interesting times for a young woman in Bombay. The tentative beginnings of freedom for women, plus, in my mother's case, her plunge into artistic 'bohemian' life, were the backdrop to a new drama. The Second World War would change their lives. British forces from the UK and the colonies poured into India, mostly through Bombay. Soldiers on leave roamed the streets and partied in hotels and clubs, when not breathing fresher air in lovely hill-stations.

Women volunteered to help in canteens and hospitals. I found, tucked amongst her papers, a scrawled handwritten note, on browning, tatty paper, dated December 1942. It says:

My Dear Young Lady,

Would you object if I sat in my lonely seat and just keep gazing into your beautiful eyes. Never have I ever seen such a beautiful girl ...

It is torn off at this tantalising point, but on the back, in my mother's hand, it says an American soldier wrote it to her when she did voluntary work in a canteen.

Being interested in writing and books, Pearl applied for a job at The British Censor Office:

I had to sit a test. One question asked the name of the British Ambassador to Egypt. How or why someone in Bombay needed to have gleaned this bit of information I don't know! But thanks to my reading of Tatler magazine, I was able to name [and she still remembered at the age of 92!] 'Sir Miles and Lady Lampson'. I got the job.

Because I was single, it was thought inappropriate to be censoring letters written by soldiers in case I was shocked by their language or intimacies. So I was assigned to censoring books and magazines for anything that might inadvertently or deliberately reveal anything helpful to the enemy. Time and Life magazines were my special responsibility. Anything deemed anti-British had to be dumped. I think we had to sign the official secrets act and also swear not to reveal what we were doing or where we worked.

I was in the Press section so, for the first time in my life, I was reading the writings of Indian political intellectuals and seeing India from the Indian point of view. At my various schools we had only learnt history from the British side: the Black Hole of Calcutta whitewashed! But — being wartime and the start of anti-British riots in India — political sensitivities meant that anything in the press that was anti-British or inflammatory had to be stopped from appearing in the local newspapers. I'm afraid I was as zealous as anyone in stopping it.

Because I loved writing I enjoyed having to write synopses of books, manuscripts or articles. Before long I was 'head of my table', the youngest member of the section, so I felt enormously important. I often wonder what Beverley Nichols, a well-known English writer of the day, would have thought if he had known that a twenty-one-year-old Anglo-Indian girl had passed his manuscript of 'Verdict on India' for publication. Though he was lucky as it was particularly cruel and inaccurate about Anglo-Indians!

Apart from a British soldier standing discreetly at the entrance of the old building we occupied near the docks, there was nothing to suggest anything secretive about what we did. We wore civilian clothes and it was easy to blend with the general population. This was not to last. As censorship grew from mainly military into political, so did the scope of the office. As anti-British riots worsened, any anti-British material going out or coming into the country also had to be banned.

We were moved to a building near Flora Fountain and given a khaki uniform to wear. We were mostly women workers and the uniform consisted of a dress with patch pockets and epaulettes and a forage cap. It was hardly flattering! The cap sat very uneasily on the fashionable hairstyle of the day: two rolled-upward sections of hair and the rest rolled under to collar level …

But, from being anonymous, there was suddenly great interest in the Greek-inscription badges we wore on the epaulettes. Although we couldn't decipher the lettering ourselves we were told that it said 'We Work in Silence.' Why in Greek, or why anything at all, I don't know. I used buses to get to and from work, and I was rarely in a bus queue without being aware that others in the queue were trying to read what my badges said. On one occasion it was too much for the American soldier standing behind me. 'Excuse me, Ma-am,' he said, 'what does your badge say?' I replied very primly, 'I'm not allowed to say.' 'Well, don't then,' he said, 'I can see it says "South Epsom Salts"!'

I have these badges safely in a drawer at home in Melbourne and when I look at the one saying 'We Work in Silence', in Greek lettering, it does indeed look a bit like 'South Epsom Salts' …

But back to mixed blood. Something has fascinated me

since our first visit to India: being a watered-down Anglo-Indian, a mixed-blood descendant of (whiter-than-white) Sir James, appears to be a 'no-go' subject to Indians we meet on our trips. Across two decades of visits, when I mention that I have some Indian blood it causes an awkwardness I am yet to fathom. Indian friends and acquaintances ignore my India connection and never follow up with a question about whence it came, why or how. Charming and courteous as always, they move on to other subjects. I am curious and want to find out what lies behind this response. Something I could explore now we had a reason to keep returning to India.

On the other hand — there is so much else to discover and learn about India. Our own (less bohemian) business adventure is to take us now to Kolkata (formerly Calcutta), a challenging and fascinating experience.

Kolkata

Victoria Memorial. Calcutta was then the capital of British India. The Viceroy Lord Curzon commissioned this memorial after the death of Queen Victoria. Started in 1906 it was completed in 1921, by which time it had been announced that New Delhi would be the new capital. Constructed of white marble, the building obviously aimed to implant the imperial stamp upon India. It houses galleries and the main museum

One of India's most famous clubs, the Tollygunge Country Club (est 1895 and known as the 'Tolly') is one of the oldest in the world, located only 7 kms south of the city centre. Originally an indigo plantation, its 100 acre spread includes indoor and outdoor swimming pools, tennis and squash courts, an equestrian centre, residential facilities and the famous 18-hole golf course

A typical Kolkata intersection: tramstop, taxi, cycle-rickshaw, human rickshaw, fresh vegetable stalls, small shops. And people. All jostling for space.

The flower market in Kolkata. An unmissable experience in any major Indian city is a dawn visit to the flower market. The colours, the scents, the chaos… Fresh flowers, such as jasmine, tuberoses, are woven into women's hair, form offerings at temples, are crafted into garlands to hang around the neck or in dwellings from humble to grand. For weddings, funerals, celebrations of all types, flower garlands are integral. The arts and crafts of India have been inspired by floral motifs for centuries. And fresh marigold or rose petals, often changed daily, float decoratively in water at entrances to hotels, shops and homes

11: Stitching Things Up in Kolkata

Preparing our first business trip to India, we decided to investigate *kantha*,[10] an embroidery style typically found in Bihar, Bengal and Bangladesh. Sometimes known as sujani and, in its simplest variant, as gudri stitching, *kantha* consists of simple running stitches, very densely worked, often depicting Indian motifs: flowers, birds, religious symbols, scenes of daily life and so on.

We wanted to see if we could interpret *kantha* through a more Western and more minimal filter. Internet searching back then was less productive, but luckily we discovered Shamlu Dudeja in Kolkata. She was very responsive to our emailed enquiry and immediately invited us to stay with her. Feeling this was too personal, too soon, we opted for her offer of putting us up at the famous Tollygunge Club — more of which later.

For most Westerners, Kolkata's image is linked to extreme poverty, beggars, destitution, illness, Mother Teresa, traffic and trams. True as these aspects are, in this city of over 15 million people, it is far from the full picture. It is certainly teeming and

10 *Kantha* began as a technique in which poor women re-used worn saris. Threads would be taken from the sari borders and used to patch together old saris in layers, with simple running stitches, to create quilts, bedcovers, wall hangings and other garments.

chaotic. On our very first day we did get caught in its infamous traffic, we did see a dead body being carried past our car, we did find ourselves stepping over sleeping emaciated bodies when entering the apartment of a well-to-do contact.

But we also marvelled at its stock of decaying Art Deco and Art Nouveau buildings, originally a nice yellow ochre colour but now besmirched with decades of grey/black pollution. It has lovely trees, leaves thick with dust. Then called Calcutta, it was the capital of British India, until the seat of power was moved to Delhi in 1911, so it has fabulous British colonial buildings. Kolkata's central park, larger than New York's Central Park, encompasses Fort William and the extraordinary Victoria Memorial building, a vast white marble meringue around which the central city pivots.

Kolkata also has a proud intellectual and cultural heritage. Bengalis see Kolkata as the intellectual capital of India. Of names well-known in the West, it has spawned the Tagores, Satyajit Ray, Amartya Sen and authors such as Vikram Seth and Amitav Ghosh. Books, films, art are taken very seriously. As is food. As are its clubs. The British established the full gamut: the Bengal Club was the social pinnacle, the Saturday Club less so (trade!), The Royal Calcutta Golf Club (the oldest in the world outside the UK), The Royal Calcutta Turf Club, the Bengal Rowing Club, the Cricket Club, and on it goes. They are still central to life in middle- and upper-class circles today, with hefty membership fees and lengthy waiting lists.

It is easy to smirk at what seems now a parody of Britishness. But we too have many such parodies in Australia. They remain as part of our shared British colonial history, elitist, but providing pleasurable social and cultural interactions to those who can afford the fees. In Kolkata we've been taken to several of these places by kind residents. We've enjoyed events, dinners and cocktail parties in the clubs as well as in private houses. In fact the party round in 'Cal' (as it is still affectionately known) can be quite exhausting. It's also a bit incestuous — despite the large population overall, the social 'A list' is relatively small — and possibly rather gossipy, even bitchy at times.

On our first visit we accepted Shamlu's offer to arrange accommodation at the Tollygunge Club, usually referred to as just 'The Tolly'. We were glad of this club refuge, as we soon discovered that our visit coincided with a state election. The city streets seemed like the Wild West with competing political rallies, untamed fireworks, gunshots, the odd murder, a curfew and an alcohol ban. This version of democracy in action was a bit daunting for innocent Australians on a first trip to India. After slightly nervous exploration of city sights, we were glad to retreat to the green respite of the Tolly, another of the world's oldest golf clubs.

In the 18th century, Major William Tolly widened an old creek to form a canal (a 'gunge') to open up river-borne trade with the hinterland. The Tollygunge Club, situated on land that was once an indigo plantation, is slightly out of the town centre, and certainly peaceful. The main building was the garden house of WW Johnson, a late 18th century indigo planter.

We drew up under an elegant front portico. Rather dark rooms, where we signed in, were crowded with heavy Victorian furniture. There were adjoining pavilions housing bars and restaurants, a huge indoor swimming pool, plus a large equestrian centre and horses. All set in undulating lawns, brightly flowered garden beds and rather serious-looking golfers. In midday heat we watched from a verandah as rounds were completed before whisky and soda in the bar, seemingly more caddies than golfers, holding umbrellas to shade their players from blistering sun.

Our room, where we hoped to be cocooned in lovely natural fibres, perhaps dyed with indigo, instead had nasty bile-green synthetic bedcovers that slid off the rock-hard beds. But we could have Chinese food in one restaurant, English in another (macaroni cheese), Indian in another. All incredibly cheap and with eccentrically random service. We discovered that there was an early large Chinese community, still living many generations later in Kolkata's Chinatown and where we were tempted by a restaurant quaintly named 'Don Giovanni Chinese Restaurant'. We enjoyed the Tollygunge Club a lot. From this base we made our first contact with Shamlu, who had already rung to make sure we were safely settled.

12: Servants and Shamlu

Shamlu is credited with helping to revive the craft of *kantha*, nurturing and promoting it in India and internationally, winning several awards for her work. She runs an organisation engaging the women stitchers directly, working from their own homes in villages, and at their own pace. As the Grameen Bank and other similar enterprises have shown, seeding small businesses for women can lead to very effective benefits for children, for families, for communities.

When we met, Shamlu was in her mid-sixties and Chair of The Calcutta Foundation, which, amongst other ventures, supported an orchestra for people who had grown up in British-run orphanages and had learned Western classical instruments. The foundation arranged for visiting international conductors and helped support performances. It continues to provide famine relief, supply building materials after natural disasters, while also running an orphanage for the children of leprosy sufferers.

It was Shamlu who famously put a note under the hotel room door of Steve Waugh, then Australia's Test Cricket Captain, suggesting he visit a home for the sons of leprosy patients, called Udayan. She was keen to get his support to raise funds for an additional home for the daughters of leprosy patients. This led to a major commitment in time, energy, and fund-raising from Waugh over the ensuing years, leading to the opening of Nivedita House in 1998.

The attractive Shamlu was once a model, had been a maths lecturer at the famous Loreto Teachers' Training College, and is the author of a major series of maths books used by many primary and middle schools in India (and a later series for Pakistan), the royalties from which continue to support her now. She and her husband had two children, but she was widowed at fifty, a year after her son had also died. Not one to wallow in her grief, it was then that she engaged Steve Waugh in her charity projects.

On subsequent visits to Kolkata each year, we tried a couple of hotels closer to the centre, and then began accepting Shamlu's kind offers to stay with her. This was such a pleasure. A spacious ground floor apartment with that rare commodity: a large, green back garden with beautiful trees, colourful bedding plants and an expansive lawn. We have been fascinated with all aspects of life 'from the inside', albeit a relatively well-to-do life.

Visiting India over the years, we noted that middle-class Indians discussed servant problems a lot. When we first started doing business in the subcontinent, we used to roll our eyes (inwardly, if that's possible) and think 'What are they fussing about?/They don't know how lucky they are/They don't know how hard it is for us to run professional careers with children and virtually no help,' and so on. But gradually, as we've come to know their lives better, we see how complex having servants can be.

First, there is no privacy: servants are always there, padding around silently on bare feet. But they are very present. Young friends say they can never have a decent loud argument in case the servants hear. Ayahs take the young children to play in the park or to birthday parties and, like English nannies, they meet for gossip regularly. Nothing remains secret for long.

In a typical start to the day in Shamlu's house, there are instructions to be given, plans to be conveyed: 'I need Anil (the driver) to take me to the tailor, but first he has to pick up the dry cleaning. Tell Ramesh to take the dog for a walk before the vet gets here. I'm expecting someone for morning tea, so we need some fresh biscuits and sweets. The graphic artist for the new maths book will be here soon, and tell the driver I'll be going to a cocktail party this evening. We will pick up my friend Alka on the way. My daughter's driver is bringing the grandchildren over after school — they'll need a snack and a cuddle while I brief the *kantha* embroidery girls about the photo shoot tomorrow. Bring some tea now, please. My sister-in-law is staying, but friends from Australia have arrived, so her bed can be moved into my room and make up the spare room for the visitors. Tell cook to come and see me about the meals. Alfonso mangoes are in season and I know Sue and Val love them, so get some for breakfast tomorrow. There are a couple of other friends dropping in for a drink. One is a doctor — I'll just check the servant's radiography results with her ...'

That was not an exaggeration; just one day in the life of Shamlu. And I haven't even mentioned the landline phone interruptions, nor her constant use of a mobile phone. Whether in business discussions or in the homes of all our Indian friends, the interruptions never end. You think you have their attention, but then you realise eyes have flickered in the direction of a passing servant who needs to be told something. It is very hard to feel sorry for them when they complain about the servants. But we do understand now that the constant presence of others can feel oppressive. And is very distracting.

These days, the newer-rich and younger Indians are less inclined to have servants living in — 'My husband says he doesn't want a cook sitting on his head.' This apt alternative for 'under his feet' expresses perfectly the amount of mental space servants can occupy. Live-in servants used to be an integral part of the family. Their health and welfare, as well as that of their families back in the villages, were all part of an employer's responsibility. They would pay for children's education expenses, grandmother's operations or medicines. Even if they complained about it, a good employer would genuinely care about the welfare of staff and their extended families, usually living huge distances away. The health and happiness of one depended on the same in the other.

But less likely to be resident these days, servants have to fend for themselves outside working hours. And today's younger generation of employers may know little or nothing about their servants' families. Even an enlightened employer may know very little of the personal details of live-in staff. Staying once in a friend's apartment in Delhi, we were shocked to discover that our elderly host had had the same personal servant living with her for 30 years yet did not know how old he was or when his birthday was. She was unsure where he slept, waving vaguely in the direction of the roof when we asked.

Equally fascinating, there was clearly a mutually-dependent symbiosis between them. He hovered anxiously over her at meal times — serving food he carefully cooked according to her instructions each day — encouraging her to eat a bit more, nagging her even. He was genuinely concerned about her welfare, which was also his welfare. We once found him sitting on Sue's guest bed watching daytime TV, one of the perks of his rather restricted life. The poor man leapt to his feet when we unexpectedly arrived home early. We didn't mind at all, but we knew he might be in trouble.

We learnt too about the careful delineation of tasks as we noticed he didn't empty the wastepaper baskets in our rooms. Not his job. A male 'sweeper' swept the outside areas, a female cleaning servant did inside, but Raj's job was to look after his 'madam', which included banking and shopping, and cooking and washing up. But, as we should have realised, not house guests' wastepaper baskets!

We have heard many tales of servants stealing, having shadowy affairs, disappearing without notice. Sometimes there is a sinister note to the stories. Shamlu's recently widowed sister-in-law, now on her own in her house, became nervous of her own servants, feeling they resented her while knowing too much about her movements, her possessions. Would she be murdered in her bed? The Booker prize-winning novel *White Tiger* did not seem to go down too well amongst our acquaintances in India, often dismissed as over melodramatic and unlikely. ('What's more,' they added, 'what would the author know? He doesn't live here!') But we did note traces of this Pinteresque fear of a servant's power.

On top of her *kantha* work and her charitable foundation duties, moving in Shamlu's orbit in Kolkata involves a lot of socialising — an absorbing succession of cocktail parties, lunches, dinners. Anticipating this, we packed some of our best 'going-out' garments and some good jewellery, ready for the social whirl.

Preparing for an evening party, we repaired to our respective rooms to dress in our finery. We took the trouble to look our best, which is why we bothered to bring evening clothes from home. Shamlu came to inspect us. She stood at the doorway to our bedroom, looking a bit alarmed, and said, 'But didn't you bring anything dressy?' Deflated, we finally went out adorned in her jewellery. At other times we wore her glorious hand-embroidered silk saris. Dress-ups. At the parties we found people very welcoming, much more so than at an equivalent gathering in Melbourne. And there's always a feast of flashing diamonds and scintillating silks, garden settings a-quiver with massed tea-light candles, twinkling bud-lit trees and hedges. Plus plentiful deep-fried nibbles ...

One magical evening was spent on a platform barge, moored on the Hooghly River. It began with a music and classical dance rendition of Rabindranath Tagore's poetry. The weather was balmy, the barge festooned with fairy lights and colourful paper lanterns. The performance was entrancing. Then drinks and nibbles and milling around making small talk. One young man, with whom I struck up a conversation, told me there had been 5,000 guests at his recent wedding. He only knew a small percentage of them, and a servant had to be rescued after she got 'walled in' behind a vast pile of gifts.

When I asked another young man what work he did, he said he was a banker. Then he added, somewhat hesitantly, 'Actually, I like to write film scripts'. I asked why then was he working as a banker and he replied that his father wanted to be able to say proudly: 'My son, the banker.' 'Oh, well,' I responded lamely, 'perhaps writing as a hobby?' He replied modestly that one of his scripts had been turned into a film recently. What was it? Only *Monsoon Wedding*!

We adapted to these cocktail parties quite well. Like us, Shamlu was happy to go home and have a soothing bowl of cereal for dinner (brought by servants on a trolley, of course). Her long-time personal servant, gentle Meera, waited for her return and massaged her feet before bed every night. What bliss.

But we adapted less well to the Indian way of dinner parties. This involves arriving at about 8 pm, then sitting awkwardly around the edge of a room (chairs were often arranged around the edge) making desultory conversation for what seemed like tummy-rumbling hours. The dinner is not usually served until 10 or later. Delicious dinner, usually several courses and many side dishes, then dessert. As soon as it is finished, everyone leaps to their feet and departs. Perfunctory goodbyes, no more small talk, just out the door. And home to bed on a very full stomach.

13: One Partition Story

As with everything in India, there are layers of story and history. Shamlu Dudeja's life is full of achievements and full of interest, all fascinating to the outsider. But these are the graphic images of the start of what was to be her family's exodus from Sindh, now part of Pakistan:

> Shamlu clutched her mother's sari as she watched from the balcony of their house. A ring of blazing fires encircled her known world. Through flames and smoke she could see local workers looting nearby houses, the booty placed in a pile for anyone to share. She sensed that something very different was going on. This was not just one bad apple, nor was it a band of opportunistic looters. This was a systematic and almost disdainful appropriation, without personal acquisitiveness, detached, impersonal, cold ... and much more frightening ...

Sixty years later Shamlu was describing her experience of the 1947 Partition of India. Sitting in her sister-in-law's comfortable apartment in Delhi, fan gently stirring the air, she was reflecting on what her parents had suffered and overcome. Shamlu's father was a Professor of Mathematics in Karachi, from a respected well-educated family, her mother with a BA, unusual for an Indian woman of her times.

Her father had enjoyed amateur dramatics, performing in a variety of Tagore and Shakespeare plays, straddling cultures with ease. Shamlu had been encouraged to take tertiary studies in mathematics, the full weight of fatherly expectations placed on her as the eldest child after the still-birth of a son. Another daughter and son completed the immediate family.

Although they were Hindus, Shamlu's father was guided in his spiritual life by a Muslim Sufi guru who became not just a mentor but a close friend. When looting and violence developed and many Hindus began to flee, her father consulted his guru who encouraged him to stay and offered him protection. As the situation worsened, Hindu friends and extended family had gathered in their home compound, terrified of the conflagration around them, wondering if they should have gone.

Then there was a knock at the door. 'My guru's men have come,' said her father. There at the door were: 'Two Muslim men with pistols to protect us,' as Shamlu described the scene to me more than half a century later. 'Men outside were threatening to kill us. We had put our jewels in little handkerchiefs to be handed over in the hope they'd take them and leave us alone ... but we were okay, as these guards sat with us until a curfew was imposed and some order was restored the following day.'

But the violence continued. News came that many of their relatives had already been killed and most had fled their lands, leaving with almost nothing. Shamlu and her family sat, father praying, they were all watching the fires, wondering what to do ...

Eventually, her father again contacted his guru who this time advised that they leave. Immediately. They knew they were leaving everything — their heritage, their stories, their land, their houses and all their possessions. Both parents had inherited estates, with large bungalows, all of which would be lost.

Only one suitcase per family was permitted, so they took two sets of clothes per person, their bed quilts and their Pfaff sewing machine wrapped up in the quilts. In its instrument box they hid two pieces of family jewellery: a diamond bracelet, and an emerald and diamond ring. And remember that in India jewellery is more than decoration or vanity. It is a store of wealth, a measure of status, a vital part of one's inheritance.

They arrived at the docks just in time to board a ship to Bombay where they had managed to reserve a cabin. From the crowded deck, their eyes searched the dockside anxiously for a friend who said he'd bring them a meal in a tiffin carrier, in which would be more of the family jewels. But he never came.

The ship set sail for Bombay. The seas were rough, the ship was crammed with people, most standing all day and all night, every inch of deck-space occupied. Some fell overboard when the ship rolled. Shamlu recalled the smell of fear and desperation. And the seasickness.

They were to stay with Shamlu's uncle who was already in Bombay, his apartment then housing six people per room. Here they lived for two or three months while her father went off to Delhi to look for work. Eventually, he got a job with the Government of India in Delhi, then sent word that the family should come and join him. He had found a room above a horse stable. The children were excited at the prospect of living with horses.

They set out eagerly by train, realising that this would be basic housing, but at least the family would be together.

Fortunately, just that very morning her father had managed to find space on a roof terrace. It comprised two rooms, semi-covered, with open terraces and mattresses to sleep on under the stars. There were relatives next door, everyone sharing their few possessions: pots, pans, old crates for tables. But no water. It was a far cry from the privileged life they had once enjoyed in Karachi. Father's job was low status but at least he had one, and was paid. Luckier than most of the millions of dislocated, traumatised victims of a brutal Partition of India who, on both sides, Hindu and Muslim, had to re-create their lives.

Her resourceful mother found she could buy cheap bags of fabric pieces and so the Pfaff sewing machine was put to work making frocks and school uniforms for the two girls and converting father's old shirts into clothing for the little boy. Shamlu recalled that she couldn't speak English like the locals and was teased for her Sindhi accent. But she did well at school and went on to university, following her father's footsteps by majoring in mathematics. Her father progressed into more senior positions, eventually retiring as Secretary of his department. They later moved to Bombay, where he became Head of the Handicrafts Board.

Shamlu recalled no sense of grieving or grievance, that they accepted everything with grace and thanks, knowing it could have been worse. People helped each other, shared what they had, cared for those with less. Despite scarcity, her mother always cooked for an extra person, someone on the street in need. Shamlu's family, like many others who had lost everything, counted themselves lucky. Active outreach to the less fortunate has been a continuing theme in Shamlu's life. Now, in her eighties, she is still raising funds for flood victims, providing resources for the *kantha* stitchers in their villages, and maintaining the momentum of her charitable foundations.

Shamlu's sister-in-law told me a similar story, of leaving everything — land, house, jewellery — in Lahore. She said she didn't really miss anything except her African grey parrot. Some years later, she decided to write a letter to her old address in Pakistan and explain her loss, not expecting that it would be of any use beyond feeling she had tried. One morning the doorbell in Delhi rang and there, on the doorstep, stood a courier with a cage — her beloved parrot had been returned.

14: Finding my 'Touch of the Tar Brush'

That Partition story is but one of millions, most with far less positive outcomes. Although the statistics vary, the baldness of mere numbers belies the horrors those numbers represent: up to 15 million people were displaced, up to 2 million killed, 75,000 raped. Partition is one of the major reasons the British are not regarded at all fondly in India. So I could understand if having British connections might not be endearing. Yet English visitors are treated with the customary courtesy, at least at superficial levels. But I continue to notice that my touch of Indian blood mixed into a British heritage is in some way discomfiting to people. I'm not imagining it. Sue noticed before I did — and it is often she who mentions my Indian connection to see if it provokes any response.

My thin grasp of the Creed family story also needed exploring. Sue and I decided to include a visit to Bangalore where I knew the family was based at one stage and where my great-grandfather, Louis James StClair Creed, great grandson of the original Sir James, lies buried. I had a photo of the headstone in hand.

Dripping with sweat, we stepped tentatively through straggling weeds around decaying headstones. We were in the

Bangalore Christian cemetery, centrally located in this now booming city, one of the IT hubs of India. Traffic-laden roads encircled the graveyard, the roads lined with lovely old trees alight with bright orange blooms.

It was very hot, despite this being a 'hill town' where, in British times, exclusive private schools were built and soldiers, including my father, came for respite in the cooler air. We placed our feet carefully as we traipsed up and down the rows of headstones, skirting dog and human excrement, tagged by mischievous urchins cackling and cavorting to get our attention.

When we eventually found the right tombstone, I stood and contemplated. This was it: the crucible of my mixed antecedence. It matched the headstone photo I had in my hand, retrieved from the blue suitcase. The headstone was dated 1917 and, as in the photo, it read: Louis James StClair Creed, son of Henry Gordon Creed and Cecilia Aurelia de Bourbel de Montpincon [the French blue blood clearly proclaimed]. I supposed the headstone was placed by Louis' widow. But there was no later addition of her name nor, after searching up and down the rows, did we find any headstone for his wife. His Indian wife.

This was the story I'd been told: The Money family, who ran a tea-estate next to the Creeds, had given refuge to an Indian child found wandering alone after a violent thunderstorm had killed her parents. (Another version suggested a cholera epidemic had taken her parents.) She was given food and shelter. But having been fed meat as part of the British family's diet, she was no longer acceptable to her Brahmin Hindu extended family. I don't know if she really was fed meat — it would seem crass and unlikely with long-term India hands. But even if she hadn't actually eaten meat, she had now lived in close proximity with meat-eaters. Her own relatives would not take her back and so she grew up within the British family next door to the Creeds.

Young Louis Creed became engaged to Henrietta, the daughter of the Money family, but she was killed in a riding accident. Meanwhile, the Indian foundling had grown up, love had blossomed (presumably, or was it just propinquity?) and Louis married her instead. She had been given an English name — Mabel Money. Oh dear, what an awful name! I often wonder about her original name — hoping it might have been Shakuntala or Priyanka — and I wonder too at the lack of imagination (and lack of musicality) that gave her such a drab, stolid name. Especially in contrast to the melodious name of her French mother-in-law as described in such fulsome detail on this decaying headstone in Bangalore cemetery. But what a scandal it must have been. 'Quelle horreur!' as the French relatives probably exclaimed — marrying a local, and coloured!

When I returned to Melbourne after this trip I was keen to get back to the suitcase under the bed at my parents' house. Could I find anything more about Mabel? I wondered what she looked like? A few years had passed since I last opened it, and I expected silverfish, or moths to flutter out. But all was well. My mother had sorted things into large manila envelopes, texta-labelled in her distinctive hand: 'Creed Family', 'Don's family', 'School in Poona', 'My Work'. Opening the 'Creed Memorabilia' envelope with eager anticipation, I found what I had been hoping for: a photograph of Mabel. I am slightly disappointed to discover a stout, dour, rather plain woman, not the willowy Indian beauty of my imagination.

Despite my best efforts, I found nothing more about great grandmother, Mabel. There were more manila envelopes so I decided to keep searching and have since contacted a cousin in Canada who might recall something. I found letters indicating that Mabel's fair-skinned British husband, Louis, was unsuccessful as a tea planter and apparently equally unsuccessful in other business ventures.

But Mabel Money was the origin of my 'touch of the tar brush'. This expression, describing people of mixed or 'coloured blood', was widely used in my youth. Clearly derogatory in its original use, where it referred to Afro-Caribbean — or sometimes South Asian — people with visible signs of colour in their antecedence. It is, of course, completely unacceptable these days. But, in my own experience, it was more often employed teasingly, even slightly enviously. For example, in the 1960s, we teenage Aussie girls would lie on the beach, slathered in olive oil, trying to get a tan. My skin always tanned faster than my friends'. They'd say: 'You're so lucky, but then you've got a touch of the tar brush!' (Was I missing an underlying sneer? I don't think so, but ...)

Louis and Mabel had four children, two boys and two girls, all with darkish complexions. The eldest was my grandfather Edward StClair Creed, who was therefore half Indian, one-quarter British, one-quarter French — his middle name entering the family from a French godparent. Edward spent his early working life in Bangalore, where he later met my part-Italian grandmother and they subsequently moved to Bombay.

Which is where my mother, Pearl, was born in 1921.

15: War (and Love) Break Out

Fast-forward to 1938 and a tall, slim, young man could be found practising the organ in a beautiful Wren chapel in Cambridge. The surface of the pond outside shimmered with gently circling ducks, the grass was green and lush. This was my English father, who had won a scholarship to Cambridge — organ scholar at Emmanuel College — to study music, maths and modern languages.

But ... in 1939 war was declared and he was whisked off to the jungles of Burma. This is an exaggeration — he wasn't called up immediately and there were some months of training in England before they were shipped out to India. He was in the Duke of Wellington's regiment, and would be part of the famous Chindits,[11] led initially by the mercurial General Orde Wingate. Wingate was a 'Lawrence of Arabia' figure, who had led Jewish irregular forces in Palestine before the War and later in the Abyssinian campaign against the Italians.

His plan, enthusiastically supported by Winston Churchill, was to insert regular British soldiers deep behind the Japanese

---

11 Named after a mythical Burmese lion or *chinthé*. Also references the Chindwin River in Burma. Badges and insignia featured this lion. My sister and I have one badge each, as well as other Chindit memorabilia.

lines in Burma to wage a guerrilla war. The forces would be supplied by air, including by gliders. It was successful as a morale-booster at home — taking on the Japanese at their own game — but was not very successful militarily. The conditions were brutal: mountainous jungles, monsoonal rains, rampant disease and a highly effective enemy. The casualty rate was appalling. But the lessons learned were to later underpin General William Slim's decisive victory in Burma.

So my father's war played out in these treacherous jungles: heat, humidity, monsoonal rains, mosquitoes, mud, malaria, dysentery, leeches and lice — plus a ruthless enemy. A far cry from playing the organ in quiet, leafy Cambridge. I find this almost incomprehensible — picturing my own children at his age leading their student lives and then suddenly ... their worlds upended. How did he cope? He was a classical musician, a prodigy at the keyboard and blessed with perfect pitch. As a teenager his teacher had toured him around England to give piano recitals; he performed at Royal Albert Hall; he had his own compositions published before he turned twenty. He wasn't sporty, or outdoorsy, he was studious, with a quiet interior focus. His musician's ear for languages meant he relished cheap student trips to France and Spain, the latter being his language of study. That was the extent of his travel. But to be uprooted and transplanted to India and Burma, far-flung outposts of Empire ... it's hard for us to comprehend in these days of easy travel and relative peace.

Although it was a tough and often tragic time, he took well to army life. He turned out to be the wiry, hardy, resourceful type. In one book about the Chindits, he was described as the only one still eating at a stage when everyone else in his group was brought down with dysentery. He loved Burma and India.

He loved his leave breaks in various cities and hill-stations — Bangalore, Simla, Mussoorie and Nainital. He ended the War as Major Britton,[12] and was Mentioned in Despatches.

In the midst of all this, and quite unexpectedly, he fell headlong in love. Whilst on a two-week leave in Bombay in 1943, he was invited by a married friend to a dinner party. There he found himself seated next to a lively 22-year-old Anglo-Indian woman, my mother Pearl, who was already engaged to a fellow Anglo-Indian, 10 years her senior. It transpired that her fiancé had left for the War a couple of years before, but was missing. She'd been writing to him regularly, but had received no replies. His parents had tried to trace their son through the Red Cross. Nothing. A terrible uncertainty for a young woman, barely out of her teens. Was he rebuffing her? Was he not answering her letters because he had changed his mind? Had he been captured? Had he been killed?

Pearl was only 18 when the Second World War broke out, and 19 when she became engaged. I suppose that the prospect of his going to war might have led to a formalisation of the relationship sooner than if life had proceeded normally. But off he went and Pearl was formally hitched. This meant she couldn't join in the lively wartime social life that was going on around her. Dances, soldiers on leave, a new dimension in the life of a city, a new freedom for women, the general loosening of social mores that war injects.

---

12 Later in his life, as a school's Director of Music, he was also in charge of the Cadet Corps. He was promoted to Lt. Colonel after completing a gruelling jungle-warfare training course at Canungra in Queensland. (Although one wonders why this was necessary when he had spent those years in Burma! Perhaps he volunteered for it. He was older than most others on the course and came through unscathed, which was apparently unusual.)

Pearl's life was limited by convention: it was considered unseemly that a 'spoken for' woman would participate in such activities. She went to work each day but, unable to join her female friends in their exciting social rounds, she was restricted to sedate dinner parties held by married couples, the only respectable social life for an engaged woman. But one such dinner party was where she met my father, having not heard from her fiancé for almost three years.

Some of this background story came from my mother. But only the minimal version: she had been engaged to someone else before she met my father. It was a few years after Pearl had died that I was finally brave enough to open a parcel of letters she had saved, in a manila envelope labelled: 'Private: Wartime Letters from Don'. It's hard to ignore 'Private'. However, she had stored them in the suitcase with all the other family memorabilia, knowing that we would eventually access it all. Perhaps she had forgotten they were there. Or perhaps she recognised that letters like this are of historical interest, well beyond the personal.

Nevertheless, I'd been reluctant to open them, not just because of the 'Private' label, but because it seemed too intrusive, too intimate, too uncomfortable to read love letters written by one's parents. We had been quite a private family, not given to outward displays of emotion, definitely more British than Indian. Three times previously I had pulled out the manila envelope, only to put it away without investigating.

One day, home alone, I opened it. Inside, I found the letters squashed into a man's wallet, the leather cracked and dry. It's a one-way correspondence — just my father's letters to my mother, none of her letters to him. A pile of little square-ish pale blue or cream envelopes, addressed in my father's very neat handwriting.

As well as the address, on each small envelope he had inscribed 'On Active Service' and 'Written in English'. I suppose this was required by the censors who had duly opened, then ink-stamped each letter and resealed with much sticking tape.

They were in random order. I spent some time trying to sort them chronologically. I wrote the dates on the outside of the envelopes, so my sister would find it easier to read them in sequence. Delaying tactics. I felt a little shaky at the prospect of opening this correspondence. What would I discover? Was my father as reticent as he had seemed to us girls growing up? Would it be a stiff, formal romance — a not-very-romantic romance?

The letter paper was transparent, like rice paper, the handwriting was small, perfectly suited to the intricacies of music notation, but quite hard to read. He wrote on both sides of the thin paper. Some were in pencil, making it even harder to decipher. Several were long, up to twelve pages.

But once I delved in, it was absolutely clear that my parents-to-be were instantly smitten. The very first letter, written after they had only known each other for three days, said: 'You are so lovely! You overflow with grace. It is sheer joy to watch you dance, to watch you walk. I have never felt so proud as I was with you.'

Perhaps surprisingly, the letter revealed that in the three days remaining of his leave, after the fateful dinner party, they had been for a ride together in a horse-drawn cart, or *gharry*, had been caught in the rain while sitting on a bench chatting, and — more outrageous — had danced together at the Taj. Openly flouting the conventions of the time.

Another letter showed that he had stayed with her family, who had moved to live by the sea in Mahim:

My stay at Sea View was heavenly. I don't know when I have ever been so contented. To live in a house with the roar of the waves outside; to sleep in your room; to see the signs of your art all around; to feel so at home with your delightful parents and, above all, to know that you were in the same house; all this was absolute bliss.

(One assumes her parents put him in Pearl's room while she slept elsewhere? I couldn't imagine propriety would have allowed co-sleeping in the family house.) But clearly, in these very early days of their relationship, Mum had already side-stepped the restrictions of being an 'affianced' woman. Her parents had been hospitable and friendly but what did they really think? This wasn't seemly, she had a fiancé bravely away at war, somewhere unknown. I could imagine my grandmother tut-tutting in private to my grandfather.

For me, the letters were a revelation. Here was an entirely different man. I uncovered a passionate, emotional side to my father that I had thought was displayed only when he played the piano, especially his favourites, Rachmaninov and Schumann. He said himself, in the letters, that he was reserved, like his father, and couldn't show emotion except through the keyboard:

I have been brought up to feel that emotion-expressed is cheap. I know differently inside me, but my environment growing up allowed me one outlet only and that is music. If only people knew what a tumult goes on inside me when I am playing.

He ended his very first letter with these words:

82

It only remains for me to take my courage in both hands and say to you something which I have no right to say and that is to whisper, rather bashfully, that — I love you ...

I'm amazed. And after only three days together...

My mother, in her letters, must have been asking him to tell her more about himself, and his relationships. He described the shock of being called up:

When the War came I was just beginning to make a name for myself at Cambridge. I was in full charge of all the music at the College; I had been invited by other College societies to play at their concerts, a rare honour; I had music published; I was conducting the whole Cambridge University Choral Club and I was in a life and surroundings that I absolutely worshipped. Then I had to cast it all aside when, like a bolt from the blue, I was called up. One Monday I was rejoicing in this life, forty-eight hours later I had said goodbye to all my friends.

Then, with the possibility of death at any time, billeted with colleagues with whom he had nothing in common, he had withdrawn into a sort of emotional 'blankness' and he worried that it might be permanent.

Though clearly not — Pearl seemed to have transformed him. In his love-struck condition, these letters showed him expressing love, admiration, vulnerability, and insights into his own character that he spelled out with a startling frankness and accuracy.

I am very sorry to tell you that I still find people rather uninteresting. They become interesting only when you are present because, I suppose, as a background they are rather blessed with the sunshine of your presence.

He is completely different from my mother, for whom people were constantly interesting.

A love affair by post is always a bit fraught. But in wartime the logistical difficulties were manifestly multiplied. In another letter he wrote:

I am spending a night at a Rest Camp about 60 miles from my destination. Tomorrow I go to within 10 miles of my destination and then heaven knows how I reach my Camp! A day or so after that I shall be sent off to where my Company is at present. It is a place where I spent 6 weeks last year; in my opinion, the filthiest and most unwholesome spot in India ... I have some fears about the facilities for posting letters. So I am writing this while I can.

The wartime context brought urgency and intensity to the romance. For the next few months they exchanged letters and got to know each other via erratic mail. Pearl asked him to tell her about his childhood, his sister, his parents. From his replies I learned things I had never heard before. He admired his stern father, an Inspector at Scotland Yard, but he didn't feel close to his mother, though she adored him. He felt extraordinarily bad about this and stressed that he tried hard not to let it show.

He and his sister Eileen, two years his junior, had been competitive as youngsters. She was clearly very bright, but he said he didn't like her very much at the time (he certainly wasn't hiding his flaws from Pearl!) His sister was also musical and was accepted into the Royal Academy of Music, for singing. But when the War began, she joined the War Office. Fortunately, before he was shipped out to India, they were stationed quite close to each other, near Cheltenham. Their social lives intersected and their relationship improved so that he felt a new warmth towards her.

In fact it was due to difficulties of getting to visit his sister that he bought his first car. It was a bright yellow Hudson Straight Eight, an American classic, rather flashy for a man like my father. Aged 20, it didn't occur to him that he might need a licence and insurance. In his excitement, he took it out for a spin immediately. Having given his batman-orderly a turn at the wheel, at night, in blackout conditions, they crashed head-on into a RAF bus. The driver wasn't injured, but Dad was hospitalised for a few days with facial lacerations. He lost his two front teeth, wrote off the car, incurred many costs, had to replace his uniform, pay lawyers and narrowly avoided serious charges.

All this information was contained in long letters written to Pearl in 1943. Then, throughout 1944, there was relative silence, very few letters. Perhaps they have been lost or perhaps he was in the thick of some Chindit action in Burma. The censors would not permit locations to be revealed for fear of assisting the enemy if mail were intercepted. I hoped that his passionate letters were not censored in the Censor Office in which my mother was working. I think not. And I gathered from the correspondence that they managed to meet a few times when he had leave.

At some stage there must have been a proposal of marriage, but it was not in the letters. It probably happened during one of their infrequent meetings. But then I opened a small pile of letters dated from early 1945. The tone changed: there was despair and urgency. They were in the midst of an emotional and logistical tangle. By mid-1945 there were letters written every few days, trying to navigate a pathway to a marriage. There were so many hurdles. It emerged that they had decided not to tell Pearl's parents of their intention to marry until they knew that it was even possible. The Army had to give permission. But Dad's Commanding Officer was away on leave in England and out of contact.

Hovering in the background was the daunting task of telling the parents of Pearl's former fiancé. This had to be done soon, but Pearl's parents must be told first. As was customary, Dad wrote to them asking their permission. They were not pleased. They must have told Pearl they felt deceived by not knowing what had been going on. And they felt that the couple were rushing into it (which they were). They didn't disapprove of the match. They liked Dad. But he was very different from the happy-go-lucky first fiancé, who was from their own Anglo-Indian community. And they knew that ditching someone who was away at war, albeit perhaps not alive, was a serious transgression. All of them would have to weather the societal disapproval. Above all, the sadness for Pearl's parents was the sure knowledge that they would lose their beloved daughter to England once the War ended.

Pearl undertook the agonising task of visiting the ex-fiancé's parents. I gleaned how this went from Dad's responses. In one letter he said he was 'So relieved that the visit went well and that they were kind to you.' In another, he referred to the difficulty for you of 'dealing with his things'. Meaning what? Had he left prized possessions with Pearl until his return? Were there gifts he had given her that she felt obliged to return to his parents? Was there an engagement ring? Or did his parents ask her to help sort out his things at their house, presuming after years of silence, that he was dead? I don't know the answers to any of these questions.

There were also Dad's parents in England to be informed via slow and unreliable post. Pearl wrote to them too. They each anxiously awaited his father's replies. I gathered that he responded rather coolly — not negative but not hugely enthusiastic. Dad reassured Pearl that this was just the aloof Britton manner, that she shouldn't take it personally (how could she not?!)

An added pressure was that troops would be repatriated back to England as soon as the War ended. They all knew this was imminent. If they were not already married, Dad would be shipped back alone and Pearl would have to travel to England later, by herself — if she could get a passage — to marry there. A risky proposition for a young woman who barely knew her husband-to-be. And who had never left India. It would mean marrying in England without the family and friends with whom she was very close. And Dad's family didn't sound particularly welcoming.

Dad applied for an extra two weeks leave to visit all the affected people in Bombay and to make proper arrangements for a wedding. His leave application was knocked back. He applied to stay on in India for an extra two weeks before being repatriated. That was knocked back.

So, all was on tenterhooks: telegrams, letters back and forth, letters crossing, misunderstandings. And presumably the backdrop remained: his military duties, in harsh billets, with harsh weather. The uncertainty, the tenuousness, the emotional strain was enormous. I'm guessing that, for a reticent man, he was unused to the explicit and turbulent emotions he was experiencing. He was literally collapsing with worry. He was admitted to a field hospital for a few days, given tests for his symptoms — no appetite, loss of weight, not sleeping. The field doctor proclaimed it a 'nervous collapse'. He said the only medicine he could prescribe was marriage and happiness. Dad wrote to Pearl saying he needed her not just for his happiness, but also for his health ('no pressure', as we would ironically say today).

On top of the emotional pressures, there were other practical matters. If there were to be a church wedding, banns had to be read three weeks in advance, and a special licence to wed obtained. The timing was crucial with the repatriation date looming. Dad bravely chose an engagement ring and somehow had it delivered to Pearl. It consisted of nine alternating little rubies and diamonds in a flat, square setting that he decided would suit her petite frame and long, slim fingers. He was right. I have this ring and have just passed it on to my daughter who has long, slim fingers. A wedding dress had to be ordered and made, a reception organised. Most of all, Pearl's parents needed to be placated and reassured.

The pile of anxious letters flowing from Burma, or northern India, via post box addresses in Dehra Dun or Simla, then on to Bombay, revealed the heartache and confusion they were each suffering. At one stage Pearl was clearly so distressed by the strain that Dad wrote to say he couldn't bear to think of her so unhappy, nor her parents so unhappy. He suggested that perhaps he should do the 'honourable' thing and withdraw from the scene and disappear back to England. Broken hearted.

Then I found a letter that alluded to another potential spanner in the works. Pearl's father asks whether Dad had told his parents in England that his wife-to-be is Anglo-Indian. The sub-text, as Dad spelled out in his letter, was that they should know the potential for a throw-back, dark-skinned grandchild. This was the very same spanner we were to experience in 1954 when we applied to come to Australia. But I was surprised to read it coming from her half-Indian father. It showed how sensitive an issue it was that a father would be anxious for his daughter, going off to be with strangers in England, that they may not approve, may not treat her kindly. He was anticipating a possible problem, as parents often do for their children, worrying for her future happiness.

Things teetered on a knife-edge for months, then weeks, then days. But in the end, it did resolve. Dad was granted two weeks leave after all — it would take him at least two days to get to Bombay, the same again to get back to his regiment afterwards. That would allow, at most, only 10 days to finalise arrangements, be married and be together before parting again. It worked out. They were married on 30 August 1945 at St Mary's Church, Parel.

The reception was at the Taj Hotel in what is now the Sea Lounge, on the first floor, overlooking the Arabian Sea. This is where Sue and I had a cool drink on our first day in India. In the blue suitcase I found the menu for the wedding lunch — all the dishes were French, presumably a nod to cosmopolitan sophistication. The wedding photos showed a good-looking couple cutting a traditional three-tiered wedding cake, my mother slim and elegant in white silk crepe in fashionable forties-style, my father in uniform, looking handsomely Errol Flynn-ish. For the last four years of his life, in an aged-care home in Melbourne, Dad had a silver-framed wedding photo in pride of place in his room. When he was dying in hospital, we brought it to be beside him.

After a few days in Bombay, my father returned to his regiment as required, awaiting repatriation (with his new wife) to England. But he told his Commanding Officer that he would like to stay on in India for another six months. He felt that they should be together in Pearl's territory for a while, acclimatising to married life before the extra strain of a new country. We know he loved India and was a bit reluctant to return to England. He was in luck:

> I think my CO owed me a favour or two for looking after his girlfriends in Mussoorie. More than once during the War he'd said to me: 'I say, be a dear old trout and go up to Mussoorie and take Edith or Ann out to a dance for me.'

So my parents-to-be went to Mussoorie, in the foothills of the Himalayas, for an extended honeymoon. My father had been appointed Military Commandant, thanks to the good offices of his philandering CO. They lived with seven servants and my mother had her first experience of snow. Dad hired a piano and for the first time in years began to play again. He told us of Italian prisoners of war in tears of joy when he played Italian arias. And Mum found companions for painting and drawing expeditions in the beautiful surrounding hills and mountains.

One afternoon they went to see a film at the local cinema. They were the only people in the audience but, because my father was the Commandant, the cinema manager felt he couldn't cancel the showing. Instead, he screened it at double speed, including standing for God Save the King at the end!

Lt Col Henry Gordon Creed, 1812 - 1877, grandson of Sir James Creed, MP, Director of East India Company. Henry's twin brother Richard was killed in action in India

Aurelia Cecilia Creed, 1829 - 1905, eldest daughter of Marquis de Bourbel de Montpinçon. Henry and Aurelia had ten children

Son Louis James St Clair Creed, with his Indian wife, Mabel, and four children, Charles (top left), Edward (Pearl's father), Nellie and Etty

Mabel Creed with her two daughters, Nellie and Etty. These studio portraits were taken in Bangalore. Mabel was an orphan rescued by an English family who lived near the Creeds

Searching for a Creed headstone in Bangalore Christian Cemetery, 2002

Headstone of Louis James StClair Creed, born Herts. England 1853, Died in India 1917. His mother is here referred to as Cecilia Aurelia while on other documents, such as the French family tree and painted portraits, she is named as Aurelia

The Creed family, Pearl at far right, aged about 18, half-sister Blanche on left, younger brother Louis and youngest sister Hope

Pearl, 1940, aged 19, with her mother and young sister, Hope. I wonder if this outfit was copied from English Vogue and made in the tailor's shop below their apartments

Wartime Pearl, aged 22

The badges issued to Pearl during the War: at left, in Greek, 'We Work in Silence', issued for British Censor Office Staff. An American serviceman, in a bus queue beside Pearl, decided it read 'South Epsom Salts'! The other badge, Bombay Women's Volunteer Corps (BWVC), was issued when she helped in a canteen for servicemen

Pearl wrote and illustrated regular pages for The Illustrated Weekly of India, one of the largest circulation papers in the world. When she looked back at them later in life she described them as rather 'childish'. She was only 20 at the time! She wrote under a pseudonym for FilmIndia as her parents would have disapproved. The advertisement for Geralds dates from her time as an art school student and unpaid apprentice at Protos Advertising

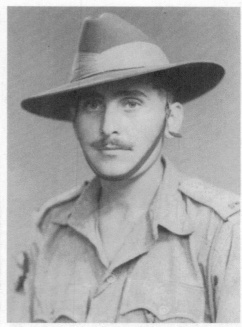

Donald Britton, Captain in 2nd Duke of Wellington Regiment. Bombay studio portraits. Soldiers had photo portraits taken for family back home, in case of their death. These were taken early in his War years

Now Major Britton, the bloom of youth and innocence has somewhat faded. Taken 1944, thinner but still handsome

Wedding photo outside St Mary's Church,
Parel, Bombay, August 1945

And a lighter moment!

Cutting the cake at the wedding reception, Taj Mahal Hotel,
Pearl's father Edward Creed on left

Honeymoon and posting as Military Commandant in Mussoorie in the Himalayan foothills. This photo was taken at Chaubattia, another military rest station nearby. The six-month sojourn in the hills might have helped Pearl acclimatise, ready for the bleak post-War winters ahead in England

16: The Whims of Whiteness

Inevitably, the six-month honeymoon in the foothills of the Himalayas came to an end and my parents had to return to England. They were still very young: Pearl was 24, Donald 26. The adjustment can't have been easy for either of them. It meant a return to being an impoverished university student in 'digs' in Cambridge, my father now six years older than when he left his studies, carrying a few battle scars and a new (and foreign) wife.

For my mother, as someone of British-Indian upbringing, England was the backdrop of her imagination. The images in her head, the poetry, the art, the history — all were British. She was about to live in the very city in which the school exams she sat — far away in an Indian school in Poona — had been created and marked. The lure of the 'home country' was probably quite exciting for a young Anglo-Indian, despite removal from her family and everything she was accustomed to. Nevertheless, she had to leave a demonstrative, warm and fun-loving family. Maybe her boarding school experience helped her make this break? And she was with a man she loved.

Cambridge is beautiful but also known to be a cold, windswept part of the country. The immediate post-War years in England were particularly cold, food rationing coupons were needed for staples, while many foods were simply unavailable. My parents were in student accommodation in Emmanuel College, not heated, on the third floor of an austere red-brick late-Victorian building. The elderly Professor in the flat below was kindly in his gruff way. They attended the famous May balls and parties where charades were played in Latin.

Pearl had no idea how to cook and had barely been inside a kitchen. That was the servants' domain. My father had to teach her how to boil an egg. Her first attempt was simply to pour boiling water over it. Then she had to learn to make stews from indeterminate bits of gristly meat, bulked up with potatoes and turnips. Ugh … it must have been ghastly after the plenitude to which she was accustomed.

And I wonder if she suffered slights, remarks about her olive colour and her Anglo-Indian accent. She joined art classes, made friends. One was Irena Newton-John whose husband, Brin, had a wonderful baritone voice and he and Dad often performed Lieder together. He was a fluent German-speaker and had been in Intelligence during the War. He returned to Cambridge with a German wife who possibly found it more difficult in post-War Britain than my mother. Anyway — there was a bond that led to both families later emigrating to Australia on the same ship.

At Cambridge, when I was born, there was something of a stir. I was the first baby born to a married undergraduate living in College. Where could a washing line for nappies be placed? Could my pram be parked on a Fellows lawn when my father was only an undergraduate? Perhaps there were notes on these weighty matters in College Council deliberations in October 1947. The parking of the pram mattered because these were the days when new parents followed the advice of a Dr Truby King who declared that, after regular four-hourly feeds, babies should be wrapped warmly and placed in a pram at the bottom of the garden. Regardless of the weather! Rain, hail or snow were all acceptable. Only fog was deemed bad for their health — then babies could be brought inside.

After obtaining a double first, my father took up a teaching position at Winchester College. Again, new friendships were forged and the community of a public school provided instant support. My younger sister Cara was born during this time. We loved hearing Dad's story of becoming accidentally locked in Winchester Cathedral at night where he had been practising the organ. To attract attention, he depressed the loudest organ stop, wedged a match into it to keep it playing, clambered down from the organ loft, and waited until someone heard the horrendous din and came to unlock him.

The War had opened horizons that made my father restless in England. After the heat of the East, he hated the gloomy cold of England and suffered terribly from chilblains on feet and hands (disabling for a pianist and organist). He applied for a job in Australia and, after being interviewed by Sir William McKie, an Australian who was then Organist and Master of Choristers at Westminster Abbey, he was appointed Director of Music at Melbourne Grammar School, a leading boys' private school in Victoria, Australia.

That was 1954, when the reality of the White Australia Policy intervened: Mum's Indian blood was an impediment to their emigration to Australia, overcome only by her paying full fare. Ironically, my mother was later employed by the slightly Orwellian-sounding News and Information Bureau, an Australian Government body tasked with telling the stories of successful Colombo Plan migrants, most from Asian backgrounds. In the 1980s, and still officially a British citizen, I belatedly applied to be 'naturalised' in Australia. I was interviewed and approved by a very nice man who was 100 per cent Indian. The form had asked for mother's place of birth. Like my father three decades earlier, I put 'Bombay'. With a happy smile he said, 'That's my city,' accompanied by the characteristically Indian sideways nod of the head.

Some years ago, in a further twist, I applied to the Indian Consulate in Melbourne for status as a 'Person of Indian Origin', or Overseas Citizen of India. I was effectively told I didn't have enough Indian blood! My mother had had too much! How the wheels turn. Such are the whims of immigration laws. I am still stewing over this, since the guidelines say that having a parent, or even grandparent, born and raised in India provides grounds for eligibility. My mother was patently born and raised in India and I have all the documentary evidence required. She clearly had Indian blood, one-quarter, blood that caused her to be penalised by the Australian authorities (who had upped her Indianness to one-third) under the White Australia Policy. She had been proudly part-Indian all through her personal and professional life.

Yet each time I submitted the required evidence, all duly JP certified, to the Indian Consulate in Melbourne I was told there was a new obstacle. Their first response was: though my mother was 'born and raised' she might have been 'just a resident Britisher'. Then I was told my records didn't go back far enough to prove the Indian blood (i.e. my elusive great-grandmother Mabel). Then I was told my mother's birth certificate doesn't have her name on it (it doesn't — her parents seem to have decided on a name when she was three weeks old — yet her name appears on her baptismal certificate, which I have also submitted).

Then they said: 'If only you could supply either her Indian passport or a wartime Ration Card.' Since ration cards were only issued to Indian citizens, they would apparently count as decisive evidence. To my amazement, I did find her Ration Card in the blue suitcase. To their amazement too, it seemed, because finally I was told of a new reason for rejection — 'Aha!' they must have thought, 'she can't argue with this one' — as I was born in 1947 this was outside some cut-off date for applying for overseas Indian status. Why didn't they tell me this from the outset? It would have saved me an awful lot of time and trouble.

Since my mother died, I have felt more strongly about trying to keep alive the family connection with India. Although my claim is legitimate, it's clearly more sentimental than essential. It illustrates the quixotic and capricious nature of identity. Too much, too little, not coloured enough, too coloured, right documents, wrong documents. If this was hard for me, who didn't really need it, consider the plight of refugees, lost in a bureaucratic maelstrom without any papers at all.

17: Westernisation and Miracles:
Pearl in India after a Nine-Year Absence:

Moving to Australia in 1954 was made more enticing for my mother because the trip by sea from England enabled a stop in India to be with her family again, nine years after leaving. After a few days ashore, my father sailed on to Australia to start work and find us a house, while we broke journey to stay with my grandparents for three months. My memories of this time are vague, mostly prompted by small fading photographs: two fair-haired English girls, aged three and six, with a snake charmer, or playing with the servants, or getting new frocks made at the tailor, or posing more formally with grandparents, squinting into the sun with lush-looking plants as backdrop.

Among other photos and documents in the blue suitcase, I found a large 'Golden Jubilee Edition' of Filmindia magazine, dated April 1954. Inside, I discovered a long article, with illustrations, signed 'Hyacinth', which I knew was my mother's pseudonym. Referring to Indian Independence, gained in 1947, her article was entitled 'The Post-Freedom Indian She?':

Eight years spent in an orderly Western country had left me thirsty for the insanitary charms of an Indian street: the suicidal wanderings of the Indian pedestrian; the discordant cries of the vendors; but above all for the sight of Indian women going on their modest way, self-consciously elegant as only they can be. To think of living again in an India made more Eastern by virtue of its independence! Oh for the wonderful hazards of dodging misplaced paan juice again!

Bombay, here I come …

And what did I find? An India even more Westernized than the one I had left behind. Here was Bombay, here was the familiar dirt, the dust, the seething masses, but here also were bigger and better Cadillacs; more and pinker Europeans, and over everything a pseudo Anglo-American veneer.

The touch of West was on everything — but more especially on the women. Where were the delicately shuffling Indian women, their carriage made more graceful by the restraining sari? Here were women stepping out in the unmistakeable longer stride of the long-emancipated — here were Indian, and particularly Parsi, girls wearing dresses and shorts, and when they were wearing saris, wearing them in a more figure-revealing way.

The article spanned three full pages and was interspersed with her illustrations. It went on to discuss the use of cosmetics — 'It's almost a conceit to think one's face looks good enough without it' — and, under the subtitle 'Mass Uplift', she commented on a 'uniform voluptuousness' of bosoms. She wondered if the government was adding something to the flour, illustrated with a sketch of a glamorous woman in a sari, swathed lightly over an hourglass figure and cleavage-revealing *choli*.

She commented on the Indian proclivity for dressing the same way, following the same fashion from hair to toe. It interested me to read her views then, because Sue and I often comment on something like this even now. That there are relatively few templates in women's dress — if they stick with Indian garb — two main outfits: either the sari with *choli*, or the *salwar kameez* (the 'pyjama suit'). Details matter a lot within these templates, and this does create variations. But there is still a sameness to the basic outline. It is a lovely sameness: we would be happy to dress in salwar suits ourselves, as they are comfortable and compassionate to figure imperfections.

In the bigger cities this is changing, especially in the last five years, as more women are wearing jeans and *kurtis* (a tighter, shorter version of the traditional Indian *kurta*). Indian men have long given up on Indian dress, opting in the main for European trousers and shirts, often in rather nasty polyester-looking creams and browns. This is such a pity as men in traditional, crisply starched, long white *kurtas* — often paired with black Nehru-collared waistcoats — look terrific. And surely they must be more comfortable than their majority counterparts in Western trousers, belts, shirts and ties.

Dotted among the pages of my mother's article were also paid advertisements. One was for a face skin whitener — a revolutionary new miracle beauty bleach that made you fairer in four weeks. (Shades of my Creed ancestor's white lead, mixed with vinegar, lethal, but oh so lucrative!) Unfortunately, skin whitening persists over the centuries, and over continents, to remain a big business.

There was an ad for Castophene compound castor oil chocolates, a delicious laxative. And on an earlier page I found Mammytone — a modern bust-builder, a 'hormone-vitamin' treatment. It didn't say whether you rub it in or swallow it, but it 'never fails to beautify your bust to fascinating form'. It developed, lifted, rebuilt, rejuvenated and remoulded the contours to exotic curves. Not only that, but it went on to offer five different versions for varying breast deficiencies — one mixture to develop and swell a flat bust 'to perfection', another to tighten and lift sagging and flabby bust, also to perfection, another mixture would reduce over-developed bulky-heavy bust. Miracles indeed.

I wondered if her parents knew by the time of this visit in 1954 that Pearl was writing for the film magazine? They had disapproved of her film reviewing when she was young and single, during the War. Perhaps a decade later, it was more acceptable: the film industry more mainstream and their daughter now a respectably married woman. But Pearl stuck to her earlier pseudonym and I wondered if readers welcomed her back.

It also interested me that, as a girl of six, I hadn't noticed that my mother was working when we were visiting India, presumably meeting publishers' demands and deadlines. One wouldn't expect a six-year-old to notice, let alone recall later, but it did make me reflect on how little my own children know about what work I managed to do while they were young, with few childcare options and no grandparents living nearby to help. I think how little, in general, one's children know about parents' early working lives, apart from the 'highlight' episodes that are told and re-told as family stories. Or told at funerals.

Sue and I have started a late career that takes us to India. Our now-adult children will remember this part, but they are unlikely to remember anything much earlier, I suppose. Unless we bore them with stories. Or write them, as my mother did. The written episodes from her life are wonderful to have, but it took me until my late fifties to appreciate them. I have spent years trying to find a way to meld her stories with my own experiences of contemporary India. Some say our writing styles are so similar that it is hard to tell who is talking if I don't make it clear. I'm not sure if that is true, but would be happy if it were.

But back to Bombay in 1954. After full immersion in Indian life for a few months, the wrench of leaving family again must have been painful for my mother. And a new set of adjustments awaited in Australia. She was young, of course, and my father was eager for our arrival. It was an adventure, but it still required courage to set off across the world to a fairly unknown continent in the '50s, a very long sea journey away.

I seem to recall we clambered aboard a ship in Bombay Harbour, mother and two daughters, with calamine lotion and make-up covering our chicken pox. Do I really remember this or is it a story I've been told?

18: India Routines and Charming Irregularities

The business Sue and I started has developed its annual rhythms. We invite a mailing list of customers to an annual two-week event in a rented shopfront each November. Such ventures hadn't been labelled 'pop-up shops' back then, so we were trail-blazers of a sort and had a lot of trouble persuading estate agents to bother with us.

Throughout each year, interspersed with research projects (me) or architectural projects (Sue), we work with pattern and sample makers in Melbourne until we feel we have the garments and the range more or less right. In late February, we pack the bottom of our suitcases with these rather heavy paper patterns, plus some made-up samples, some clothing and footwear for ourselves, and gifts for our Indian friends. A major item in our suitcases is a bulky pharmacopoeia of 'what-ifs?' — what if I get this or need that? — covering all possible adverse health events. And, most importantly, a couple of cardboard casks of Australian wine. With all this checked in, we collapse into the seats for our annual flight to India.

A central part of the business is the use of handwoven fabrics. These are woven for us, to our colour specifications, mostly in the village of Mangalgiri, about 200 kilometres from Hyderabad.

The lead-time can be several months, so it requires careful planning. The cotton yarn is first dyed in boiling vats, then turned and twisted by hand so the colour is evenly distributed. The yarn is dried, then dipped in starch, which helps cement the colour and also gives it a slight sheen. The yarn is then polished by stringing it across large frames in the red-dirt laneways of the village. Family members rush up and down the yarn in pairs, holding either end of huge polishing brushes. Yarn is then spun on spinning wheels, made famous by Gandhi and featured on the Indian flag, a reminder of a fast-disappearing ethos. Finally, these coloured threads are woven in pit looms: men sit with their legs in holes in the ground, working the foot pedals while their hands play nimbly above the ground on ancient-looking looms. Like playing a church organ.

These are important artisan skills, passed down through families, skills that risk being swamped by synthetic yarns and power looms: faster, more efficient, more consistent and with predictable outcomes — that's what most big buyers want. By contrast, handcrafted goods require patience and tolerance. All sorts of things delay production, the weather being the foremost. Dyes won't set if it's too hot or humid or wet. Polishing can't be done in the rain. Monsoons interrupt for weeks on end. Family weddings take out more days. Illness. Births. Deaths. Festivals. A never-ending list of interruptions.

Mangalgiri fabric is usually woven in *thanns* — the word for a piece of running fabric, about 10 to 12 metres in length, folded. When these arrive and are unfolded, it's a bit like a soil core sample: there may be variations in the colour, or in the tension of the threads, or we find bits of fluff, the odd chicken feather or grain of rice. We picture the family occasions that have interrupted weaving, the power failures, the spicy lunch breaks. Lives lived. But we do need to have the fabric washed before it's made up!

All the vagaries of the weaving process and of the weavers' lives result in what we describe as 'charming irregularities' on the MOTI swing tags we attach to each garment. We think these variations add to the charm, and certainly the authenticity, of handwoven goods. A more florid label at Fabindia reads: 'Handloom means a glorious uncertainty when it comes to uniformity.' However, there are times when the irregularities are not especially glorious or charming and are just plain faults that render a portion of the fabric unusable. Working our way around these is one of the many challenges we have learned to deal with.

Handmade goods are humbling. We once queried why some resin bangles were taking so long. They featured an intricate 'cut-out' pattern. We had assumed they would be pressed out in a machine of some sort. 'Madam,' our supplier said gravely, 'they are carved with a very small saw by hand. He can only do two a day.'

We sometimes use pintucked fabric or meterage that has been machined all over in parallel rows. In Western countries, and probably in China, there are machines with seven or eleven needles that can stitch multiple parallel rows in one go. In India our suppliers do it with a single needle, guided by their hand and their eye. If the rows are not quite straight, it adds to the interest. Or so we believe. Some of our fabrics are stitched all over, by hand, using a simple running stitch, which renders them a bit like that stalwart of old-fashioned summer clothing and bedcovers: seersucker.

We stocked linen gauze stoles that took a week for the cord-work embroidery to be completed on each piece. The *kantha* shawls and saris from Shamlu's girls in Kolkata can each take months to embroider.

We began by importing the handwoven fabrics from India and getting our clothing range made up in Melbourne. This went on for our first two years, when we were rag-trade neophytes and thought it best to keep an eye on things. It was also at a time when the garment manufacturing industry in Australia was going through tough times, with most people outsourcing to China. We wanted to support local manufacturers and thought they might welcome our business. But instead, we found it induced nothing but irascible complaints: 'too few', 'too complex', 'too fiddly', 'sorry, but we won't be able to do it again next time'.

So we went offshore as well. But finding a suitable manufacturer in India also proved difficult: we were too big for a small tailoring person and too small for the larger manufacturers. Eventually, through various introductions, we were delighted to find Sheila — more of whom later.

19: A Missing Nightie, Wiring and Other Practical Matters ...

Regular trips to a country like India enable endless fascinating insights. On our first trip, we visited the famous laundry ghats in Mumbai and marvelled at how clothes could emerge white and pristine from greenish-looking greasy soapsuds set in the midst of rampaging traffic and fumes. Mostly, they do return looking thoroughly clean. With the inconvenient exception of my white nightie that disappeared in the Oberoi Hotel's washing system.

Front-desk girls, looking elegant in beautiful saris, were not especially helpful. We have continued to notice this in India and imagine it may be a symptom of the 'carefully calibrated hierarchy of status' I quoted earlier. Do they see themselves as a cut above the rest of the staff? And apparently some of the guests too? But we enjoy the names on their enamelled name tags.

This particular morning at the front desk, Twinkle was telling me that they doubted my nightie could possibly have disappeared from their very superior hotel system, but they will lend me a replacement. Next morning it was Dipti's turn to haughtily dismiss the problem. Was it still circulating in the ghats? I imagine it has found a good home somewhere ...

After the first few years we sought out three-star-ish hotels, less exorbitantly costly than the five+ stars. Business hotels more appropriate to our new status as business people.

Once, when taking the lift to our rooms in a hotel in Hyderabad, I noticed a brass plaque that read: 'Hotel for The Profound Businessman'. Every day we wonder if we are Profound Businessmen. Is it possible to put these two words even in the same sentence? It seemed that the hotel thought so, as the brass plaques graced all the entrances and every lift. There was a pianist playing vaguely familiar Western cruise-liner music in the lobby — just vaguely familiar because the piano was completely out of tune. This is the sort of eccentricity we like ...

Several such hotels later, I can report that we did feel a bit irritated when we had to prop up the hairdryer plug on two books on the floor so that it remained in hopeful contact with some electric current. Once, when we asked for a non-smoking room, we were told that: 'All rooms are smoking and non-smoking both.'

We complain when there is only hot water coming out of the shower (not terrific when it's 40 degrees Celsius outside). In one hotel there was no water at all coming from the taps in my room. The desk told me, 'Only ask us, madam, 10 minutes before you want water and we will send same through the pipes.' Now I understand why hotels often say in their advertising: 'hot and/or cold water 24 hours'. You have to learn not to assume.

I took some friends on a trip to India. Accustomed mainly to plush five-star hotels and first-class travel, it was not easy for them to cope in Jaisalmer where, as bad luck would have it, it rained hard and solidly for all three days of our visit. Liquid cow manure ran down the narrow streets of this spectacular Fort City in the Thar desert near Pakistan.

We were staying (against heritage advice) in a small hotel set into one corner of the fort, each room idiosyncratically different. Narrow, winding stairways were cut into the fabulous yellow Jaisalmer granite and sandstone. The hotel consisted of only seven rooms plus terraces with spectacular views. But our friends copped a rat in their room, then the rain found its way in to soak their bedding and, to top it off, the power shorted and there was a fire. Oh dear ... charm sometimes doesn't quite cut the mustard (as the Indian newspapers would say, fond of charmingly old-fashioned turns of phrase).

Mouldering carpets, ear-shattering air-conditioners, a hotel room with no windows — these can all be par for the course in India's three- and four-star hotels. But if your food waiter asked you this: 'And who is your dinner, madam?' I would guess you've never been asked such a philosophical question in a Western restaurant. Of course, he meant, 'How is your dinner?' He went on to ask, 'Why were you born?' After a momentary pause, I knew I could forgo an existential discussion and answer with my place of birth ...

Dripping taps and smelly carpets are worth putting up with for these moments of delight. Does this sound patronising? It's not meant or felt that way. There is genuine joy in language slip-ups and I must be making many in my pathetic attempts at Hindi.

Electrical wiring could be, and probably is, the subject of a dedicated photo essay — spaghetti is more orderly. It's a miracle that the power works at all. It's more of a miracle that you don't see people, especially children, fried on wires.

In the rain in Jodhpur, we lurched down a slippery, wet, cobbled alleyway, reaching out instinctively until we realised that it was electrical wires we were hanging onto for balance. We've seen wet laundry hanging out to dry on exposed wires.

We feel quite sophisticated in our mastery of 'the electricals' in India: we have even graduated to sticking a pencil into the power point to override the earth and enable our appliances to work ...

It is said that, in Delhi, 35 per cent of the power is pirated. Apart from the ethics and economics of this, the dangers of gimcrack amateur wiring are too awful to contemplate. People living on the streets or in shanties sling a wire with a hook onto nearby powerlines to run their TV sets overnight, then decouple in the morning. Tim Flannery reports in his book *Atmosphere of Hope*,[13] that in Old Delhi people modify their TV remote controls to switch power meters on and off to avoid electricity charges. The widespread installation of cable TV has made the wiring blight even worse. Installers simply drape wires over trees, over neighbouring houses, across streets, with no compunction or restraint. As long as the connection is made, a fee can be charged and the customer can access more than 850 TV channels available in India. Everyone is content.

Even legitimate paid use of electricity is whimsical. In one major blackout in 2013, 660 million people were left with no power. In many cities, power is routinely rationed, businesses tying their output around using computers or machinery when it is their turn. This leads to the ubiquitous use of rackety back-up generators. A visit to somewhere like Lajpat Nagar

---

13 Text, 2016.

market in Delhi can be overwhelmingly noisy and fumy as each stallholder powers up ancient machines to generate power and light.

In an upmarket showroom in Sharpur Jat, looking at lovely cashmere gauze scarves, we had to 'chase' the power around the room. We were all set up with goods to admire on a table at one end of the showroom when the lights went out. No windows with natural light to help. But there was a light still on over another table. So we moved a pile of beautiful scarves, plus our handbags, water bottles, notebooks and calculators to that table, only to have the same thing happen there. Three moves later ... it is hard to be efficient in India, much less reach 'Profound Businessman' status.

20: Please Be Signing Your Backside

On our first visit to India we were, like most tourists, overwhelmed by this huge and chaotic country and especially the confusion that reigns in airports. Delhi airport in those days was a disgrace for a national capital. Ceiling panels missing, loose wires hanging out, dirty walls, dirty immigration booths, completely charmless surroundings. And charmless personnel too.

Our flight arrived quite late, but one of the treats on our itinerary was to stay at the famous Imperial Hotel. Built in the 1930s, The Imperial has a wonderful driveway lined with 24 elegant king palms. This entrance sweeps off Janpath, formerly known as Queensway, second only in importance to Kingsway (now Rajpath) in Sir Edward Lutyens' grand vision of New Delhi.

The Imperial Hotel has been the venue of choice for visiting Royalty, heads of state and other dignitaries and celebrities. On its famous verandah, with its turquoise-tiled columns and capacious wicker chairs, one can imagine confabulations between Jinnah and Gandhi, Nehru and Mountbatten, as they nutted out plans for Independence and the Partition of India. This was, as the website puts it, a rare space for 'an Indo-British rubbing of shoulders'. Photographs on the walls attest to this fortuitous friction. We learn that Lord Willingdon inaugurated the hotel in 1936, the same person who later ordered the arrest of Gandhi and after whom my mother's family apartment block in Bombay was named.

Staying at The Imperial for two nights was a part of the travel package we negotiated in Australia, and we knew it was an expensive part. By the time we got to the hotel, it was well past bedtime and we were exhausted. We were ushered into our room, two nice plump-looking single beds, bedside lights warmly glowing, a big bathroom with marble floors and a huge claw-footed bath. It all looked welcoming and enticing. We unpacked and finally clambered into our beds at about midnight for some quiet reading before sleep.

Knock, knock, knock. Constant, slightly muffled, knocking noises. Impossible to ignore in the quiet of night. We kept reading, hoping it would stop. It didn't. Like tinnitus, it was a regular noise that can't be ignored once one is conscious of it. It seemed to be coming from outside our window. We drew aside the heavy curtains but could see only blackness. As our eyes became accustomed to the dark, we realised that what we were looking at was not a nice view of the famous hotel gardens but sheets of corrugated iron flush up against our window. Renovations in progress.

But why noise at this hour? We rang the front desk. 'What is the knocking noise? It's two in the morning, it's impossible to sleep. Can you get it stopped?'

'There is nothing, madam, no building works happening at this time of night.'

The knocking continued. Another hour. We rang again.

'There is nothing, madam.'

111

We demanded to speak to the Manager. We asked him to come to our room and listen.

So an immaculately uniformed man appeared, ready to confront two tired late-middle-aged women in their nighties who are imagining noises. But he reluctantly had to admit there was knocking. With no explanation or apology, he made a dignified exit from our room.

We gathered that he sent staff to investigate and they informed us that a husband and wife, what we would call 'brickies labourers', were cleaning bricks ready for the next day's work. It would be stopped. I think this was supposed to conjure up a nice simple human story.

But we threw on jackets and went outside, where we discovered a large construction area, complete with floodlights. Bricks were certainly being cleaned and a major renovation project was in progress. Many people were working, in the middle of the night! Had they closed the rooms nearby or were other guests trying to sleep without complaining?

Eventually, the Duty Manager offered us another room. By then we were too tired to re-pack and move our toiletries and clothing. So at 3 am we padded barefoot in our nightclothes down the corridors — the width of the corridors is one of the fabulous features of this hotel — to another room to finish off an unsatisfactory sleep. Not an ideal solution, but we had been dealt with for the night.

In the morning we scuttled back to our original room, still clad only in nighties, while elegantly attired tourists and well-dressed businessmen looked askance. It was an undignified start to our first day in Delhi. But we sat for breakfast in a beautiful internal courtyard with sumptuous arrays of patisserie and fruit, including huge glass bowls of glistening pomegranate seeds. A sweet scent pervaded The Imperial Hotel, wafting from magnificent urns full of massed tuberoses.

We were informed that there was someone to see us in a waiting area near reception. There we found an agitated man, literally sweating with anxiety. His hair was that strange orangey colour you sometimes see on grey-haired Indian men who dye it with henna. It emerged that he had changed our travellers' cheques at the airport when we flew in the night before. He had accidentally given us an American-dollar exchange rate instead of the Australian dollar in which our cheques were denominated. The Aussie rate was then significantly lower than the US rate.

No wonder he was distressed — he would have to personally make good the extra rupees he had given us in error, a major impost for a foreign-exchange employee. Shamefully, we hadn't even noticed our bonanza. We had been too entranced by his words when he asked us to sign the back of the cheques: 'Please be signing your backsides.' Now, overcome with gratitude at our not hesitating to hand back the money, he said, 'God bless you both,' and rushed back to his office.

Some years later we were staying at a hotel called The Claridges — we always liked the added definite article — a four-ish star hotel built in the 1950s. We had taken to this hotel as moderately priced, not too pretentious and conveniently located. We were told that The Beatles once stayed here. A classic structure with a nice curved staircase, an attractive lawn and garden and plenty of comings and goings.

Again, before we learnt to use guest-houses, we would book it as part of a package via a large Indian travel agency. This seemed to mean allocating us the worst rooms in the hotel: rooms with no windows, noisy rooms, tiny rooms — all varieties of inconvenience. But as we became more assertive, we insisted on being moved. And hence we graduated to nicer rooms overlooking a central courtyard with pool or facing the pretty gardens.

One year we were housed on the second of the three storeys. In the middle of the night, we were awakened by loud banging and knocking. It went on and on. We rang the front desk: 'Are there renovations going on? It's the middle of the night. Would you ask them to stop, please?'

'No, madam, no renovations happening in the hotel.'

'But we can hear it.'

'No, madam, you must be mistaken.'

We've heard this story before! Sue took off up the stairs in her nightie and saw jackhammers at work, arc lights on. We rang the front desk: 'Please come to our room and listen.'

So once again we had the Hotel Duty Manager dutifully sitting on a bed in our room in the early hours of the morning having to acknowledge that there was indeed something going on. Not acknowledging in so many words. No apology. He just bowed slightly and left. And maybe an hour later the noises stopped. In the morning we investigated and there was a major renovation taking place.

This was an update that resulted in the hotel's prices going up in line with a new five-star designation, precipitating our search for alternatives. It seems obscene that the cost of a hotel for one night can be so disproportionate to the wages of its employees. Or in such contrast to the poverty beyond the grand entrances of India's wonderful hotels. But that's life. And it's not only in India.

The hotels perform a central role in the life of big cities

because Indian wedding festivities often take place in these multi-starred hotels. Weddings are a feast for people-watchers. One's status and income level are aligned with the status and cost of the hotel chosen. And the number of guests matters a lot. We have often been pressed to join in. For reasons we find impossible to accept, foreign guests (especially, sadly, white ones) add some extra cachet. The Indians always look fabulous while we, and most Europeans, look dowdy and colourless by comparison. Why would they want us there? But they often insist, to the point that it seems rude to demur, and they make us feel very welcome. And just as my mother says in her writings, in India it is fine to stare. So we do. And enjoy every minute of it.

21: Life in an Indian Hill Station, 1957

'Get up quickly,' I called to the children, 'I'm going to show you Bombay."

This is my mother speaking, invited to give a radio talk soon after we returned to Melbourne from six months living in India in 1957. She continued:

I had been roused by the waking sounds of the neighbourhood. It was 5.30 am and my first morning in Bombay after years living abroad. I lay awake listening to the cacophony of yawns, mouth-rinsings, sleepy talk and children suddenly boisterously awake. Getting up, like going to bed, is a noisily public business in an Indian city.

The night before I had stood on the balcony watching the same people going to bed. The block of apartments opposite our hotel would have delighted any peeping Tom: no demure lace curtains, no discreetly turned-off lights. The very plump Goanese woman had crawled into a vast bed to lie fanning herself to sleep beside her equally plump child. The Hindu musician in the room next to hers had played a last tune on his small Indian harmonium before curling up beside it to sleep on the floor.

On the street, charpoys were brought out by some pavement sleepers. A customer sat in a tea shop, sipping his tea luxuriously from the saucer. It was midnight and a few sleepers were already on the pavement, cocoon-like in their blankets, heads covered against the heavy night air or perhaps against the spluttering noise of the car-repair business which flourished day and night in the street.

But now the sluggish night had passed, its heat tempered by the gentle whirrings of the ceiling fan. Here was morning, the crows at their early squawking. I felt a tremendous rush of excitement for this great, hot, noisy, dirty city that is Bombay.

This was the transcript of Pearl's radio talk, part of a series called Armchair Chat. We had been in India for six months staying with my grandparents while my father was on a concert tour in Russia. He would join us later. We had travelled to India by ship from Melbourne, via Sri Lanka where, in a startling introduction, I saw a man run across the Arrivals Hall with his throat cut. There were 'troubles' in what was then Ceylon. Next, we landed in Bombay, the ship's gangplank disgorging us into a different world. Three years since our first visit, my sister and I, aged six and ten, were now more conscious of the excitement, confusion and exoticism.

My grandparents had left Bombay and retired to a hill-station called Panchgani. Known for its boarding schools on the lines of the British public schools, its name refers to the five hills which surround the town. Also known now as the place where Freddy Mercury of Queen, a Parsee Anglo-Indian, went to school. Situated in the Western Ghats, the scenery is beautiful and the air is fresh. Pearl continued:

But Bombay was only one stop on our journey. We were on our way to one of India's beautiful hill-stations and to the warmth of long-missed home and family. A train trip first to Poona. One exciting part of a train journey in India is a visit to the cloakroom provided for each coach [in my own more recent experiences of toilets on trains, adjectives other than 'exciting' come to mind]. Here we were confronted with an alarming notice which read: 'Beware of thieves asking for permission to sleep on the floor of the carriage. Please don't accept food, drink or tobacco from strangers. These may be doped.' So the children then sat tight-lipped, daring anyone to offer them the smallest opium-tainted toffee!

At Poona, once a stronghold of English pukka-sahibry, we stayed at a hotel where I used to be taken to dinner as a once-monthly outing from my boarding school. In those days dinner was a solemn affair where British officers wined and dined their ladies in the manner befitting officers and gentlemen. Dinner on this occasion was equally solemn. We were the only diners in the vast room. Poona still seethes with khaki, the tropical grey-green khaki of the Indian Army. But Indian Colonel Blimps have deserted the 'dry' hotels for their regimental messes and clubs where alcohol still flows, if a trifle less freely than in British days (there was prohibition in Bombay State in the 1950s).

Our suite of rooms rattled with antiquity. Each time we crossed the room the cupboards set up a jig. The heat outside was dry and scorching so it was with some relief that I stepped into the enormous white porcelain bath. After my bath, I pulled out the plug only to find that I was marooned in a sea of soapy bath water. There was no outlet pipe. When I complained to the manager, he smiled gently and replied, 'Better luck next time!'

But neither Bombay nor Poona is the real India and as we drove through the cotton-growing area of the Deccan, we got our first close view of the real India, rural India. Here the crude wooden plough pulled by oxen still works soil impoverished by centuries of cultivation and women work in the fields beside their menfolk.

The soil turned to red as the car sped further, climbing higher to our hill-station, Panchgani in the Western Ghats. The air grew cooler, the scenery more wooded, we were there at last, 4,500 feet up and looking down on the sweltering valleys chequered with cultivation.

Many hill-stations grew up as holiday resorts for Europeans in British days. Here now in the 1950s the British are actually missed. Boarding schools still flourish as the children of India's prosperous come to be educated on English public school lines. But hotels and guest houses languish for lack of customers. A faded picture of Queen Victoria holding court with Indian princes hangs in a hotel lounge; a moochi, or shoe-maker, presents a certificate from an English Captain dated October 12, 1929. It says: 'I have always found Mahadeo to be a capable moochi. He has made five pairs of sambha leather boots to my satisfaction.'

The focal point of a hill-station is the bazaar area. Here my daughters and I spent many fascinating hours. We were a source of much puzzlement to the shopkeepers; me with my foreign-looking clothes and fair-haired children, but speaking reasonably fluent Hindi. For the first month we were taken for many a commercial ride in the arguing, bargaining game that is the bane of the tourist in India and the sport of the shopkeeper.

Later we were to become good friends. I could then say to the enormous woman who sold us vegetables, 'You gave us a bad papaya yesterday. I want another.' She would hand me another, her mountains of flesh heaving and trembling as she made a laughing reply. Gadekar the cloth merchant would tell us the local scandal: 'That man there with the pink turban, he pretends he is very poor but he made a lot of money on the black market.'

Rightoo, the tailor, complained bitterly about how little the government was doing for the 'respectable middle classes'. He had meant to be Right-O, as a symbol of prompt service, but the sign-painter had misspelled the name and Rightoo he had been forever after. He made us many dresses, copied faithfully from pictures in magazines. He cut his patterns in newspaper and could make a dress in a day. Only once he let me down. 'I am sorry, Madam,' he said, 'your dress is not made because a cow put its head in my shop and ate the pattern.'

We once stepped over a dead panther to buy our loaf of bread! The local baker was the only *shikar* of the district and whenever a marauding panther took a local goat he would set out at night to hunt it. On this occasion the panther had been laid out in front of the showcase containing buns and biscuits for all to admire. My younger daughter crushed her bun to her chest in excitement as she gazed in awe at her first panther!

We went to every local festival and there were many. These were occasions of great excitement. People from surrounding villages would swarm in to the bazaar area. Booths would be set up selling bangles, brass and copper cooking utensils, simple toys and delicious-looking pink, white and yellow sweets. My daughters would stare enviously at the children eating these sweets with complete disregard for the dust and flies. There would be music and dancing. The drummers set up an infectious

120

beat, the dancers would tie on anklets of bells and join in. We would long to join in too ...

We attended the wedding of a young servant boy whose father, Kishaba, was the chief butler at a local boarding school. He was a man of some consequence in the area. His dignity was heightened not only by his fine bearing and the number of 'chitties' or letters of recommendation he had from previous masters, but also by his set of magnificent false teeth. These added enormously to his prestige and he would discuss them or flash them on the slightest provocation.

His son the bridegroom was only 15 and the bride only 13. They drove to the wedding in a much-decorated hired car, an amazing number of women and children squeezed in with them. The less important friends and relations rode behind in bullock-carts or walked. The ceremony was held under an awning outside Kishaba's hut. The bride sat, small and frightened, a pathetic figure in her new sari, while the groom (obviously quite a wag) sat beside her grinning widely and greatly enjoying being the centre of attention.

There was a hum of conversation all through the ceremony and occasionally a brass band would break into music and be silenced as quickly by a stern look from the priest. He conducted the ceremony in Marathi but when a small boy started to argue loudly with his mother, the priest let out a tremendous 'SHUT UP!' in English. This I suspect was for our benefit ...

On matters of etiquette at weddings or festivals I would consult our ayah Kissy. She was only 26 but her family had lived in the area for generations and she was au fait with all local customs. At this tender age she had four daughters and the eldest, Bikki, was already married. Bikki lived with her husband's parents, but whenever this life irked her she would contrive to come gathering firewood near our house so she could slip in and see her mother. She was only 12!

Our servant boy, Sadhu, was only 11. He was playful and sharp, in the manner of children who have to earn a living at an early age. He and Kissy would skirmish over who should have the larger mug of tea or bigger plate of rice. Kissy would throw off all sense of decorum and race with him to get the choicest helping. We grew to love these two during our stay. They epitomised for me all the contradictions of my country. The easy laughter that transcends the poverty and fight for survival, the child-like simplicity and the instinctive wisdom. When we climbed into our taxi on the first stage of our long journey away from India, Kissy stood with tears streaming down her kindly face, while Sadhu, struggling to look suitably sad, stole surreptitious glances at the hand in which he clutched our farewell gift — a small wad of notes!

Aged 10 at the time, I remember quite a lot from this 1957 visit. I had my first experience of Tandoori chicken, served at The Napier Hotel dining room in Poona on our way to Panchgani. It was an unforgettable sight. The waiter brought the whole chicken to our table, glistening deep red, nestled in a basket lined with a blue-check gingham napkin, to be dissected into its succulent fragrant parts. And two well-behaved little girls were encouraged to eat with their fingers! It seemed just like the promiscuity described by our ancestor, Richard Creed, in his notes from Afghanistan in 1878.

Once settled into my grandparents' Panchgani house, Kashana Cottage, we would wake to a queue of men holding the bridles of their horses and hoping to earn a few rupees taking the 'missy-babas' for a ride along the hill-top paths. I was always a sook, and frightened of horses, so had to be cajoled into clambering onto the often decrepit animals standing forlornly outside our gate. Though I never enjoyed it, I put up with these excursions until a horse fell over, pinning my leg underneath, fortunately with no real damage to horse or child.

My sister Cara, though younger, was definitely braver and more adventurous. She recalls the excitement of the dead panther in the bakery, though she remembers it as a tiger. Perhaps we saw both. She had a narrow escape from one of India's most venomous snakes, the Russell's viper, that dropped down from the roof of a shed just beside her. She saw Grandpa and the servants batter it to death. The servants beheaded chickens for our dinners, there were rides on hired bicycles (Cara recalls coming a cropper when brakes failed down a hill), picnics in the nearby hills with wonderful views from precarious metal viewing decks. I recall that a young teacher, Mr Bhattacharia, used to take me on day-long bicycle rides into the valleys where we distributed sweets to village children. (Would a parent allow a ten-year-old these days to do anything like this? I presume my grandparents knew him! And certainly nothing untoward happened.)

Food features strongly in childhood memories and we both recall the crunchy *channa* (fried chick peas) served warm by street vendors in cones of newspaper. Cara says Granny made a memorable creamy milk coffee and she loved watching eggs being fried, with smoking-hot ghee spooned on top of the whites so they bubbled. We watched the pots being washed on the ground outside, supple Indian servants sitting on their haunches scrubbing until the pots gleamed to Granny's strict standards. All the fresh vegetables were washed in Condy's crystals that turned the water purple and apparently protected us from germs. Water was boiled and boiled again for drinking. Milk was boiled and left to cool, covered by a little white net cloth edged with beads. Looking back now, I suppose it must have felt quite a responsibility to keep her granddaughters healthy. I can't recall ever falling ill when we were there.

We lived in Panchgani for almost six months, home-schooled by mother, under instructions from our school back in Melbourne. Granny felt sorry for us having to sit and do school work so, through a small serving hatch into the dining room where we sat, she would quietly pass us snacks on delicate English bone china plates. My favourite was the small chunks of sweet Indian brown sugar called *goor*, or jaggery, that melted in the mouth as we rehearsed our times-tables.

A succession of deliveries and services were at the doorstep each day: the fruit wallah, the vegetable wallah, the *doodh* wallah (milk) all heralded by their unique cries. There was the knife-sharpening wallah, equipped with a leather strop and a grinding wheel on his bicycle, who would work on the knives until they were wafer thin and ferociously sharp. Kissy had a favourite one that she guarded from anyone else. We thought it a very amusing trick to hide it from her. She would obligingly chase us around the house and garden until we revealed its hiding place.

Kissy and Sadhu were kind, sweet people, devotedly caring for my grandparents until they left India and moved to live with their son's family in England in the 1960s. Being an unaware youngster when I had lived with them at Kashana Cottage, I was fascinated to read about their lives when, years later, I found the transcript of that radio talk, delivered by my mother soon after our return to Australia.

Donald returned to undergraduate life at Cambridge in 1946, after 6 year War absence, now with a young wife. At a May Ball, 1947, Pearl pregnant with me

Pearl as young mother in Cambridge,
rugged up for the very cold post-War winters

At a wedding in Winchester,
Don now teaching music and
Spanish at Winchester College

At my sister
Cara's baptism,
Winchester, 1951

Pearl with her two daughters, Cara and Val, in Winchester garden, 1953

In 1954 family moved to Melbourne, Australia, for Don to take up position as Director of Music at a leading private school. Photo from series of Pearl taken by close family friend Brin Newton-John, 1956.

Living in the Indian hill-station, Panchgani, for six months with our grandparents, 1957/8. Two girls, aged six and ten, gazing longingly at Indian sweets in the local market

Sadhu, our grandparents' servant boy (and willing playmate for us girls) sent to buy a new brass cooking pot

Kissy, the main
household helper, dressed
in her finery for a
wedding

Val and Cara dressed up in saris for Cara's
seventh birthday

At Poona (now Pune)
railway station. Pearl
pensive, farewelling India
and her parents. En route to
Bombay to catch ship back to
Melbourne.

Pearl and Donald in Melbourne, 1964

Don in photo by Brin Newton-John, trademark bow tie, Melbourne, 1968

After Don was appointed to a new post in Brisbane, Queensland, 1971. Pearl in her garden, photo by close friend Irena Newton-John

The Britton family, Christmas in Melbourne, 1999

22: Darshan, Our First Driver, His Story

Sue and I have our version of the kindly servants my mother had described. We have our driver, Darshan. To have a driver is not as luxurious as it sounds to Western ears. If you're not young and adventurous, or impecunious, tourists and business people usually have a driver in India. As do most well-to-do Indians. A driver drops you more or less exactly where you want to go, parks in improbably difficult spots, and waits for you. Waits as long as you want.

When we first started travelling in India, we were always dashing out of shops or tourist attractions, concerned that we were keeping our driver waiting. Indians looked at us incredulously. This is what you have a driver for. To wait for you. Actually they should be called waiters rather than drivers, since there is usually more waiting than driving in a day's excursion. While we are occupied they usually fall into a deep sleep. Sometimes they go off to get the car fixed, especially the air-conditioning which often breaks down. Or so they claim. We're never sure of the truth here because we know they don't like driving with it on. They tell us it gives them coughs or sore throats, but of course it costs more to run the car with air-conditioning on.

For a few years as newly minted business-women, we had

opted for another three-star-ish business-type hotel in central Delhi, not far from Connaught Place. Looking out of the hotel window, its ledge occupied by murmuring pigeons, we could see what Lonely Planet described as 'a strange collection of salmon-coloured structures'. They loomed large — each about 10 metres high, like fossilised hard-edged dinosaurs, at once ancient and futuristic, if that's possible ...

It is the Delhi Jantar Mantar, an observatory built by Maharaja Jai Singh II in 1710. It comprises a series of huge brick structures, one a sundial, another measuring azimuth and altitude, another tells the time in four other places in the world when it is noon in Delhi. Incredible that this could be achieved 300 years ago, and without a smartphone! Jai Singh was obsessed with astronomy and had five such observatories built, the largest being in Jaipur, seat of his power. In the context of modern Delhi, the Jantar Mantar looks bizarre, marooned amidst chaotic circling traffic and new office blocks.

But what I am really interested in is the hotel car park below. This is where our current taxi-driver-of-choice lives. He lives in his car. Darshan's car is called an Ambassador. Both driver and car have stories to tell. First the car: it should be included in the list of great British legacies to India, along with democracy, bureaucracy and cricket. Hindustan Motor's Ambassador was spawned in the 1950s, based on the British Morris Oxford, and was the first car to be manufactured in India.

Unique to India, the Ambassador cars are the vehicular equivalent of a slightly portly ageing bachelor uncle. I've actually seen them described in devotee chatrooms as 'fat aunty' due to their lumpen shape with smallish windows. Some still have foot-operated windscreen wipers. In Mumbai most taxis seemed to be a different variety, not as endearing as the Delhi and Kolkata ones. There was a fashion amongst the Mumbai taxi drivers to re-line the interior of their cabs with garish '50s cinema-carpet-like fabrics, sticking a large fluorescent tube where once there was a discreet interior light. Very flashy. Just the way the rest of India sees Mumbai.

Up until quite recently, new models of the Ambassador continued to be made, their external appearance hardly changed in over 50 years. You could even order an armour-plated model or a stretch-limo model. They are still the official government vehicles, used by politicians and senior bureaucrats — usually plain white, with flags and sometimes curtains, to signal the importance of their passengers.

But the aspiring classes don't want such a relic from India's past, so the plant has finally shut down. Nippy little Japanese-brand hatchbacks and bigger SUV's have now taken over India's city streets. It is a great pity that Ambassadors have almost disappeared, as their idiosyncratic ordinariness swam against the tide of planned obsolescence and global marketing homogeneity. Someone in Delhi recently told us that their sturdy resilience, combined with some nostalgia for things Indian, is creating a small resurgence of interest in Ambassadors for private use.

But when we began our regular Indian trips in the early 2000s, the Ambassador taxi was ubiquitous in Delhi and even more so in Kolkata where there were a staggering 33,000 of them. They were yellow and black in colour, bruised and battered by their constant engagement in the madness of Indian city traffic. Their beetle-like black and yellow colour, and even their bulbous shape, made insect-plague analogies seem apposite, large swarms swirling around the city roundabouts.

Somehow early models kept going, no doubt with all sorts

of gimcrack, Heath Robinson contrivances to keep them on the roads. We twice had to help push them off busy freeways — to the chagrin of our driver and shocked amusement of passers-by. Indian women of our middle-class ilk wouldn't be seen dead helping to push a car. In fact we almost were dead at the end of it, due to risky traffic and even riskier traffic fumes.

Back to our hotel. There was a row of Ambassador taxis parked down below our window. It was early morning. The drivers were rubbing their eyes, rubbing their cars, smoothing the white (varying degrees of whiteness) antimacassars on the seats. If you are lucky your Ambassador will have un-noticeable springs in the upholstery of the back seat. But more often than not the springs are uncomfortably noticeable. We have spent some long trips seated almost below the window level because our springs were so collapsed. Others up so high we can barely see out. Come to think of it, one always seems to be in the wrong position vis-à-vis windows in these cars.

Having said that, though, there was something comfortingly solid and loveable about an Ambassador. It deluded us into feeling safe and contained. Our Indian travel agent in Australia was always surprised when we specified an Ambassador as our vehicle of choice. Sadly, it is rarely an option now as we step into Toyota Innovas which, it has to be said, are much more comfortable and practical, but entirely lacking in charm.

Now to the story of Darshan who had become 'our driver'. The large hotels have taxi car parks and some have washrooms for drivers, and even meal areas. The hotel's major-domo, handsomely resplendent in *sherwani*, turban and excessively unctuous manner, was stationed at a lectern outside the hotel entrance. He used a clip-on microphone to call your car number.

Darshan's was 5351. We requested this number, the major-domo tweaked his curling moustachio and bellowed the number through his microphone. Black and yellow beetle number 5351 emerged as if from a crack in the wall.

No matter where you wander, your driver always finds you, miraculously sensing your whereabouts. We are their bread and butter for the day. Maybe tourists and business-people in India are entirely predictable in their movements. But, even in the most unlikely spots, or the most crowded places, and in mega-cities of over 16 million people, somehow your driver keeps tabs on you — word seems to go out that two European women have emerged into the street again.

Darshan's father sent him off to Delhi from his home in the Punjab at the age of 13 with 100 rupees in his pocket. That's about two Australian dollars at today's values. Darshan is a solid, slightly shambling Sikh, with large blood-shot sloe-eyes, the shape seen in Mughal miniatures. Some say the Sikhs in India are like the Irish to the Poms — the butt of unflattering 'dumb' jokes. But they are often the most handsome and elegant of Indian men. Tall, tough and strong — there's something about those turbans, the steel bangle, and the hidden knives ...

Darshan is not, however, of the dashing ilk. His English is only adequate and we're never quite sure if we've made ourselves understood. But he is eager to please, totally reliable and honest. When we ask, 'What do we owe you?' The answer is the predictable, slightly irritating, 'What you like, madam.' We probably pay less than tourists, but a lot more than the basic going rate for locals. So we know it may only be commercial good sense for him to look after us. But we think he likes us and we certainly feel very warmly towards him.

We learn that he has two children, a girl and a boy, and he is in his early thirties. He looks older. We are both old enough to be his mother! (What does he make of us gadding about the world on our own and at our age?) Each year we have handed over small gifts for his children. After several years of this, we discovered that the children are not his. They belong to his sister and her husband. He is a devoted uncle, but Darshan and his wife are 'not blessed', as he puts it, with their own.

We learned this from his brother-in-law, Jaspal, also a taxi driver, who was deputed to look after us one year. We had sent a text message to Darshan from Australia to say we were arriving next month. No answer. But when we arrived in India, a phone call came from Jaspal. He would pick us up instead. What a good system this was!

The taxi drivers always line up outside hotels, sleeping in their taxis for a few hours overnight, in between trips to the airport, or perhaps delivering young Delhi swingers to and from the booming nightclub scene. They catch up by sleeping in the car whenever they get a chance by day. When you return to the car from a meeting or shopping they are often so dead to the world that you wonder how they snap into life so quickly — and whether they can possibly drive you safely.

We speculate about Darshan's bloodshot eyes. Is it lack of sleep? Or is he on something? He swears: 'No drink, no smoke, no drugs.' He always looks immaculately clean, a neatly pressed shirt, changed each day, and so does his turban. The car smells fresh.

Once, Darshan unexpectedly stopped by the side of a road and leapt out of the car. We wondered what was going on. He came back about two minutes later, only slightly sheepish, having bought himself a pair of shoes. 'Very good value, madam, since we were passing...'

In the time we have known him, Darshan has progressed from living entirely in his taxi to renting a shift in a bed. This involved a tiny room with a narrow bed, shared with two others, each having 8 out of 24 hours access to it, depending on their occupations or their workshifts. Time-share beds. But Darshan has worked long hours, seven-day weeks, eleven months a year, just one trip back to his family in the Punjab by train each year. He has done well enough to rent a flat in west Delhi. Now his wife has joined him and they live together with his sister and brother-in-law and their kids. The latest news was that his sister and brother-in-law were going to have a child especially for Darshan and his wife to rear as their own. This would overcome the shame that can go with childlessness in India.

Darshan and his wife know they are fortunate to have children living with them. A lot of children grow up cared for by grandparents in villages while the parents are off making a living many miles away. Their mothers may be ayahs to someone else's children, witnessing other children's milestones, loving someone else's children as if they are their own, returning to their biological children only for a couple of weeks a year. It's a heart-breaking reality of economic life for so many in India.

Darshan is entirely trustworthy and helps us achieve so much more in a day than we could under our own steam. In fact our lives and work in India would be quite impossible without a driver. We discovered that we can entrust him with tasks on our behalf. Instead of waiting for us, we may ask him to pick up or deliver parcels while we are otherwise engaged. We once sent him off to a pharmacy to buy anti-DVT stockings for the flight home. It seemed quite an intimate errand in a way. Imagine asking a taxi driver to do this here in Australia. We gave him the details and the cash. He brought back stockings and the change.

He delivered some beautiful silk scarves to a courier when we were running out of time to do it ourselves. He lends us his mobile phone when ours won't work. We leave all our parcels in the car in his care. We feel self-conscious, even ashamed, about the quantity of stuff we buy, even though most of it is for our business. It began to rain one time when we were out, and he appeared as if from nowhere with an umbrella to cover us as we walked across a small uncovered space. He hovers anxiously when we visit a market in search of unusual buttons. We learned that it is a market deemed unsuitable for women.

What gives us any right to be so well looked after? Such a luxury and such a privilege to have this. We know we are paying for it, but the relationship seems more than money can buy. Darshan comes when we ask, does what we ask, without demur, with flashes of humour sometimes. I needed a luggage strap one Sunday, flying back to Australia that night. I didn't know if he had understood what I wanted. We went about our business for the day. Then I noticed we were driving back to the hotel a different way.

We pulled up in a scrappy area outside a dusty awning. 'Come with me,' he said. A shoe repair and luggage 'shop'. Two straps for 70 rupees. He talked it down to 60. I only wanted one — but it'd be churlish to say so, especially at that price. And maybe 60 rupees was still well above the going rate for a local. As we got back into the car with two luggage straps wrapped in old newspaper, Darshan said, 'This is tension-free shopping!' Such a Western idiom, a surprise coming from someone whose English is usually rudimentary. But spot-on.

23: Two Unforgettable Bedtime Stories

'The Sikh religion is not very old,' said our guide, 'only about 400 or 500 years.' He explained that observant Sikh men do not cut their hair (hence the beards and turbans) and must wear some symbolic items: a bangle, a small comb, under-shorts of a certain type, and a small knife.

We were on our way to the famous Golden Temple in Amritsar in the Punjab. We washed our hands under a row of taps, then walked through a large, shallow marble pond of water to wash our feet. It was dark, about 8.30 pm, and the Amritsar streets were abuzz with people of all ages making their way excitedly through to the Temple. Turbans bobbed joyfully in the crowd, like tall multi-coloured mushrooms bursting up from the ground. Husbands accompanied their wives and children, all in their bright Sunday best.

The Punjab State in north-west India is the homeland of the Sikh religion. Chandigarh is the capital and Amritsar, one of its major cities, is the site of this temple. Sikhs believe in one God, and, amongst other precepts, the equality of all (no caste system) and service to others. It is based on the spiritual teachings of its founder, Guru Nanak. Since his demise, there have been nine subsequent leaders. However, the tenth Guru decided that the

135

Sikh scripture would be his successor. No more human leaders. The scripture itself would be the eternal spiritual guide. Hence the importance of a nightly ritual we were about to witness.

The pristine marble paving inside the temple area was balm to tired feet, as this glamorous temple, covered in real gold, came into view. It seemed a chimera, glittering under lights against a dark sky. It was mirrored by its own shimmering reflection in the waters of a surrounding lake. Amidst this glamour, we were here to see a book being tucked into bed.

The Golden Temple is the pinnacle temple of the Sikhs. Sikh temples are open to all, regardless of religion, gender, race or caste. At the Golden Temple this involves a crowd of many, many thousands, some of whom have queued all day to get into the actual temple building, where, if they are lucky, they will proceed in the queue around an internal circuit, then exit. Over 100,000 people visit each day. Some have to queue until the next day to get in.

Being tourists, we seemed able to avoid some of this queuing and joined a crowd pressed against barriers, located outside the entrance to the temple itself. We were waiting for the book to be ceremoniously brought out from inside the temple. Turbaned priests in white robes chanted in expectation. We glimpsed a gold palanquin arriving. It was set down, miraculously right in front of us, thanks to our guide. The attendants began to prepare a bed inside the palanquin. Sheets, blankets and a pillow were each held up and misted gently with a rose water spray, then placed tenderly inside. They then festooned the palanquin with garlands of fresh marigolds, and they blessed it. We awaited the book. It arrived, carried aloft by an attendant. It was placed lovingly in its bed, like a most precious newborn baby, and tucked in carefully.

The palanquin was lifted on the shoulders of the turbaned, robed attendants and carried up a flight of stairs to an adjoining temple where it would spend the night. In the morning at 4.30, the ritual is reversed. This takes place every day of every year in the Golden Temple and, in similar ceremonies, in every other Sikh temple in the world.

Another central practice in Sikh temples is the community meal: anyone can come for a free vegetarian meal, all comers seated together and served by Sikh community volunteers. At The Golden Temple we were told they serve 50,000 meals PER DAY! With only a few paid organisers, this is carried out by volunteers and the provisions are mostly donated. There's a machine cooking 9,000 chapattis an hour. Reinforced by a team making thousands more by hand every day. Standards are high. Misshapen ones are put aside in a basket to be fed to cows or other animals. Vast vats of lentils, of rice, of a vegetable or two, are stirred with huge wooden paddles. The vegetables are varied every hour and a half. I took a turn stirring *gobi* and *aloo*, cauliflower and potatoes, mixed with fragrant spices.

The preparation and cleaning areas were busy and incredibly noisy: groups of women seated in a circle were peeling kilos of garlic cloves for the dhal and vegetable mixtures; another huge hall housed the volunteer dishwashing brigade where the clatter of metal is deafening. People lined up to receive a metal *thali* (a platter with sections for each element of the meal) and then streamed past the servers who gave them a generous dollop from each vat. Plus a freshly cooked chapatti. They sat in long rows on mats in a large hall, eating relatively quietly.

We were offered a cup of chai, served from a series of steaming urns, and we wondered, as we sipped, how many millions of mouths had supped from this very cup before us (and we couldn't help wondering if we'd pick up some dreaded bug).

A bit like the Muslim Hajj, Sikh people try to visit the Golden Temple at least once in their lives. There is a specially built structure in which women can splash themselves in the lake surrounding the temple. Some men wade into the waters, some fill containers with the water to take home, as Hindus might take Ganges water. Or Christian pilgrims at Lourdes.

The whole scene seemed utterly innocent, benign and cheerful. It was hard to conceive that any violence could occur. But there was a bombing in 1984. It was an attempt to dislodge a militant Sikh leader and his followers, housed in the complex. Ordered by then-Prime Minister Indira Gandhi, it incurred the wrath of militant Sikhs and she was later assassinated by her own Sikh guards. We were told there were plain-clothed police mingling with the crowd. But for a visiting tourist it seemed nothing could disturb this joyful scene.

Also on the historical dark side, there is the infamous Jallianwala Bagh massacre of 1919. This eight-acre garden is just around the corner from the Golden Temple. The British Army opened fire on a festival gathering of picnicking families (as well as some peaceful protestors), after cruelly blocking off the garden's main entrance. Walled in on all sides, there was no escape. Many perished in a deep well into which they had plunged, hoping to avoid bullets. Hundreds died: men, women and children. Its brutality is cited as a key factor undermining British rule and lending impetus to the Non-Cooperation Movement and Quit India.

As someone of British origin, it is hard to stomach the process of describing what happened here. I've only set out the bare facts above. The details are even worse. I found it difficult to be there. It was crowded with Indian tourists, so we felt conspicuous and hoped we wouldn't be judged for the sins of our ancestors.

The next evening we went to the India/Pakistan border, only 30 minutes drive from Amritsar, to witness a different bedtime event. Here, every night, the two countries' flags are lowered at sundown in an extraordinary ritual. Our guide prepared us: 'You will have to walk about one kilometre, you cannot take a handbag, only your phone or camera. And your passports.' We have to leave everything else in the car in a large car park area where the guide and driver will remain.

Unfortunately, in the flurry to debouch from the car, other vehicles tooting and crowds pushing by, we stupidly left our hats and water. We joined the throng and strode out in full sun, no trees to shade the road. We reached a barricade where foreigners showed passports and everyone walked through screening devices. It was rather hot — 4.30 pm and the temperature was in the mid-thirties.

We eventually arrived at the entrance to a huge stadium, a semi-circular edifice with tiered rows of concrete bleachers. Like half an MCG, but with less comfortable seating. It was quite unlike what we had expected. We tried to decide on a good vantage point amidst the thousands already seated. We were looking down on a wide 'roadway' where there was an MC bellowing through a microphone. Deafening pop music emanated from loud speakers. Spruikers plied the crowd with flags, ice-creams, drinks. We were parched, having no water nor money to buy it. We even considered begging from strangers.

It was a very festive, good-natured atmosphere, comprising groups of young men, young women, large families, all ages. But

I feel uneasy with nationalistic crowds, whatever the nationality. It was a whipped-up, exaggerated nationalism, deliberately roused to fever-pitch by the MC with slogans and well-known Indian songs. 'Jai Hind, Jai Hind!' ('Victory to India!') they shouted. Women were encouraged to come down onto the road and dance, handed Indian flags to join in a vast group, waving arms, hips swaying to the music in a jolly cacophony.

At the end of this road, there was an elaborate, tall, decorative gate and on the other side, in a similar semi-circular tiered stand, was the Pakistani crowd, fewer in number and far less raucous than the Indians, but yelling their own versions of similar mantras.

We had been there about an hour, dripping with perspiration in full sun, lips and mouths so dry we were barely able to speak (anyway it was too noisy to hear each other). Then there was some anticipation below. Soldiers were lining up. Someone in a beret received many salutes as he smartly inspected something, military swagger very much on show. On orders from the megaphone-bellowing MC, the dancing crowd of women dispersed and dutifully returned to the bleachers.

Then followed something I can best describe as human-sized rutting peacocks performing a New Zealand haka. Soldiers appeared in high-goose-stepping groups, all wearing a type of turban with a long colourful tail and a veritable cockscomb atop. The same was happening on the Pakistani side. When each group reached their side of the gate, they gestured at each other with belligerent fist-pumping and chest-thrusting. This aggressive charade went on for some time. Eventually, as the sun sank, the border gates were closed and the flags of India and Pakistan came down for the night. They were ceremoniously folded and put to bed.

24: Living Public Lives — Shocking Disparities

We find ourselves seated in cars too much in India. But walking in the cities can be difficult. Footpaths may be non-existent, or potholed, or crumbling into precipitous fissures. Puddles are large and, one suspects, potentially lethal. Streets are crowded with pedestrians, cars, bicycles, carts, rickshaws, sellers of stuff, sleeping homeless, beggars, mangy dogs, cows, little shrines, sewage, spit — everything. One has to concentrate on treading warily. It would be easy to step in something nasty or to break an ankle. And that would be hugely inconvenient.

It would be even easier to trample on a life. Lives are lived publicly, amid noise and chaos, but still with some dignity. Westerners (and well-to-do Indians) take up profligate amounts of space in every sense. On the streets in India we feel lumpen and ungainly, dispensing minor largesse like awkward leftovers dumped on the wrong continent. Poorer Indians seem able to fit into tiny spaces, walk lightly on the ground, sit neatly with limbs tucked under, sleep soundly amidst all kinds of ruckus and din.

Accustomed to being unnoticed, the poor are often so thin, so slightly built, they appear to be a different race. It shocks us to learn that, as India prospers overall, the differential in body size between rich and poor is actually increasing, not decreasing.

Worse still, the disparity in IQ is also increasing. The number of Indians who are obese or overweight is rapidly increasing. Along with the concomitant problems of diabetes, cardiac disease and cancers. In Western countries the problems of obesity, and its related illnesses, are disproportionately represented in lower socio-economic groups. In India it is the reverse. The middle-class, a growing cohort, can now afford fast foods, they do little exercise (drivers take them everywhere), little housework (servants), their paid work is often sedentary, and TV-watching at home is their leisure. It will be tragic if the over-fattened middle to rich cohort garner a greater share of health spending than the under-nourished poor.

The acceptance of 'the way things are' by all parties is distressing. It bothers us that Indians simply don't make eye contact with the poor in the streets, or with waiters in restaurants, or baggage carriers, or any of the other myriad service-providers. We are constantly smiling, looking grateful, saying 'thank you'. This is too craven, we gather. It is also a bit exhausting, because service is so constant.

Australian author Sarah Macdonald, in her book, *Holy Cow*,[14] describes an Indian friend asking her why she has to be so 'sucky-crawly'. We've adopted this, and abbreviated it to SC, but we haven't managed to give it up. A deep discomfort with inequality causes us to overcompensate — it's just normal politeness we say to ourselves — but it does sometimes seem we are being over-ingratiating or condescendingly charming. A friend said when she comes to India she finds herself 'too easily in touch with my inner memsahib'!

---

14 Penguin Random House, 2002.

And we wonder what the waiters at breakfast, or servants in the houses of friends, feel about us being all thanks and friendly engagement. Do they find it embarrassing or simply tiring? India is so densely peopled that perhaps it's essential to stay unengaged, to keep one's distance as much as possible, especially in daily personal interactions. When the young bell-boy hefts our overweight suitcases into the boot of the car, we know it is not only because it is his job. In India, role assumptions are based on centuries of history, of caste and knowing one's place.

Being in a car insulates us from many realities of life in India. But no visitor to India can resist describing the traffic. Novelists, travel writers, letter writers, all have a go at capturing the noise and the danger, the chaos and that sense of impending doom.

I know Sue, my travel partner, will dismiss this as fanciful, but there are times when I experience the Delhi traffic as almost beautiful. There is something symphonic about a glissando into an intersection or roundabout, barely altering speed, gliding across six notional 'lanes' of multiple vehicle types — small three-wheel auto-rickshaws buzzing noisily with billowing fumes, large flashy 4WDs with tinted windows, lots of small Japanese cars, many now made in India, dangerously lurching overburdened trucks, bulging buses, a politician's white Ambassador, bicycles, motorbikes, the odd tractor, camel or elephant, varying octaves and decibels in their motors, their horns — and then emerging from this chaos mostly without accident, mostly without anger, as if a conductor has miraculously brought together the various instruments of an orchestra in a complex musical score ...

The fact that it 'works' in its own fashion certainly doesn't have much to do with the occasional traffic policeman, ineffectually flapping a tired hand, his uniform and (presumably) his lungs blackened by fumes. Nor to traffic lights either, as once we crossed an intersection and I asked Sue, 'Wasn't that a red light?' To which she replied, 'I think it's in the eye of the beholder.'

Driving in a rural area, we were curious as to why at intervals there were sheaves of wheat across the road. Then we discovered that the wheels of passing vehicles were being used to thresh the wheat. This seems to epitomise something about modern India — the contrasts, yes, but it is the *accommodation* between the old and the new, the primitive and the modern, the poor and the rich, that is so striking.

In recent years it has become compulsory for all cars to have seat belts in the front seats. However, no sane visitor wants to sit in the front. Often the back seats appear to have belts fitted and we instinctively reach to do them up. But it's an illusion — only the shoulder straps. No housing for it to click into. (Where are all those absent housings? A pile of them somewhere? Sold — but for what?) So we sit unbelted and resigned to our fate ...

Out of the cities, on highways and country roads, teetering trucks and buses defy what architects know as 'the slenderness ratio'. A given width will take only so much height before tipping over. On a recent trip of about 80 kilometres, taking three hours, we passed five freshly overturned trucks. People and contents spilled across the road. Along the route many more truck carcasses lay dismembered and rusting at road edges. That was on a good highway!

Trucks have Sanskrit messages painted on backs or sides, translating as: 'India is Great', or 'Because of a mother's blessing I bought this truck', or 'If you have an evil eye on my truck your face will turn black'. All written in lovely Sanskrit script. I've heard the script described as looking like washing hanging on the line. But that belies its beauty.

Trucks also have the words 'HORN PLEASE', usually in English, painted on the back. This is novel for a Westerner, not used to sounding a car horn unless extremely pressed or extremely angry. In India it is expected that you sound your horn, a courtesy (supposedly) to let other drivers know you'd like to pass, or just so they know you're there. As a consequence, drivers hold the steering wheel with one hand, thumb permanently on the horn with the other, changing gears only when forced by the juddering engine. One arrives at destinations exhausted by the journey — there has been so much to look at, so many near-misses, so much noise of horns, so many sudden lurches.

In Delhi, in the lead-up to the 2010 Commonwealth Games, there was a Government-funded campaign to stop drivers using their horns, knowing how distressing the noise is to foreigners. It was moderately successful at the time but, as each year passed, horn use began to rise again. And with growing affluence, car use is rising dramatically, causing terrible traffic problems in all major cities. Ruining them, actually. And the pollution is appalling.

Flying in to Delhi at night, one looks down upon a very dimly-lit city (compared with, say, Bangkok) due to pollution haze, plus the low wattage and intermittent electricity of the nation's capital. And there may be a smoky smell entering the aircraft. Accompanying me on one trip, my husband thought the plane was on fire. But no — just the air in which we were about to immerse ourselves.

Over a decade ago, Delhi mandated that all buses and tuk-tuks must convert to Compressed Natural Gas (CNG). This had a noticeably beneficial effect on air quality. But the benefit has been wiped out by rapidly increasing numbers of vehicles as the population increases and the middle classes grow. We are relieved that Tata's Nano car hasn't been a huge success in the cities. Accessibly cheap cars are a wonderful thing, but Nanos, with their petrol engines, would dump ever more pollution into the city environment.

Recently my favourite bright silver earrings, which had never needed cleaning in eight years of wear, turned black, oxidised, in one Delhi day. The inside of my lungs must look like the Australian-government cancer warning picture on our cigarette packets. The benefit of the Delhi Metro moving travellers underground will likely be negated by population growth and the status of owning a car (or three) amongst the burgeoning Indian middle classes. And, more sadly, the hegemony of the car means that Delhi has now banished cows, camels and elephants from the roads.

146

25: Adventures in Sainik Farms

On each visit to Delhi, Darshan drives us to the place where our clothes are made. It takes at least an hour to get there, through hectic traffic, to a semi-gated community called Sainik Farms. These tracts of land, once rural, have developed into sprawling middle- to upper-class housing estates, outside the city centre to benefit from fresher air, more space.

The whole place was unauthorised: it was simply commandeered by those with the right contacts and money. There are some very large ugly houses, a few very large interesting houses, but little of architectural merit. Grecian columns meet French chateaux. Or so we guess from the glimpses we get over high walls, gates often ostentatiously labelled with the owner's name and title, many of them military: Rear-Admiral Sethi or Brigadier Bhalla.

But there are plentiful trees and lush gardens, some perfectly manicured lawns and a few shops in the narrow meandering streets and laneways. Too many cars now, causing hair-raising encounters, but demonstrating the imperturbable ability of Indian drivers to wend in and out of each other's way. There is no apparent logic to the numbering system: we are looking for Block N, which seems to abut Block W. But it does feel slightly rural and a pleasant contrast to the hectic centres of both Old and New Delhi.

We are told that each collection of about six houses has its own water system, its own power generation, its own security guard. And its own committee of management, each with a president and a vice-president. Though technically illegal — the land and the utilities have simply been 'appropriated' — in recent years it has become regularised and partially connected to official grids. But since the official supplies are erratic at best, residents continue to operate their own wells, generators and so on.

As an aside, it seems that every system requires a back-up in middle-class India. For instance, households install their own generators to cover for power outages, rooftop rainwater tanks to cover for water shortages, and all have water purifiers in their kitchens as tap water is not potable. If you have one cook, you must have another cook because your main one might disappear to his village for a while, either notifying you or not, and there's nothing you can do about it. So, you have understudies ready to step in. (Heaven forbid that you might have to cook for yourself!) Same with your drivers, dog walkers, cleaners, stitchers, embroiderers. Whether in business or private life, everything needs backing up. It is a complex, time-consuming, energy-sapping country to live in.

The house we go to in Sainik Farms is charming in a low-key way. The office and the workrooms for machinists and embroiderers are mostly on-site. We clamber up a precarious external spiral metal staircase and spend hours working through patterns and samples with our friend, Sheila, who runs the business. As always in India, there are endless distractions, making it hard to concentrate. Fans and air-conditioners demand constant vigilance to keep paper under control, as draughts lift and mix things in unplanned and often undesirable ways.

Our eyes feel sore and dry and our throats are affected by fabric 'dust', a slightly toxic mix, one suspects, of floating fibres and chemical dye residues. Phones ring (everyone has at least one mobile phone, as well as landlines), servants need instructions, workers come for items to be checked. Even the Bank Manager comes by to conduct some transactions.

There is another client on the scene, staying with Sheila, from Rome. She has collected leaves from Indian trees, peepul and gingko, and is having the shapes printed onto fabric for doona covers and placemats. Samples are produced for her approval. Then she leaves with a driver, who needs instructions from Sheila, to find fabric. Another client-cum-friend is here from England. In between clothing samples, she has been having her teeth fixed for a fraction of the cost back home.

There's such a lot going on! No wonder we are exhausted at the end of a day. Somehow we have to remain business-like, checking our own patterns, trying on samples — the seams are half-inch instead of one centimetre and it's making a difference to the sizing. Do the fabrics work? Will it be too see-through? Will we remember that a colour that looks wonderful here won't translate back to Melbourne weather, Melbourne skin colour and Melbourne's propensity for black.

Masterji — the Muslim master tailor — pops in and out with adjustments. We duck into an ante-room to try on samples in case he is confronted with one of us semi-dressed. He would 'die of shock' says Sheila, amused (our own feelings of modesty seem to matter less). The mirror is rather too small and a bit dusty. Everything in India gets dusty so quickly. We notice that in houses with servants the chore of dusting is never-ending. Delhi as a whole is rightly proud of its treed streets, but the leaves are often covered in thick dust, presumably washed off in the monsoon season.

Today at Sheila's we are marooned in a sea of white froth consisting of 3,000 skirts, each one made from 12 metres of hand-printed white voile, destined for Barneys in New York. At the bottom of the spiral stair there is noise and dust as a small private well is being dug to access more water. In Australia this would need permits, inspectors, safety barriers. Here it began when we arrived and is finished by the end of the day. God knows what effect it will have on the water table. Already water shortages are causing major problems in Delhi.

We have interesting conversations apart from business. Sheila is well-read, well-travelled, has clients in Europe and the US, and is an astute observer of Indian ways. Maybe because she is of Nepali descent, she also has the sharper eye of the semi-outsider. She attended a famous boarding school, La Martinière in Lucknow, and has an MA in linguistics. We like to pick her brains about speech idioms and the nuances of life in India. We share a similar sense of humour and intense interest in fiction. We swap notes about novels. When we first met Sheila, we were surprised to find she had read the novels of author David Malouf, a respected writer in Australia but hardly mainstream. She out-reads two avid readers!

While we are working, Darshan puts in hours of sleep in an empty block of land next door. I have a photo of him, or rather of his socked feet, as he sleeps across the front bench seat of his Ambassador, his feet poking out of the open passenger door.

He loves it — a day in the country, all expenses paid! When we point out to him that while we are busy working, he sleeps peacefully in his car — his bedroom at Sainik Farms — he says, 'Yes, room 5351 for me!' (His taxi number.) He tells us his 'lubberly name' is Manga. (A 'loverly name' sounds even more affectionate than a 'pet-name'.) Maybe he is quite a wag — if only we knew more Hindi ...

26: The Puzzle of Mixed Blood

Entwined with my now regular visits to India is the continuing puzzle of why a silence usually falls when I say I have some Indian blood. Since fair skin in India is much sought after, surely an easy shortish-cut would be to inter-marry with a Caucasian? Beauty shop shelves are groaning with skin-whitening creams and even underarm-whitening deodorants. The marital columns in the daily newspapers list 'fair' or 'wheaten' skin as one of the most desirable attributes, often ahead of wealth and education.

But it seems that to confess to having a bit of coloured blood is, well, beyond the pale. And to think that I have always been so proud of it. In India they admire Sue's pale skin (which she hates), and are quite indifferent to mine. I rather like the description of Anglo-Indian women as Chutney Marys — in fact we considered using it as the name for our mixed-race Indian-Australian clothing label. But back in British times (and maybe still today) it was used pejoratively. I mull over why I should expect any interest. Am I being overly self-absorbed? But Sue's curiosity exceeds mine, so I often leave it in her hands to mention my connection, or not.

Every now and then, when there's time between our

business commitments, I try to do a little research. On one occasion I was taking tea and cake with the brother of a supplier at The International Centre in Delhi. He was a Professor of English Literature at a leading Indian University. I told him that I remained mildly puzzled by the attitude I felt to Anglo-Indians.

He talked about Anglo-Indians in terms of religion rather than skin colour. He told me about 'rice-Christians', the term used to describe Indians brought into the Christian fold by missionaries in exchange for a bag of rice. He suggested novels and writers I should read, amongst which is Tagore's *Gora*. I later read and enjoyed this great novel, but it seemed more about religious differences, with skin colour an aside, or at most an under-layer (or is it an unspoken layer?) It was interesting, but I didn't feel I got any closer to an answer.

I also discovered that many low-caste or poor Indians converted to Christianity to escape the Hindu caste system. Hence, other Indians may regard Christians as poor, uneducated, or otherwise low-caste people. Anglo-Indians, being mainly Christians, get lumped into this category as well. Perhaps that is why Indians might find it odd that I would draw attention to being Anglo-Indian?

We know that mixed blood people all over the world may suffer the awkwardness of being neither one thing nor the other. In India, a country that calibrates status so carefully, Anglo-Indians remain outsiders to both sides of their bloodlines: barred from the top echelons of British society and regarded as casteless outsiders by Hindu society.

On top of that, social and psychological distances, both large and infinitesimal, are a daily fact of life in India. The social system is 'irredeemably hierarchical'. Sudhir Kakar[15] said in an interview that: 'Indians are perhaps the world's most undemocratic people, living in the world's largest democracy … one Indian typically looks at another through a variety of filters — including gender, caste, religion, class — all aimed at answering the question, "Is this person superior or inferior to me?"'

Geert Hofstede,[16] a Dutch cultural anthropologist, developed interesting tools for measuring cultural differences. One variable he used is Power-Distance, a measure of the extent to which the less powerful accept, even expect, that power is unequal. They accept hierarchy, accept that everyone has a place and there is no justification needed. India scores high on this index. This is part of the context in which Anglo-Indians, along with everyone else in India, jostle for a place.

We met up with an Anglo-Indian family in Kolkata. Most of their relatives had left, but they had never been able to get visas to their countries of choice, having neither desirable skills nor money. The atmosphere in their apartment felt claustrophobic and fossilised. Dowdy Western clothes, crochet doilies everywhere, an upright piano with peeling walnut veneer, faded Axminster carpet. They were kind, jolly and extremely friendly. But I found it depressing. The carpet reminded me of a story about my grandfather: he used to freshen up the pinkish tones in the Axminster in their Bombay apartment by adding a few drops of Mercurochrome mixed with water in a 'flit' can and spraying!

---

15 Sudhir Kakar and his wife Katharina are the authors of *The Indians: Portrait of a People*, Viking, 2007.

16 G. Hofstede, *Culture's Consequences*, Sage, California, 1980.

Perhaps I am over-projecting. There is an All India Anglo-Indian Association and, judging by its website, there are happy, optimistic Anglo-Indians leading successful lives in many different occupations in today's India. I discover from the papers in the blue suitcase that my grandfather was for a time Vice-President of the Bombay branch of the Anglo-Indian Association. And my mother, as a young woman, also served on the committee.

There is confusion of terminology too, because British-India-philes or long-time India hands, with no Indian blood, are often described as Anglo Indians (minus the hyphen). People of mixed blood were for a time called Eurasians. British Raj regulations made a distinction between Eurasians and Anglo-Indians, depending on blood percentages and on whether the coloured blood derived from mother or father. A British father was assumed, of course, and most likely the case. But usually now, to be Anglo-Indian (with hyphen), means to be of mixed British and Indian blood.

Whatever the mixture, especially prior to and immediately after Independence, mixed blood people in India found their loyalties divided. And, because of this, Indians often regarded them as disloyal, even traitors. In my mother's descriptions of her life, we can hear her emerging awareness of this identity conflict. The Creeds set themselves apart from the Anglo-Indian community in many ways, yet they were literally immersed in it when they lived in Willingdon House, situated right opposite a large Anglo-Indian residential community. Although their outside life often revolved around this community — Christmas functions, cricket matches, concerts, fairs and so on — they were not fully part of it, as she described here:

155

For some reason my parents didn't allow me to visit any of my friends in 'The Blocks' which is where the railway families were housed, three huge three-storey blocks of flats made dark and grimy by proximity to the rail yards in the days of dirty steam engines. We were members of the Railway Institute, a Club, and made full use of its facilities. When I was old enough to free my sister Blanche from the odious task of 'taking Pearl for a walk', I was able to visit the Institute by myself.

The most exciting time was at 5 pm (although my parents didn't like me going then) because the hundreds of railway workers would pour out of 'The Gates' at the end of their working day. Standing at the entrance to these Gates were the 'Money Lenders' waiting to waylay those who wished to borrow and certainly those who had not paid back. The money-lenders were Pathans from the North-West Frontier, huge, light-skinned men who wore their tribal dress: very loose pantaloons, large loosely-tied turbans and velvet embroidered waistcoats. If my mother was with me she'd say 'don't look', and I realised when I was grown up that this was because she pitied the poor workers for their public shaming when they were in debt. To me 'don't look' always suggested something exciting, so when on my own I would give the money-lenders a wide berth, but staring all the while!

The Railway Institute consisted of a main clubhouse, tennis courts and a bandstand where a brass band of Indian railway workers played under the baton of Bandmaster Bond, a very fat Englishman. The bandstand was a rotunda with wrought iron decoration. It was here where Father Christmas appeared each year to give presents to the Railway children and to those of us who were ex officio members. I can't recall that there were any others who were non-railway families.

The members comprised mainly middle-rank railway workers, usually Anglo-Indians, Indian Christians and Goanese, but overall a preponderance of Anglo-Indians and just a sprinkling of English families. The Club was very active in that there were tennis tournaments, billiard tournaments, regular Saturday night dances, a football team, with matches played on the maidan that Willingdon House overlooked.

Anglo-Indians by nature are very friendly and hospitable people and love a party and having their kith and kin around. I have observed both in England and in Australia that these habits continue. And wherever they congregate they are more than happy to include anyone from their adoptive country. They are chameleon by nature and have settled well everywhere.

The Club House consisted of the billiard room on the lower floor — one had to pass through it to go to the floor above — an awesome experience for me, rather like walking through a men-only church: absolute silence from the spectators sitting on tiered seats, only the click of cue against ball to cover my footsteps. There was a handsome curving staircase to the top floor where the main rooms were: a dance hall with a stage, and my goal, The Reading Room. I would brave the Billiard Room to rush up the stairs to this haven. It seemed to be full of 'old' gentlemen sitting round a large central table reading the English newspapers and magazines or lolling back in planters chairs reading their books. Where were their wives? Perhaps it wasn't seemly for them to be there?

The magazines on the central table were bound copies of out-of-date English papers and magazines (several months at sea!) and my favourite for its animal cartoon 'Pip, Squeak & Wilfred' was the Daily Mirror, bound in a yellow paper cover. I would wait, and wait for some 'old' gentleman to replace it on the central table. While I waited I would pick up my second favourites, The Tatler or The Sketch.

There must have been some innate snobbery in me because I would pore over photographs of glamorous English socialites, or read reviews of the latest shows in the West End so that when I went to England as a young bride I knew nothing of the nitty-gritty of living: how to cook, or sew, or clean a house, but I did know about Ivor Novello's rise to fame and when I read now [in 1989] about the very elderly and notorious Duchess of Argyll, I remember clearly that she was once Miss Margaret Whigham, the most beautiful debutante of her year, later to become Mrs Charles Sweeney! There was nothing I didn't know about Hunt Balls and being presented at Court. And all of that while I waited for my chance to read 'Pip, Squeak & Wilfred' in the Daily Mirror, in Bombay, as a ten year old!

While my mother was absorbing English social nuances and enjoying this Anglo-Indian version of an English Club, members of the English community in India, though not all upper class by any means, were possibly smirking at her mixed blood appearance and slightly chi-chi accent. But Pearl was a proud Chutney Mary, with a clear eye for snobbery. And not immune to some of her own!

27: Chutney and Cream

Sheila invited me to lunch with an old school friend of hers who is Anglo-Indian. He attended the famous boys' boarding school, La Martinière, in Lucknow, brother school to hers, and they have remained lifelong friends. Good-looking and amusing, we have an entertaining time in The Garden of the Five Senses. This is a rather strange concoction of shops and restaurants set in gardens outside town in south Delhi. It was fashionable for a bit but already feels in decline, many of the shops now closed. And with a Metro station under construction nearby and other large building works about to commence, it looks as if it won't be 'out of town' much longer.

We sit in a pleasant courtyard and enjoy 'fusion' food: Thai fishcakes, an Anglo-Indian curry, a glass of wine and fresh lime sodas. Sheila and her friend explain that there were many Anglo-Indians at their schools in the 1960s, but there were 'class' distinctions within the Anglo-Indian community itself. Some were poorer, less educated and/or darker skinned. They were sometimes awarded scholarships to these prestigious, expensive private schools and referred to as 'foundationers'. They kept to themselves and were not much accepted either by Indians or fellow Anglo-Indians of a better 'class'.

I realise more and more that, from a larger Indian perspective, Anglo-Indians are just one of many 'other' groups. Perhaps no-one mixes much outside their groups? After Independence, the Indian Constitution tried to deal with non-mainstream groups by designating them as SCs, or Scheduled Castes. These include dalits or untouchables, TCs (people from Tribal areas), and OBCs which stands for 'Other Backward Castes'. What a dreadful designation! Our Western sensitivities find it hard to accept this official use of the word 'backward'.

We also squirm at the official description of those who rise out of the backward class, bettering themselves through affirmative-action programs and then gaining higher incomes or good professions. These are referred to as 'the creamy layer'. A judgment by the Indian Supreme Court in 1992 explicitly used this terminology: 'Just as the cream rises to the top of the milk, this "creamy layer" should not continue (nor their families) to be eligible for preferment and assistance programs available to the Other Backward Castes.' Since OBC's comprise at least 25 per cent of a very, very large population it affects a significant number of people. The income limit for being creamy is officially defined and is set currently at 8 lakhs per annum, a lakh being 100,000 rupees.

When the Indian Constitution was drafted in 1947, seats were reserved for Anglo-Indians because it was thought they needed 'protection' and would never have the numbers to achieve an elected spot. This seat reservation continued until very recently, even though their numbers had dwindled, and did give Anglo-Indians some political influence, especially in the shifting coalitions that can secure government in today's politics.

I arranged to talk to an Anglo-Indian newspaper editor at

The Press Club of India in New Delhi. In its noisy, somewhat decrepit Clubroom, over glasses of very peppery chai, we ranged over all the possible reasons behind negative attitudes to Anglo-Indians. Some I had heard before, some were new to me. The superficial things were obvious: they set themselves apart by their British dress, British-style cooking, English language usage and Christian religion.

They also thought of, and even spoke of, Britain as 'home'. And the fact that so many left India after Independence in 1947 to go to Britain, or to Commonwealth countries such as Canada or Australia, seemed to prove the point. Most Anglo-Indians left. It smacked of disloyalty in Indian eyes. Those who didn't leave, often wished they could. They were sad. They knew there was little future for them in India. They felt unwanted. Some felt it beneath their dignity to mix with Indians, there was some arrogance I was told.

Under British rule the Anglo-Indians had been used as a buffer between the British and the Indian population. One could almost say they had been deliberately 'bred' (encouraged) for this purpose: to provide a third tier, to form a transitional group between the ruling Brits and the awesome mass of the native population. As Gloria Jean Moore[17] pointed out, Anglo-Indians were more hardy than the British: being born in the country they had better immunity to exotic diseases, and they cost nothing to ship out. They knew the country and its customs, they were literate, efficient, reliable. Some claim they were 'the bulwark upon which the British Empire rested.'

They were protected and preferred for jobs by the British.

---

17 *The Anglo-Indian Vision*, AE Press, 1986.

But — and this is a big 'but' — the British never allowed Anglo-Indians to reach the top jobs. They were stuck at middle management level in the Railways, Police, Customs or Telegraph offices. As a result, Anglo-Indians were often the gatekeepers — the officious ones who administered orders from above, denied your requests, knocked you back. So they were resented by the native population for their preferment by the Brits and then resented again for being the people who administered unpopular or inconvenient regulations.

Since Independence there have been some notable exceptions to the 'glass ceiling': several Anglo-Indians have reached the top echelons of military command, for example. But, under British rule, they would never reach any higher than middle levels, no matter how good they were at their jobs. This must have been frustrating and depressing for those with talent or ambition.

There were also other stereotypes to deal with. One image is of Anglo-Indians as fun-loving, happy-go-lucky, sociable, musical, sporty. But the other is of Anglo-Indians as 'wasters', unambitious, lazy. With job opportunities curtailed before and after Independence, those left in India sometimes turned to alcohol or drugs. Some wives turned to prostitution to help make ends meet. This all contributed to a picture of Anglo-Indians as feckless, or worse.

The simple fact that Anglo-Indian women wore Western dress, even went out to work — albeit in seemly occupations such as stenography — was regarded as 'loose' behaviour. And it hasn't changed much: today this is how many Indians still regard girls from states such as Nagaland or Assam who come to work in the bigger Indian cities. Like the Anglo-Indians before them, they are more Westernised in language and dress, are often Christian, and live away from their families in rented accommodation. Even today, they suffer harassment and negative attitudes as a result.

Perhaps mentioning the fact that I, of British heritage, have some Indian blood is a reminder of a colonial past that people prefer to forget or ignore. I am a relic of an unwanted past. Perhaps it's more than about crossing boundaries, about people not keeping their place, within their race or caste? Do Indians subconsciously still regard Anglo-Indians as turncoats, and mixing blood with the British as a sort of betrayal?

At the most basic level, is miscegenation still unacceptable? Could this be so in the 21st century? The visible proof of sexual transgression — across caste, colour, class, race — possibly this remains discomfiting, better not talked about. Literally unspeakable: the 'original sin' of the British tea planter hooking up with 'a native'.

28: Quit India: Stirrings of Nationalism

Despite being half-Indian, my grandfather (Pearl's father, Edward Creed) had grown up with a stern Anglo-Scottish father, steeped in British ideas of how a 'true gentleman' should behave and dress. So her half-Indian father also wore pinstriped suits, spats and a topee. As mentioned earlier, Pearl had been raised and educated in a very British colonial style.

But India was increasingly restive during the War years. The Indian Independence movement had been building for some years and was gathering further momentum, with Gandhi and Nehru its eloquent, charismatic spokesmen. Lord Willingdon, then-Governor of Bombay — and after whom their apartment block had been named — had ordered the jailing of Gandhi. Anti-British riots were growing in intensity. Pearl stopped wearing her uniform to work in the British Censor Office as it indicated her allegiance so clearly.

As an observant person, and from a family who were friendly to all — black, white, rich, poor — the growing divisions in society would have been confronting. Here is what Pearl wrote in 1989, looking back on this time of questioning and doubt:

Quit India was the slogan for independence and although

Mahatma Gandhi preached passive resistance things inevitably got out of hand. Britain had been at war with Germany for some time and was now at war with Japan. The War was close to India now. Britain was in a vulnerable situation. It was the time to strike for independence.

History books have recorded all that [and I should add here that many thousands of Indian soldiers were fighting and dying with British troops in Europe and Africa]. But it was a time of questioning for me. Anglo-Indians had always been intensely loyal to the British. One was only an Anglo-Indian if the English ancestry was on the father's side. If one had an Indian father and a white mother, one was an Indian. Anglo-Indians followed the heritage of the father's side and, since our English-style education fortified this, we were very pro-British as a rule. And from this perspective, Gandhi was the villain.

We lived then in Mahim twelve miles from the office, which was in the city centre, so I took the bus to work. Our house was a five-minute walk to the bus stop and I had to run the gauntlet of a poor area where beggar children collected. One boy was so horrifyingly thin I could never resist slipping him a coin or two. He had obviously told his friends so that soon I looked like a female Pied Piper with a horde of scruffy children following me as I walked to the bus each day. Worse was the fact that they chanted 'Larai-walli' (war-woman) as they followed me. Finally my mother had to send our bearer with me to ward off my growing number of followers.

Now with anti-British riots an almost daily occurrence, my uniform became the stamp of our pro-Britishness, and at my parents' suggestion I stopped wearing it and went to work in 'mufti'. Others did the same. It wasn't just a uniform that raised the wrath of those fighting for Independence: anyone in Western dress, including Indians, particularly those in suits and 'topees' became objects of humiliation. 'Take off your hat' became a command, and my father, driving home from his office had his car, a Renault, stopped by a crowd of rioters. He was made to take off his hat and then drive his car forward and back, a few yards each way, over and over again, while the crowd jeered. He was lucky to escape with no more than a humiliating experience. 'Britishness' was equated with affluence and power so it was understandable that the crowd wanted to 'put down' more than it wanted to hurt. There was no kinder nor less pretentious person than my father who was also dark-skinned and hardly British in appearance. But the clothes and the car were enough.

After his experience it was decided that it was unsafe for me to take the twelve mile bus ride and that I should take the train to the nearest rail-head, Dadar. My father would meet me there and we would drive home via a circuitous route. The very first time I did this unfamiliar exercise, as I began to cross the overhead bridge that linked the two lines, a huge crowd of screaming people rushed towards me. Someone had lit a fire at their end of the bridge. As I turned with them there was smoke coming from the end I had just left.

But it was literally more smoke than fire and no-one was badly injured. I met up with my father and finally we were safely home. My parents were probably more worried about me than they ever showed so it remains in my mind as 'another adventure'. There is a sort of unreality about people in one's own world suddenly erupting into uncharacteristically violent behaviour.

Nearer to being a frightening experience because it revealed the power of anyone obsessed with a cause, was when I was in a bus at the very heart of Bombay city, at Flora Fountain. The bus would soon stop near the Censor Office where I had to alight. But suddenly two Indian students ran out in front of the bus with arms raised ordering it to stop in the middle of the road. The mood in India was so electric that the British troops had been told not to act, or react, in any situation such as this that could easily lead to a riot.

There were two British soldiers on the bus, passengers like the rest of us, but they too remained still, waiting to see whether the next move would be to set the bus on fire or turn it over or just humiliate the passengers. One of the students ran to the door of the bus and screamed 'everybody OUT'. I was nearest to the door and had to make the first move: as I got up I looked straight into a face so filled with rage and hatred that I truly realised the meaning of patriotic fervour. And I was scared!

But that, as far as I know, was the end of the incident: traffic disrupted and a busload of passengers forced to be humble. I hurried to the safety of the Censor Office as fast as I could.

My only other personal experience of the Indian riots happened when my parents were away and my elder sister, Blanche, had come to live in the house with me to keep me company. She had one small son and was pregnant with another — who was born soon after this incident.

Our house at that time was literally on the beach: the back door separated from the sand only by a narrow wall of rocks. The waves at high tide during the monsoon would wash over these rocks and one could feel the spray in the upper balcony of the house. Noises were masked by the sound of the sea but since it was a quiet suburb the sea-noises had little opposition.

We had gone to bed early when, at about midnight, my sister and I were roused by the ayah calling 'Fire!' We looked out of the window and there by the back door was a small fire. We ran downstairs and round to the back door on the sea-side and threw sand over the fire. Only when we had put it out did we discover that someone had pushed kerosene-soaked rags under the back door. It was then that we realised the danger in the situation: whoever had lit the fire was probably close at hand and here we were, three women (one pregnant) completely exposed and vulnerable to anything lurking on that darkened beach. We hurried into the house as quickly as we could.

Disrupting traffic, arson, riots, strikes, street-marches; all these were part of the times. But by then, through my increased knowledge of the Indian point of view (courtesy of my censoring Indian books and articles) I was feeling decidedly less British and understanding the need for Indian independence.

It is interesting to feel my mother's gathering sense of her Indianness. And in tentatively trying to understand contemporary Indians' attitudes to my small tinge of it, I can see that Anglo-Indians today might be a reminder of a time better forgotten. The British can be depicted as a rapacious imperialist power intent only on maximising profit and benefit for themselves. And that is mostly true. I have several times heard it said in India that 'The Brits are the cause of all the poverty in India.' I'm not sure that is entirely true.

But it is easy to see that the British drained and diverted resources and sapped the will and spirit of the subject nation, acting almost entirely in their own commercial and political interests. As do all colonising powers. Shashi Tharoor's book,

Inglorious Empire: What the British Did to India,[18] lays it out in fulsome detail. There were horrific massacres, there was appalling neglect leading to millions of deaths in famines — Tharoor estimates 35 million people died of famine during the Raj, most notoriously in the Bengal Famine of 1943/44.

During the Second World War it was clear that the British acted primarily in their own best interests. But it is a complex picture. In those War years of which my mother was writing, Indian troops were fighting and dying for a (dying) British Empire while a rebel Indian National Army began siding with the Japanese, at the same time as my British father was fighting against the Japanese in the jungles of Burma to stop them getting into India.

Then, finally, there was the over-hasty British departure from India, leaving a bitter, arbitrary division into India and Pakistan. This was the wrenching horror of what is known as The Partition. Millions displaced or dead. Shamlu's story was but one tiny example of the traumas that affected Hindus and Muslims alike as they fled their lands, jockeyed for new places in strange parts, suffered ruination, desperation, and bore tragic losses of family members. Tharoor wrote: 'The British were heedless of the lives that would be lost in their headlong rush to the exits,' and 'No greater indictment of the failures of British rule in India can be found than the tragic manner of its ending.'

18 Scribe, 2017 (2016).

29: Still Searching for Indian Granny, Mabel

Indians are currently the fastest growing immigrant group in the state of Victoria where I live. Australia is a melting pot of nationalities, especially post-1973 when the White Australia Policy was officially disbanded. So, to be of mixed blood in multicultural Australia is of very little interest to younger generations. And in India most offspring of Anglo-Indians 'marry out' so the Anglo percentage of their mixed blood is dwindling. Just as Anglo-Indians become more 'Indian' in blood, so Indians generally are becoming more Anglo, more Westernised, in behaviour, dress, even thought. These shifts blur what were once sharper distinctions.

Maybe the non-response in modern India to my touch of Indian blood is as simple as something one encounters anywhere — people not especially interested, or not knowing what questions to ask. Whether you are a Swede in Australia or an Aussie in France or a Nigerian in Belgium, all foreigners experience something of this lack of curiosity. And, in a multiculturally mixed-up world, it's become increasingly irrelevant.

As time has permitted, I have been gradually working my way into the parcels of papers and letters in the blue suitcase under the bed in Melbourne. I have found a small pile of letters written by my great-grandfather Louis James Creed (Louis the Transgressor) to his son, Edward, my grandfather. I am hoping to find some mention of Louis' Indian wife or of attitudes that prevailed at the time.

In a distinctive hand, fountain pen and neat italic-style, most of the letters admonish his son to be a better businessman. He is outraged that his son hasn't immediately replied to his letters, saying that such laziness in personal matters of correspondence will 'inevitably' lead to bad business habits. There are hints of treacherous business partners making off with funds, and father exhorts son to take someone to task, but to do so 'in a gentlemanly manner'.

In fact, poor Edward is trying to run one of his father's failing quarries in South India and, more obviously, he is trying to earn his father's respect. Father, though stern, is clearly fair to his staff and thoughtful of their needs. He is loving too as there are many affectionate messages to his son and references to his two daughters, their new dresses, their health. He describes joyful outings with his girls. He takes them on train trips, enjoys their excitement, he encourages their reading.

But his Indian wife Mabel, Edward's mother, doesn't seem to be with them on these excursions. Or, if she was there, she isn't mentioned. In all the letters, there is only one reference to her and it's en passant. Even then she is not named. Louis says that a visitor had been to their house (presumably an English visitor) who 'made no mention of mother and the girls'. Louis then adds, tellingly: 'And I didn't ask.' I can only assume this refers to his 'coloured' wife and half-caste daughters. Poor Mabel the unmentionable.

A bit more information has very recently come to light, again translated from French and sent by my French cousin. It tells us that Mabel was only 15 when she married Louis Creed, shocking to us but not unusually young for an Indian girl at the time. (And even young women in Victorian England were deemed a bit over-the-hill when they reached their twenties.) Although Louis was by then in his early thirties, the dearth of potential partners of similar ilk did cause problems for European men. Especially when they lived out of the major cities. (And Louis' previous fiancée, Henrietta Money, no doubt deemed a suitable match, had died after a fall from her horse.)

The French document claimed it was evident from Mabel's forehead marking (an Indian *tikka* presumably) that she was a Lingayet Brahmin. This confirmed what I had previously heard about her place in the Indian caste system, the Brahmins being regarded as the uppermost level.

So Louis Creed had made a bold — some would say foolhardy — decision to marry this young local Indian girl while he was also struggling to establish quarries in India. Meanwhile, his youngest sister, Rose, had moved to France and married into the family of a prestigious music publisher, Heugel et Cie, founded in 1839. For several generations this family was at the centre of French musical and artistic life. Artists were commissioned to illustrate the cover sheets of musical scores, amongst them Alphonse Mucha and Jules Cheret. Marcel Proust's secret love, the composer Reynaldo Hahn, had his work published by the Heugel company, as did many famous French composers, including Offenbach, Delibes, Faure, Massenet, Poulenc and, the more contemporary, Boulez and Dutilleux. In 1896 Heugel published songs composed by Hahn with words by Proust.

So, at about the same time as Louis Creed was courting

disgrace by marrying a 15-year-old Indian orphan, his sister's French family was entertaining Marcel Proust to tea! The contrast between the lives of these two siblings is fascinating to consider.

In a curious parallel to Mabel's early story as a foundling after a storm, it transpired that Louis, her husband, died as a result of an infection sustained after a severe cyclone hit the Madras coast in 1916. I found an old newspaper cutting describing the scene. It was night-time, the rain and wind were howling, the roof of his house was blown off, trees uprooted and buildings torn to shreds around him. Amidst the chaos, his house and office buildings collapsing, he rescued the young daughter of one of his staff. The little girl was stuck under fallen roofing material and was severely injured. He sheltered her under his overcoat until the storm passed.

The newspaper said that he acted heroically and there were suggestions that he should be awarded a medal for his actions on the night. He was described as a hero 'with a very big soul'.

I discovered a letter to his son who had heard news of this. He responded to his son: 'I am not a hero. Just an ordinary Englishman who acted as anyone would, and with just a small soul!' But, aged 64 and prone to bronchial infections, he became ill and never really recovered. He died a year later in 1917.

Mabel lived on until 1928. The only other reference I could find was in a note of condolence written to her son, my grandfather Edward, by an aunt and cousins in France on hearing news of Mabel's death. They expressed sorrow and sympathised with his 'extreme grief' at her passing. But they said nothing personal about her. I stared at two formal studio photographs of the pair. Although they are black and white photos, Louis is clearly blue-eyed, sandy-haired and a bit chinless, while Mabel sits beside him, dark-skinned, frowning, in a pale sari with an embroidered border, some modest jewellery ...

I am pleased to learn later from my mother's cousin in Canada that his mother, who was Mabel's eldest daughter, left them where they lived in Goa and went home to Bangalore to nurse Mabel when she became gravely ill. At some time after, she must have been moved to Bombay because my aunt in London mentioned that 'grandma Mabel', also known as 'Indian granny', lived with them until she died. And this was in the apartments in Willingdon House where the journey into my Indian connections began.

30: Getting Down to Business: Exasperations and Compensations

Since my mother re-visited India in 1957, and went again in the 1980s, India had gone through decades of economic and social change. But some things, good and bad, stayed the same. She told us stories of mistakes and idiosyncracies that made us chuckle with amusement. Similarly now, trying to be profound businesspersons, Sue and I veer between annoyance and amusement, but often settle on mild exasperation.

We've concluded that it's best to deal with India in pairs. Tolerance levels vary from day to day as one becomes tired, or suffers tummy ailments, or just gets sick of the endless negotiating over goods, over fares, over destinations ('No, we do not want to go to your Uncle's emporium!') Provided one of us is feeling strong, the other can sit smiling weakly, a version of Good Cop, Bad Cop.

Early on in our business, when we were importing fabric to be made up in Melbourne, we ordered 120 metres of black silk-cotton. When it arrived, it was not black but mid-grey. When we protested, we were met first with silence. Then, after repeated emails, we were told: 'Madam, it is the Indian black.' This was nonsense as it wasn't even a dark grey. But mistakes are never admitted. The first-line response is no response. Then, there may be some story or other as to why grey rather than black. If only they would say, from the outset: 'Black isn't possible. Will grey be alright, instead?'

Tough-minded businessmen of my acquaintance are bemused by our acceptance of this being how things are: 'Why don't you get angry?' / 'Why aren't you firmer with them?' / 'I presume you won't pay,' and so on. But it's not how things work, at least not in our small-scale milieu of relationships that matter. We know a lot of sweat (and other foreign bodies) has gone into the handweaving of those 120 grey metres. We have gradually used most of it. It is lovely, even if not black.

Recently we ordered some jackets in Jaipur. We took trouble, while we were on the spot, to get samples made. We had to be sure that four key variables would be exactly as we wanted: the right colour, the right sizes, the precise block-print we chose, and the right shape of jacket. Great care was taken because our order the year before had been sent in the wrong sizes. This time there would be no mistakes, no 'goof-ups' as another supplier called them, when she sent us button-front dresses with no buttons sewn on.

The jackets were duly ordered, carefully, in writing, after approving the samples. Some weeks later when they arrived in Melbourne, they were the right colour, the right sizes and the right print. But the wrong shape of jacket. We emailed our rebukes, our disappointment. No reply. Then: 'We will make up the right ones and have them with you in a couple of weeks.' No apology. We said, 'Okay, but what do we do with these wrong ones? We don't want both lots.' Email silence for a few days.

Then we received a peremptory email instruction to send

them to someone in Canberra, name and address supplied. We googled this person and saw that she had a small business a bit like ours. Naturally, we rang her to confirm the arrangement, only to discover she had heard nothing about it. Although she sometimes used this supplier herself, she didn't want our jackets. When we remonstrated with the supplier by email his only response was: 'Well, why did you ring her?'

We were astonished by his cavalier response, but clearly he was content to have shifted the problem. He had placed the goods on the equivalent of 'ambulance bypass' until they found a home. In the end, we kept both lots of jackets. And, of course, the supplier knows this will be the outcome if he just 'blanks' us. In fact he will quite likely end up being paid for two lots of jackets. We informed him we would pay for any jackets we sold and return any leftovers (if we could be bothered stuffing them in our suitcases).

When we were in Jaipur the next year, he was surprised to see us appear with money we owed for the extra jackets sold. He had effectively doubled his order. And we had twice the number of happily jacketed customers. Good business practice all round, Indian style! And the fact that he sports a six-carat diamond ring suggests his business tactics may be worthy of emulation.

Exasperation is most often provoked by reluctance to 'tell it straight' and the habitual tendency to avoid saying 'no'. While based on a commendable desire to please, it has led to a lot of problems for us. We plead with our very Westernised suppliers: 'Please do tell us if something goes wrong or if it is not possible to do what we ask. We would much rather know. Please!' But we have rarely succeeded. And the endearing sideways head nod can be difficult for Westerners to interpret. It is often supposedly saying 'okay, yes'. But it feels a bit un-emphatic, a bit too ambiguous. In a business one hankers for certainty. They're also fond of saying: 'That should be okay.' Should be? We need 'will be'!

Although it can be frustrating, we quite enjoy the annual argy-bargy. And there is both pleasure and challenge in literally clambering over hillocks of clothing, fishing out something that looks promising from underneath a piled mass. It's not easy. It's often hot, airless and dusty in these warehouses. Our customers think we just go to India and buy. In fact it's quite hard to find things that we like and that will suit us. That's why we mostly make to our own designs. But it's also nice to buy some ready-mades, such as the ubiquitous cotton quilted jackets. If we find a garment that approximates our preferences, we order it with variations. Which then may lead to the sort of saga described before: charming, or sometimes not-so-charming irregularities...

With our regular main suppliers, we enjoy their company and all that we learn about their lives. Importantly, we trust each other — we know they won't intentionally diddle us financially. They often don't demand the 50 per cent upfront before shipping that is common practice. We pay when it all arrives. If we query an item on the bill, Sheila might say: 'Just bring what you think you owe me and pay on your next trip.' Our husbands, experienced in more hard-headed worlds, shake their heads and wonder if this is a way to do business.

On the other hand, we're not sure that our suppliers have come to understand our needs any better. We are repeatedly inconvenienced by their failure to advise us of imminent courier arrivals. They can't comprehend that there could be literally no-one at home. Even in the poorest home in India, there is always someone at home: a servant, a child, an elderly relative.

In general, we have become far less anxious, more accommodating, more philosophical. Perhaps we have become more Indian? We can see why people might be temperamentally allergic to doing business in India. But not the two Melburnian MOTI partners for whom relationships matter, enjoyment matters, and insight into India matters.

31: Beggars, Charities
and Female Disadvantage

A few years ago we visited Shantiniketan, about four hours' drive from Kolkata. With a population of only about 80,000, it is home to a famous university, founded by Rabindranath Tagore, and located around his family home. It has boasted many famous alumni over the decades, including Satyajit Ray and past Prime Minister Indira Gandhi. This small city (by Indian standards) has produced two Nobel Prize winners — Rabindranath Tagore, poet, playwright, novelist and artist, and more recently Amartya Sen, the social economist and author.

We had come with Shamlu who was taking us to visit the workplace of a group of *kantha* artisans, supported by her NGO.[19] It is in their team-leader's home. We were ushered into the living room, containing several plump couches, formal Victorian-style chairs and side tables. In pride of place amongst the furnishings was a free-standing, green ceramic washbasin, fully plumbed in. We were treated to a delicious array of foodstuffs and drinks in the adjoining dining area. Clearly, they had gone to great effort and we were grateful and humbled. We always do our best to

---

19 Self Help Enterprise Foundation (SHE).

eat even when not hungry, and even when slightly worried about hygiene (though that basin in the sitting room augured well).

The embroiderers were in a long, slightly dingy hallway, sitting on the concrete floor working. At first, we were dismayed. This wasn't what we had imagined. But then we realised it was very practical. Indian workers often choose to sit cross-legged on the floor. They have the necessary flexibility we lack. These girls were working on long pieces of fabric — mostly tussar silk — which would become dupattas or saris. Saris come in approximately six-metre lengths of fabric so, with this seating arrangement, one person can sit on one side of the corridor, back against the wall for support if needed, while another can work at the other end of the same sari, her back against the opposite wall, fabric piling in the middle. There were plenty of beaming faces as we wended our way down the corridor, awkwardly skirting this beautiful stitchery.

In an adjoining room, we watched the supervisor who marked out the underlying pattern that the girls would use as guidelines for their hand stitching. She was using stencils and an old-fashioned Reckitt's blue bag. We noticed she had only one arm. Sitting cross-legged on the ground, she held the stencil down with one foot, the blue bag working speedily and lightly in her only hand.

Back in Kolkata, each swathed in newly purchased silk *kantha* stoles, Shamlu took us to a party at the Sheraton Hotel to launch its opulent new Presidential Suite. It cost then (a few years ago now) over $1,000 per night. We were treated to 'street food' stalls (very upmarket street food!) and people milling around dressed in well-cut suits, lush saris and sparkling jewellery. But right next door was a slum sheltering Bangladeshi refugees.

It is similar in Delhi where a flashy new shopping mall, full of expensive international brand names, is located right next to a slum. It's not surprising, I suppose, that vacant land attracts both the destitute and the developer. The book by Katherine Boo[20] about the Mumbai slums illustrates this dichotomy very clearly: the slum children aspiring to work in the plush hotels alongside. But it is an uncomfortable juxtaposition for us Westerners, used to poverty being fairly well hidden and rarely hard up against ostentatious wealth.

More generally in India, one is always beset with the dilemma of poverty and beggars. How to respond? It's a 'nuisance' to be so often confronted: it's in your face all the time, and it constantly tests your sense of injustice, your generosity, your patience. At first we gave to everyone. If they need, why shouldn't they have? It is small change for us but may make a big difference to them. We always carried our 'beggar's purse', a small purse into which we placed all coins. Then we added all 10-rupee notes to the purse. Then 20s. Then, as the years went on, 50s. And 100s. This cash stash is ready to hand out easily, without the awkwardness and delay of fishing into handbags and wallets.

We have become slightly more discriminating these days, though it still feels uncomfortable to deny anyone. Our Indian friends, and our drivers, tell us we shouldn't give to school-age children, or to their parents who encourage their begging, because the kids should be in school. Government schools are free and education to a certain level is compulsory. Their parents are exploiting them and ruining their potential futures. But the family depends on the income a child can bring in by begging.

---

20 *Behind the Beautiful Forevers: Life, Death and Hope in a Mumbai Undercity*, Random House, 2012.

It's a dilemma, a moral and practical dilemma that two visitors can never hope to resolve.

For a few years we donated money to a school for street children in Kolkata.[21] The challenge, the owners told us, was to keep the parents onside. The school fed the children every day so that parents would allow their children to stop begging, at least for the morning. They brought the parents in for a meal each week to enable a regular pep-talk about the value of education for their children. Without this extra outreach they knew they risked losing the children who would soon be back on the streets.

One hears that babies are drugged by their parents so that they look listless and ill. This is horrible. But what should we do? Not give? If a parent is prepared to use such measures they must be desperate. Again we are cautioned: 'They live in a nice house round the corner' / 'They are using the money for their drug habits,' and so on. Our drivers are coldly dismissive of beggars. On one trip there was a regular beggar on the corner near our hotel. Having no legs, he propelled himself on a flat, wheeled trolley attached to his torso, just a castor-height above the ground. To us he was appallingly vulnerable as he approached cars at the traffic lights, well down below our window level. When we commented on his absence one Sunday morning, Darshan responded curtly: 'Of course not. He only works six days a week.' We were with a guide once who, needing change for a large note, went to a beggar to get it! There are certainly more matter-of-fact attitudes to money here in India, but getting change from a beggar? Beggars belief!

---

21 Tomorrow's Foundation.

We routinely give to beggars who are elderly, disabled, lame. That's if we can get our hand out of the car window fast enough before the traffic lights change or traffic jam clears. Tragically, there is no shortage of needy recipients in India and we know there is nothing much by way of welfare support. We are told that people can always get meals at temples. And we know there are a lot of charities doing wonderful work in India. But the need is so great. There is still widespread malnutrition and poverty in India despite its increasing affluence.

Our business has made contributions by allocating a percentage of profits for this purpose. Each of our suppliers is actively involved in charitable works. I have already mentioned Shamlu's chairmanship of the Calcutta Foundation and of SHE (Self-Help Enterprises). Via Shamlu, we have contributed to earthquake relief and to a tube well in the village of her women workers.

Another friend and supplier, Madhavi at Manan in Khan market, encouraged our contributions to an NGO[22] helping to feed slum children. Sheila and a close friend founded a school for the children of her workers in a very poor area of south Delhi. We contributed what we could and watched this school grow each year. On one visit, we shook hands with each child as we handed out their mid-morning snack, smiling girls and boys wriggling and giggling.

In recent years we have closely followed the efforts of young Satish, our sometime driver in Delhi. Though his family have had tough times of their own (which you will find out about in Chapter 36), Satish has regularly helped those less fortunate,

---

22 The Samarpan Foundation.

for example, raising money for shoes and socks for poor people in the cold Delhi winters.

Now, in a project that seems unlikely for a young single man, he is actively involved in a program to deal with the troubling issue of menstrual hygiene. As in many countries, there is silence and shame attached to menstruation. In some parts of India, women have to live in a shed or outhouse during their monthly periods. The wife of our quite well-educated guide in Varanasi could not be included in our photograph of his family as it was her 'time of the month'. She had to look on from another room.

Some estimates suggest that a staggering 75 per cent of Indian women can't afford commercial sanitary pads and hence use rags, newspapers, straw. Unsanitary sanitary habits lead to terrible infections and even infertility. The small number of toilets in schools, and the distressing lack of cleanliness, plus the embarrassment of the girls, means they stay home for five days every month, totalling almost two months of schooling missed every year. On top of that, their female teachers also don't turn up, for the same reasons. It adds up to a worryingly negative impact on girls' education.

However, there is also the disposal dilemma: if all those 75 per cent of women adopted commercial products, or even made their own disposable sanitary napkins, there would be a huge disposal problem. As a result, there are moves towards biodegradable pads and hygienic, anti-bacterial re-usable pads (at low cost), but it's still a very significant issue. We have paid for an incinerator in the lavatory of a home for abandoned girls in Delhi. But incineration brings its own environmental problems. An on-going challenge to add to the enormous list of challenges in India and how best to assist.

Two years ago Satish and a partner, Ambreen, founded an NGO called Uboontu[23] to continue their work in a registered (and regulated) manner. She is a qualified social planner and is Muslim. Satish is a Hindu. Their religions are irrelevant as far as they are concerned. They both just feel strongly about helping others less fortunate. They have rented premises in an urban slum that provides a space to offer the local girls certified training in computer skills, to have singing or guitar lessons, and to improve nutritional and menstrual hygiene awareness. Working with local, government-backed community health workers (called ashas), they have wisely decided to make an impact in one geographic area of need. This is actually the slum in which Satish grew up and he is proud to be contributing.

When I last visited, there was a queue of teenage girls receiving, at no cost, the Gardasil vaccine (developed by an Australian) to help prevent cervical cancer, and normally very expensive. They are also providing a nutritious midday meal at the little primary school next door and plan a similar outreach to pregnant women in the area.

Uboontu's sessions on menstrual awareness and hygiene have been extended to boys, to help dispel the many myths surrounding menstruation. On our last visit we learned they have been asked to train teachers in 600 government schools to teach their program. This will potentially reach 100,000 young women, and men. And now, in the 2020 COVID-19 pandemic, the slogan 'Periods don't pause for Pandemics' tells its own story. They have been handing out parcels of dry food staples, like lentils and rice, plus sanitary pads.

---

23 uboontufoundation.org

The efforts of these two young people, using a small team of volunteers, plus strategic coordination with other charities, are extraordinary. We were sceptical at first. It all seemed too good to be true, literally. But watching the programs in action over the past five years or so has been a revelation. How many young men in the West — with minimal formal education (Satish left school at 15) and a job driving tourists to and from the airport — would forgo a large part of their mid-career earning potential for a menstrual hygiene project?

32: Paradox, Corruption and Democracy

Sometimes the ineptitude we encounter in India is charming and amusing. Sometimes it's just plain irritating. There is abundant paradox: it seems inexplicable that a country with such fine artisans, producing intricate stonework, marble carved as finely as lace, Taj Mahal-like pietra dura work, but can't lay a straight road kerb. How is it that we get beautiful embroidery for our garments, the finest rouleaus and pintucks, yet the buttons often fall off? Why can't a light-switch panel on the wall be put on straight? Why doesn't the client demand it? Why is shoddy — *kutcha* or makeshift — workmanship so widely accepted?

Why does it take so long for roadworks — and the much-loved flyovers — to be completed? Why do we see only one or two manual labourers doing desultory shovelling when there's such a huge workforce available? Why are the roads always so bad, even when they are newly built?

Corruption, we are told. This is the root of so many problems in India. The sub-contractors don't put the right amount of lime or cement or asphalt in the mix for buildings or roads, in order to squeeze extra rupees from their payment. Paint is watered down and, as a result, it wears off quickly. The weather we are told. Harsh monsoonal climates take their toll on all external surfaces, roads especially. Buildings look grimy from weather and pollution very soon after they are completed, or soon after re-painting. Maintenance needs to be constant and hence is expensive.

Why is there so little sense of 'the civic' space? The kerbside outside a swanky boutique might be filthy, or crumbling. Enormous rotting piles of garbage lie on the ground right outside a warehouse we visit in Jaipur. Inside, the most beautiful handwoven fabrics are being carefully hand-block printed. Fluttering over the balconies overlooking this garbage are metres of lovely fabrics drying in the polluted breeze.

This is perplexing to a Westerner, knowing there's an enormous well of low-paid labour, needing work. But India is so easy to criticise. And mine isn't truly a criticism. It is more a lament. Anyone can see the enormity of the task. Like changing the direction of a vast ship. A country so huge geographically, with great variety in its regional climates, in its languages and dialects, with enormous disparities in income and education — where would one start?

And, perversely, I don't want India to change. Already I rue the shopping malls, the Western dress, the cars supplanting Ambassadors, the Ambassadors supplanting camels and elephants, Nanos supplanting tuk-tuks, tiramisu supplanting gulab jamun! I dislike that sort of globalisation. India has such a unique quality and remains its own 'person'. Selfishly, I want it to stay like that.

When my mother returned for her last visit in the 1980s, she was dismayed at how her 1930s Bombay had changed. It was dispiriting. Family all gone, emigrated to Canada, New Zealand or England in the intervening years. The buildings and landmarks she had loved were dirty and dismal, the air polluted, the traffic appalling. Similarly, the India that Sue and I began our relationship with two decades ago has changed rapidly before our red, dry eyes.

On our return from each visit, my mother would tentatively enquire: 'Did you still like it? Did the mess and decay and poverty bother you?' She wanted us to love it as she did. And I could quite honestly reply that we somehow see through it, our gaze passes (avoids) the problems. Objectively, I know the side of the road is littered, even disgusting, and heart-breaking sights clamour for attention. But we can nevertheless appreciate the abundant trees of Delhi, or sudden crumbling bits of a Mughal monument that emerge through the traffic, or the flash of a colourful sari …

Much has been achieved in India over the years we have been visiting. Many more people have moved up the economic scale. We know about the growing Indian middle class, earning and spending amounts that were unthinkable for these millions of people only a decade or two ago. And there are numerous achievements we could emulate. I can only mention a few we have personally observed. I have no doubt there are many more large and small improvements that any Indian politician would proudly point out.

For example, in Delhi about 15 years ago it was mandated that tuk-tuks and buses would change to CNG. It had a dramatic impact on air quality at the time. Similarly, Delhi successfully banned plastic bags several years ago. We have only recently embarked on this in Australia. There has to be legislative (and popular) will to do it, accompanied by successful enforcement. They did that in Delhi, now a city of almost 30 million people!

The Delhi underground was built efficiently and to a high quality. On time, on budget and is being extended all the time. Our city of Melbourne hasn't yet managed a fast train to the airport. Sadly, none of these measures has headed off increasing vehicle pollution and Delhi now has the dubious distinction of topping Beijing as the most polluted city on earth.

But the overwhelming negative for India is the pervasive corruption, beginning with the alarming statistic that in the 2014 election about 34 per cent of MPs elected had criminal cases against them, nine for murder, 17 for attempted murder. Sixty-three MPs elected for the winning BJP party had serious criminal charges against them. In fact, people with criminal charges were more likely to be elected than those without. There are successful candidates who conduct their campaigns from jail. The 2018 election was won by PM Modi's BJP in a landslide, but newspaper reports suggest almost 43 per cent of newly elected members won despite facing criminal charges. Since they hadn't yet been convicted, they were eligible to stand and to take their places in the Parliament.

They haven't been convicted because, innocent or guilty, the legal system is dysfunctional: cases may take decades to wend their way through a system that has a backlog of over 30 million cases. The police are not trusted, many take bribes. Bureaucrats can be bought, driving licences are bought, everything has a price, every system can be corrupted. Public trust in those who govern is nil. The educated classes often don't vote as they feel so disaffected. Votes are bought, sometimes with pitiful little bribes, such as a throat lozenge. That people are willing to be bought for so little demonstrates the level of corruption — but also the level of need.

We hear stories of Mayawati, ex-Chief Minister of Uttar Pradesh, spending inordinate amounts of public money on self-aggrandising statues, including one of her holding a Queen Elizabeth-style handbag made out of gold. The first version was not to her liking so she had it re-built, at vast expense. Although she was from a Dalit (untouchable) background herself, she encouraged the poor to 'donate' to her campaigns, taking their jewellery in exchange for a gift of a cheap polyester sari. She amassed enough money to buy a hugely expensive apartment in a very upmarket area of Delhi. Even if these stories are only half true, they are shocking.

The anti-corruption political movement led by Anna Hazare was initially very successful with huge crowds attending rallies, resulting in the successful election of several candidates in the Delhi Legislature. But subsequent inexperience and poor judgment have left supporters dismayed. Nationally, the ousting of the Congress party in 2014 in favour of the BJP, was a protest vote against multiple examples of Congress's corrupt politics and corrupt administration. It remains to be seen whether Prime Minister Modi and his party, elected to a second term in 2018, will be able to curtail any of it.

However, a Bloomberg article, published soon after Mr Modi's win, was alarming. It began: 'Amit Shah is on trial for ordering three murders, kidnapping witnesses, running an extortion racket and hiring criminals to shoot up a rival's headquarters. Between court hearings, he'll now be running India's ruling party, the Bharatiya Janata party.' This man was appointed President of the BJP, two months after the party was elected in the 2014 landslide with anti-corruption as one of its main mantras.

Of course, there are so many exceptions to this bleak picture: individuals, programs, policies, outreaches that are exemplary. Indian democracy is in some respects a shining light in the world. It is amazing that genuinely democratic elections are carried out with relative efficiency, with relatively little violence, given that it is such a massive undertaking with around 900 million voters, 10 million election officials and a million polling stations.

But, after their votes are exercised, Indians are often let down by their politicians. Indian friends we speak to shrug their shoulders in resignation and remain deeply cynical about politics. Unfortunately, this means they often don't vote. They say it seems pointless. Coming from Australia where voting is compulsory, we don't have the choice to opt out. We think that opting out is bad for democracy. It is sad that well-informed Indians don't vote because they are so disheartened with governments of all persuasions.

33: Feminine India?

There is another thing that I ruminate upon: why does India seem to appeal more to Western women than to Western men? Every place we visit, every place we stay in, has a preponderance of female tourists. Sue and I began our trips to India together because our husbands didn't want to go again. It's not that they hadn't enjoyed their visits in the 1960s. But that was enough.

Many of the women we meet, travelling together, in small or large groups, explain that they have always wanted to visit India but their husbands don't. So they eventually come without them, usually later in life, when free of children or after retirement. There are lots of young women too, often travelling alone, who say (despite the horrors of rapes) that they feel quite safe in India, once they get used to being stared at constantly.

Women seem to fall easily under India's spell. Like Sue and me, they become addicted. They return home and immediately begin plotting the next trip. We've also met women doing business in India who, again like us, had started their enterprises primarily for this reason: in order to return to India regularly. What is it about India that's so enticing, and especially to women?

When I asked our twenty-something driver if he had any ideas why women like India so much, he said, without hesitation and quite sincerely: 'We are very caring. We do really care about looking after people.' I think this is true. Part of what we enjoy about our trips is the sense of being looked after. Possibly, being older women helps. India is difficult, harsh, exhausting but we feel genuinely looked after. We miss that feeling at home, despite loving husbands and family. This is somehow different. Indian men seem to understand about family and accept that one puts family first. Sons know it is their duty to look after their mothers, their aunts, their sisters.

We wonder if what attracts women more than men is that India is more 'feminine' or 'feminised'? Or is it just that Western men find the teeming crowds, the noise, the dirt too hard to deal with? Women seem to cope with it better, more accustomed perhaps to crowded shopping and the small chaoses of family life with children, tiny microcosms of the inchoate multitudes in India.

There are volumes of words written and debated around the issue of 'the other', of Edward Said, of Orientalism/ Occidentalism, of the stereotypes of the East as romantic, exotic and 'feminine', while the West is rational and 'masculine'. But what I am talking about in this chapter is altogether more prosaic and literal: it's simply the reflections and observations of a long-time visitor, with a background in psychosocial research.

As a rashly sweeping generalisation, there seem to be two broad types of middle-class Indian men — the bumptious, pompous and overbearing types and the self-deprecating, charming, kind types. We often experience the latter in both women and men, but it is more noteworthy in the men as it seems rather different from Australian (and British) men. As we are now entering the elderly demographic (the one that irritatingly says '65+' on questionnaires, as if there is no difference between a 66-year-old and an 89-year-old) we are often surprised by the attentiveness and courtesy shown by Indian men at social functions. We don't experience the same thing from strangers at a cocktail party in Australia.

Staying in the restful Loharu Guest House in Jaipur, we struck up a conversation with an Indian teacher who conducts courses for American college students. He said his classes of 25 students each year almost always had about 22 women to three men. He surmised that — since students can choose courses in Europe, Africa or India — females are more interested in developmental issues while young men are more likely to opt for management/leadership courses in EU placements. Women are more likely to be involved in the 'helping' professions, to be interested in welfare, in education, in health — all areas that employ more women than men in Western countries. So a placement in Africa or India might appeal more to women than to men.

Anecdotal evidence from several travel agents in Australia, and in India, suggests more female than male tourists from the West. Women are particularly interested in textiles, jewellery and handcrafts, all of which are a lure to India, perhaps less likely to be shared by Western men. The commonly offered textile tours comprise almost all female participants. Perhaps women are more inclined to explore aspects of the spiritual, to be more introspective, sometimes following Indian spiritual leaders or gurus. Yoga schools, meditation experiences, ashrams and suchlike tend to attract more women than men.

But we wonder if there is something else? Something more intangible about Indian life, and Indian culture, that is attractive to women. It is in some respects a matriarchal society. There are certainly a few matrilineal states, though this is not the same as matriarchal. In general, men abdicate the domestic space, leaving women (often several generations of them) to exercise dominion. And Indian women can be formidable and extremely bossy. There are myriad stories of daughters-in-law, who are obliged to move into their husband's family, being horribly mistreated by their mothers-in-law.

Perhaps most significant of all is the structure of households: men often grow up with aunties, grandmothers, sisters-in-law all under the same roof. Frequently, there are more females than males in the households, due to differential gender lifespans and less freedom for women to pursue independent lives outside the home. So, ignoring the huge issue of how women are treated, there may simply be more 'female-ness' in a young man's upbringing than in the West.

My grandfather supported his mother, his mother-in-law, a widowed sister and two nieces. As well as his own immediate family consisting of a wife, two daughters and two sons. Those boys grew up with a lot of women in their lives! In our Delhi guest house, the male half of the couple who run it lives with a wife, two daughters, his mother-in-law and, until her death, a grandmother-in-law. Satish, our young driver, lives with his mother and father, his new wife, his two sisters and two young nieces. He accepts that he and his father must support all of them, an unhesitating commitment. His wife, who used to work full-time in a call centre, now doesn't work: it's a sign of 'middle class' status to be supported by her husband. And Satish feels proud of his role.

Do Western men dislike some feminine-ness they detect in Indian men? Find them too soft? The Indian cricket team had to learn some toughness, it was said, from the Aussies. They were coached in sledging and other such unpleasant practices. And it has to be said that they have subsequently been very successful.

In general, we notice that young men in India seem easy with women, and with older women in particular. Psychoanalyst Sudhir Kakar says mother-son bonding is stronger in India than in the West and the 'issue of men's inner femaleness' is more charged and active in India than elsewhere — men either cling to it, remain open to their femininity, or resist it by asserting a fierce masculinity. Either way, he sees it as one of the main issues of human development, probably everywhere but somehow more so in India. We certainly see it in the dichotomy I mentioned earlier — that Indian men either seem kind, attentive and self-deprecating or pompous, bombastic and over assertive.

In the West the individual is prime. In India (and other Asian cultures), relationships are prime, the collective is valued more highly. Comparative cultural studies have shown that India places far greater emphasis on the collective than do countries such as Australia, the US or UK. In India one sees the 'subsuming of individual identity to group interests' (Kakar). In India, it is expected that relatives or members of a group will take care of each other, whereas we in the West, broadly speaking, expect the individual to look after him or herself.

Westerners may experience this collectivism, this primacy of the family, of the group, this connectedness, as 'feminine'. Maybe this contributes to Western men feeling a bit uncomfortable. They may see young Indian men, who often walk holding hands, as a bit effeminate, whereas it is culturally normal. It must affect ways of doing business in India: why some can cope with it and others can't and why more of those who cope may be women.

This might be a reason we so enjoy our business in India. For us, relationships are definitely prime and we accept this, with all its upsides and downsides.

Indian men are often kind. A few years ago we visited Gwalior, site of the marvellously imposing Gwalior Fort. It rises from dusty plains, almost 100 metres high, partially constructed and partially taking advantage of towering sandstone cliffs and precipices. The approach to the fort has rows of Jain sculptures, each up to 20 metres high, and within the fort are palaces and temples.

In the town of Gwalior is the Jai Vilas Palace, an Italianate extravaganza, designed by an Englishman in 1872. The present Maharaja lives in part of it, but the rest is open to the public. Sue and I went there after clambering around the fort, so we were weary (I seem to say this a lot. But it is true, India is tiring). We mounted a grand, curving staircase, astonished to realise that its rails and banisters were carved entirely from rock crystal. We entered the Durbar Hall. Suddenly, I felt faint and had to sit.

Our guide naturally assumed I was overcome with wonder at the sight of the world's largest chandelier. As it turned out, it was due to nasty bacteria beginning their feverish work. I recovered enough to learn that two vast chandeliers each weigh 3½ tons and that the ceiling was tested for bearing their weight by 10 elephants trampling the ceiling from above. In the dining room, there is an almost cricket-pitch-sized dining table. Set inside its perimeter, there is a silver track with a nifty battery-operated silver train that transported after-dinner port and cigars to the seated guests.

Returning to our hotel, located in a former Maharaja's palace, I felt terrible. The dreaded Delhi-belly had set in, with attached fever (poor Delhi always gets the blame due to its convenient rhyming). I took to bed in my elegant marble-floored room. It had a huge bathroom that, in my knackered state, seemed too far from my bed. I used the bedside phone to ring housekeeping to ask for an extra blanket as the fever was chilling me to the bone.

A knock on the door heralded a young man in his early twenties, in a crisp white hotel uniform. He came in, ushered me back to bed, added the new blanket, tucked me in very firmly, turned off the light and, with a gentle pat on the shoulder, told me to rest. It was exactly the sort of mothering I needed.

Our clothing manufacturer, Sheila, once had a large shipment of garments to be sent by truck from Delhi to Mumbai for shipping to New York. A deadline to meet as usual. She sent it off on its road trip, but it didn't show up in Mumbai by the due day. No sign of it. No word from the driver. No answer to her frantic phone calls. Weeks and weeks of work by her stitchers had gone missing. A lot of income was also at stake. Had the truck driver made off with the goods?

She commissioned a car and driver to follow the route the truck would have taken. They knew which petrol stations it would have used along the way. And there, parked in a lay-by at one of these stops, about halfway to Mumbai, was the truck with all the goods still in it. There was no sign of the driver, but at least the garments hadn't been stolen. It transpired that the young man had received a call to say his mother in his distant village was ill. So he had simply abandoned the truck, after carefully locking it, and gone home. He didn't think to let anyone know! It is this sort of thing that can make doing business in India so exasperating. To many people he would seem irresponsible and feckless. But it is also a charming story of a dutiful son.

Our travel agent is Indian and we learnt that one of his clients rang him to check if breakfast was included in her hotel rate. Knowing she was on a tight budget and that breakfast was not included, rather than tell her this, he quietly paid for the breakfasts himself. He had helped my niece with her Indian travel arrangements and, when she became sick in Delhi with a severe respiratory ailment, he arranged for a friend of a relative to pick her up and look after her in his home. We often hear such stories. A well-respected cardiologist removed an Australian tourist from a hospital in Jaipur and took her to his own home until she recovered.

Once, when staying with Shamlu in Kolkata, Sue was unwell and a doctor was called to the house. She explained her ailments, both major and minor. I sat there too at the bedside. He did a very thorough examination, we all chatted. We diverted to a few general minor ailments, ranging across eye drops, sleeping pills, nasal sprays. Shamlu added a few ailments of her own and then brought in the servant girl who had a sore foot that he examined carefully. After over an hour of this, he charged a very modest, by our standards, A$20. He wrote a prescription for Sue, on which we saw that he was actually a cardiologist, with Indian and British specialist qualifications. But he was not pompous, nor was he put out by all the trivial medical matters that had taken up his time on a home visit.

In the myths and legends, embedded in the fabric of Indian society and the DNA of Indians, female figures are often strong and influential. In the early Rigveda a goddess is the essence of the universe. There are some ferocious female figures in Indian mythology, counterbalancing, even outwitting, gentle men. There are tormented Hindu male warriors, veering between love and duty. There are Mughal princes torn between fighting and poetry. Kakar says that in India maternal gods are more significant than paternal gods, as the latter are distant figures, whereas Indian men and women invoke goddesses regularly as part of their daily lives.

The most iconic building in India is a monument to a woman. The exquisite Taj Mahal was built by Mughal Emperor, Shah Jahan, as an everlasting symbol of his love for his favourite wife, Mumtaz. Her apartments were adorned in gold and precious stones, with rosewater fountains to keep them cool. It is said that her personality was 'a combination of modesty and candor'. But she died in 1631 after giving birth to their fourteenth child, whilst still only in her thirties. The Shah was grief-stricken.

This shrine to his love was constructed in pure white marble, lavishly inlaid with intricate, jewelled pietra-dura work. Mumtaz lies buried beneath. Its voluptuous dome and piercing minarets have withstood four centuries of weather, tourism, pollution and periods of neglect. It took 20 years to complete, employing about 20,000 workers and 1000 elephants. It remains: 'not only one of the most beautiful buildings in the world, but also the greatest ever material expression of love[24].

Tragically, the internecine horrors of Mughal politics meant that for the last eight years of his life, Shah Jahan could only gaze at his creation from a distance, locked away by his son in the Fort across the river. Though the poignancy of this image touches the heart — a father deposed and imprisoned by his own son — it's worth noting that Shah Jahan had himself gained the throne after arranging the murder of his three brothers.

---

24 *Architectura: Elements of Architectural Style*, Professor Miles Lewis, ed., Frances Lincoln, 2009

Unlike many Western democracies, India has had some strong female political leadership at national and state levels: it has had a female Prime Minister, a female chair of the Congress Party, a female President, and several female State Chief Ministers. In the 19th century the Begums of Bhopal ruled their area most successfully. Jayalitha, the powerful former Chief Minister of Tamil Nadu, was widely known as 'Mother'. Imagine the uproar in Australia if anyone had referred to Anna Bligh, several-term Premier of Queensland, as 'Mother', let alone attaching that moniker to Margaret Thatcher, Theresa May or to Australia's only female Prime Minister, Julia Gillard

I don't want to over-romanticise all this. The more feminised, caring side of India is markedly at odds with Indian societal attitudes to, and treatment of, women. From the deliberate murder of female foetuses and newborns, to appalling dowry killings, widespread violent rapes, and the neglect of widows — India is in reality a cradle to grave patriarchy. Or 'foetus to funeral patriarchy' as Amrit Dhillon so aptly put it in *The Age* newspaper.[25]

The rise of a new, and very large, middle class is also affecting underlying social cohesion in other ways. Young, educated women seek to live their own lives, pursue their careers, drive their own cars. Young couples don't want servants living in and may no longer look after servants' families back in the villages, as was once customary. These days, elderly parents or relatives, widowed women for example, are not always welcome to live under the same roof as their adult children. Aged care will become a big issue in India once families begin to opt out more widely.

---

25 *The Age* — a daily Melbourne newspaper — 13 February 2014.

34: Veg or Non-Veg? That is the Question

In the queues at Delhi airport, we couldn't join the one that was curiously labelled 'Diplomatic and Disabled'. But, as we dithered about which one to join, a helpful attendant said, 'Please take the shortest queue, madam. All queues are long.'

The dithering reminded me of my difficulty on plane trips in India. 'Veg or non-Veg?' a flight attendant would usually ask curtly. I always have trouble with this. In India we avoid meat so we are Veg. But I'm not used to vegetarianism being the default position. 'Non-Veg' sounds apologetic, it doesn't sound carnivorous enough to mean meat-eating. I am a moderate meat-eater at home, but it doesn't mean I'm 'non-Veg' as in 'anti-Veg'. I'm decidedly 'pro-Veg'. So I always need a pause to think which is which and which am I? I feel like answering 'both'. Given that our flights are often short, the attendant will have sailed on down the aisle before I get my head around this.

Veg as the default position is perhaps another less obvious example of the 'feminine' at play in India. Clearly when the vast majority of the Indian population is Hindu, and mainly vegetarian, it carries the numbers. And is nothing to do with gender. But, being from primarily carnivore countries, might Western men find this proclivity for vegetables a touch feminine?[26]

A significant part of the intractable differences between Hindus and Muslims is that the latter eat meat. There is genuine disgust at this practice. It was said that because my great-grandmother, the Indian foundling, was taken in by a household of meat-eaters she could never return to her Brahmin family. Even if no meat had actually passed her lips, she was tainted by its presence, by living amongst meat-eaters, and by the possible use of implements that had been in contact with meat.

At Thikana Guest House, our now-regular base in south Delhi, we marvel at the array of vegetable dishes that appear at our table every evening. One night recently there were various deep-fried bits I couldn't identify that turned out to be pieces of potato, pieces of yam, pieces of a sort of turnip. It reminded me of a friend who had three children and each one only liked a certain sort of fish. She would buy one large piece of flake (or whatever fish was cheapest) and cut it into different shapes, leading each child to think they had their own favourite fish.

However, my assorted fried bits at Thikana were each delicately different in flavour and accompanied several other vegetable dishes: chopped okra with tomatoes, fried sliced lotus roots, the ubiquitous paneer (a sort of cottage cheese) served up that night in a spinach puree. Paneer may also come with tomatoes and peas, or grilled in chunks in Tandoori ovens, or pureed and cooked with sugar and milk to form spongy balls that squeak when you eat them.

Apart from important religious or philosophical reasons,

---

26 Though vegetarianism is rapidly increasing in the West and I read recently that one in five people in Britain are now vegan.

perhaps vegetarianism could thrive more easily in a society with women who stay at home — wives, mothers, grandmothers — carefully preparing the fresh spices each day that form the basis of any dish in India. Or servants to do it. Because vegetarian eating is time-consuming in the preparation. There is a lot of chopping and pounding, dry roasting of spices, fine chopping of onions, grating of ginger, garlic, coconut and so on. Every ingredient has to be fresh. Pressure cookers seem to play an integral role in middle-class households. And noisy but hardy electric grinders. Lentils, or dhal, are an essential part of every meal and provide the basic protein intake, along with chickpeas and other pulses. When we stop for lunch at roadside cafes, drivers will always have some dhal and rice for their lunch.

The vegetables in India taste better than our over-indulged, over-bred Western ones. Perhaps hardship does them good. This seems especially true of potatoes that hold shape and flavour far better than ours. On each annual trip to India, I carry a diary in which to note business matters and other points of interest, comments made, scenes observed. In my diary for 2005 is a recipe headed 'Ramaswamy's potatoes'. He was the 80-year-old cook in Shamlu's household. Here it is: boil then peel potatoes. Chop into squares. Heat oil and fry pieces, add powdered coriander, cumin, garam masala, salt. Add dry roasted sesame seeds and serve. Simple but delicious, mainly because the potatoes themselves were sweet, firm, waxy. And the powdered spices were all freshly roasted and ground.

I adore Indian sweets, though I know they are not to everyone's taste. We often watch them being made in the streets, stirred with huge spoons in vast vats or wok-like dishes, the milk boiled and reduced over high heat with lots of sugar. Then it might be flavoured with cardamom or pistachio, or mixed with ground almonds and coated with a fine fluttery layer of real silver. Or red Indian carrots are grated, then stirred for hours with sugar to make various halvas, with nuts or dried fruits added, and often served warm. Jaggery adds a sweet, molasses-like flavour. Everything is fattening and delectable ...

Street stalls feature stacked pyramids of Indian sweets that we eye longingly. Just as I did as a 10-year-old in the hills with my grandparents. But the flies love them too, and we see the owners covering these delicious delights at night with hessian sacking, flies and all. One of my regrets about globalisation and the increasing Westernisation of India is that on Indian hotel or restaurant menus these days you are more likely to see tiramisu or crème caramel than classic Indian sweets such as gulab jamun or rasmalai.

Indians are very proud of their food and fussy about its details. And they always know exactly what will be good for you if you are feeling queezy, or tired, or bloated, or have a headache, or anything. We've had some pretty awful things pressed on us, but too rude to decline. A brown liquid of cumin water was fairly hard to swallow. My mother talked of rice water for diarrhoea. She loved drinking pepper water and eating green mangoes sprinkled with salt. Once, feeling wan and exhausted after a bout of Kolkata belly, we were served a glass of iced water with a few drops of Pudin Hara, an essence derived from fresh mint. It has a slightly bitter, minty flavour and feels efficacious and soothing.

35: At Home in Thikana

Modern Delhi is still a collection of villages. As in most capital cities, suburb fashions wax and wane, the unfashionable areas become fashionable, often led by artists and bohemians. So it is with Sharpur Jat, one of the ancient villages of Delhi, which has now become fashionable, boasting extravagant wedding-clothing boutiques, design studios and a French coffee shop selling quiches and éclairs.

Even though Sharpur Jat has become a boutique destination, it still consists of little meandering laneways where confusion (at least for foreigners) reigns. Noisy panel beating, a bicycle-chain repairer, someone boiling vats of dye and dipping a garment — all these on the intermittent pathways. Vegetable sellers' carts, motor scooters, school children, animals, large potholes, clogged open drains, they are all still here.

We regularly visited two suppliers in Sharpur Jat, one was the shawl wholesaler I described earlier, where the power kept outing and we had to move around from table to table like moths to the light source. Another was the studio/shop of Alecca Carrano, who served much-appreciated espresso coffees while draping us in the latest of her diaphanous linen gauze garments, cleverly designed by this multicultural woman who could boast Nicole

Kidman and Hillary Clinton as past customers.

Sue and I love the sense of falling upon treasures after stumbling through the hazards of arrival. But we do wonder what her more famous clients made of the surrounds. Alecca lived in India for several decades with her architect husband and three children. But on our last visit to her shop, four years ago, it was closed. We learn that the difficulties of life, and of doing business here, have finally caused them to abandon this home and move to Europe. We are sorry.

Another of Delhi's old villages is Sunder Nagar, where one can browse antique shops and visit the famous tea shop, Mittal's, described appropriately as 'small yet precious'. When we feel we need a break from the challenges of doing business, a visit to the subterranean quiet of the Rohit Kaicker Gallery, opposite the Zoo in Sunder Nagar, is restorative. This gallery specialises in early miniatures, *yantra*, and other interesting art and sculpture. It was here that the softly-spoken Rohit, son of the founder, taught us about *pichwai*. Over two decades, we became enthusiastic collectors.

Pichwai are handpainted fabric temple hangings of a Hindu Krishna sect, the Vallabhachari. The full spelling, *pichhavai*, literally means 'something at the back', because the largest in a typical set of hangings is positioned behind a statue of Krishna, much like a stage set. There are other associated pieces, some small and narrow, positioned on the riser of each step leading up to a plinth on which the statue may sit, others arched across the top, or by the sides. In this sect, worship was often in private houses rather than in temples per se, so the hangings were usefully portable.

The most lovely of them date from times before the

introduction of chemical dyes. The use of natural dyes — from plants, such as indigo and turmeric, and from stones, such as ground lapis lazuli — produces rich colours that never look garish. Typically *pichwais* feature masses of cows, Krishna being the god who is a cow-herd and is often portrayed with a brass pot of curd. Peacocks (symbolic of Krishna), *gopis* (dancing maidens) and plantain leaves also form part of these beautiful hangings, along with plump bolsters and delicate floral borders. During *Gopashtami* (the festival of cattle) dense, overlapping rows of cheerful-looking cows, adorned with peacock feathers, run rampant. Taking a purely aesthetic, non-religious approach to *pichwais*, as Sue and I inevitably do, there is something irresistibly joyous about their presence on the walls of our Melbourne homes.

Our stays at Thikana Guest House — *thikana* means 'a place to which you belong' — are always fascinating. It is located in Gulmohar Park, a suburb in south Delhi. It is a gated area and on the main gates it proclaims 'Gulmohar Park Journalists Welfare Association'. Our guest-house owner's grandfather was a well-known journalist in pre-Independence India. Delhi is made up of many such enclaves or colonies, as they are still known, some based originally on occupational groupings (e.g. Defence Colony), some named after important historical figures such as the 18th century Mughal administrator, Safdarjung.

These days Gulmohar Park,[27] like the other designated enclaves, has passed through several generations since initial establishment. Re-sale of properties means it has moved on from the occupations it once housed and become mixed. But the socio-economic levels remain because the value/cost of the housing stock in each of these areas is at a certain level.

---

27 Named for the beautiful Gulmohar trees.

Houses and apartment buildings surround communal gardens of varying sizes, some containing bits of crumbling monuments, evidence of Delhi's historic past. In Gulmohar Park, there is a decrepit-looking cluster of shops, which we suppose is meant to be a local shopping mall. At first, we thought it looked not only unpromising but even a bit scary. Now we don't notice and head there for supplies at the little grocer (dry biscuits, mouthwash, nice soaps) or to top up our Indian phones. There are beauty parlours, which we haven't tried, a dry cleaner, a vet, a bank and a place to buy fresh milk.

Fruit and vegetable vendors pushing handcarts still call out their wares in the mornings. The knife-sharpening man rides by on his bicycle cart. And in the street is an ironing man, using a large heavy iron filled with hot coals. We drop off *kurtas* in the morning and pick them up, handing a few rupees through the car window, on our way home in the evening.

The family that owns and runs Thikana lives on the ground floor, grandmother (widowed), mother (widowed), daughter and her husband and their two young daughters. A coven of women, one might think, for an outnumbered male, Atul. They are wonderful hosts and we feel immediately at home the moment we arrive. Oh, and another female — Raisin the elderly dachshund who trails around the rooms, dragging her metal lead to announce her presence.

Dogs in India are problematic. There are lots of badly treated, unhealthy-looking pi-dogs in the streets, always a worry in case they carry rabies. But they are highly intelligent creatures, literally street-smart. We have seen them crossing eight-lane highways choked with fast-moving traffic. They stand, patient but hyper-alert, crossing one lane at a time. An Aussie dog would be long gone by lane two.

Unfortunately, the Indian middle and upper classes choose to own rather badly-bred 'brand name' dogs such as German Shepherds or Labradors, often with malformed legs or serious personality disorders. A friend in Jaipur has an over-sexed Labrador, an awkward embarrassment to be near as he makes no distinction between humans and animals. Servants are especially retained as dog-walkers and one often sees them taking their charges for rather desultory walks, neither animal nor keeper expending much energy.

Staying in India's guest houses is so much better than staying in hotels, though naturally the quality can vary widely. At Thikana there are rooms available for renting on three floors above the family's own ground-floor apartment. Each floor has three or four individual bedrooms with ensuite bathrooms. There is a shared sitting area, a large dining area and small balconies at each level. At the top is a roof terrace. We share a communal table for meals, served at varying times according to individual needs or tourist schedules.

The guests are always interesting — writers, aid workers, diplomats, business people, academics — and from all over the world. The place exudes calm and is a welcome respite from the chaos outside. It is located on a busy, noisy main road, but across that road is a large area of parkland, thick with trees. We are not far from the Siri Fort, another remnant of early Delhi history. The service is unobtrusive and our hosts provide help when needed.

We sometimes retain a distinguished-looking acupressure man who, with quiet dignity and skill, gives a wonderful massage. He comes to the room and, apart from washing one's feet, one remains fully clothed. Dressed in a starched long white *kurta*-pyjama suit, he applies nimble but firm pressure. Very few words are spoken. It is peaceful and restorative.

On one visit he wasn't available and a substitute was provided. He talked more and asked after any health problems. I mentioned sleeping poorly. He suggested I should walk backwards before bed. And proceeded to demonstrate, skirting furniture and the open suitcase on the floor. I nodded seriously and thought it was worth a try. Next morning, I mentioned the walking backwards prescription to a fellow guest and found she had been prescribed the same remedy for 'her uterus'. I didn't ask for more details.

Food is cooked in the family kitchen on the ground floor or is brought in from the Gulmohar Club, a central community club for all residents who opt to join. In addition, from a small kitchen on the second floor, Gopal (or his offsider Chotu) cook the chapattis or roti that are served fresh and hot with our dinner. He makes fragrant masala chai when we get home from a day's work, or chilli cheese toasts if we've missed lunch.

Gopal goes home for one month a year. He has a wife and two sons and comes from near Kolkata. He earns more in Delhi than he could at home, so he thinks it's worth the separation from his family. He has kind and enlightened employers and (one assumes) polite and grateful guests to look after. But it is a life contained within the guest house for eleven months of the year, where he sleeps in an all-purpose staff room. This room contains a small stove, the water filter, fridge, small sink and workbench, and a desk. It stores guests' luggage when they go off on side trips and it is where Gopal pulls out his bedding at night. He always looks crisp and spruce and we suppose there is a bathroom somewhere. Other staff seem to disappear up a stairway on a side bit of the building.

A guard in a sentry box beside the front gate keeps Thikana secure. He vets any arrivals, or visitors, and takes charge of luggage and deliveries. He goes off duty at about 11 pm, leaving the gates and door padlocked. So it is Gopal inside who keeps all of us feeling safe, Gopal who admits guests who arrive on flights at ungodly hours, who cooks our omelettes at breakfast, brings snacks on request, keeps an eye on cleaners and sweepers.

When we first started using Thikana, Mary and Athing were softly-spoken girls from Nagaland who administered the place, taking turns in shifts. They handled the bookings, the paperwork. Huge old-fashioned ledgers appear when we arrive, into which Indian bureaucracy demands that we enter travel details, arrival date, departure date, even our ages. Passports must be photocopied and an inspector of some sort comes round every week to check the books, to see that all is in order.

As noted earlier, there are complex attitudes towards people like Mary and Athing who come from the north-east regions of India. Often derisively called 'chinkies' and regarded stereotypically as 'loose', because they are single, live away from their parents and wear Western clothes like jeans and tee-shirts. They are often English-speaking Christians (having attended English-language schools) and are much in demand for employment in shopping malls, call centres and anywhere that deals with foreigners. But they are another of the 'other' groups in Indian society, just like Anglo-Indians.

Shamlu Dudeja in one of the silk kantha saris created by 'her girls'. Kantha embroidery uses simple running stitch worked into dense and intricate patterns

Shamlu's girls at work. Typically they work sitting cross-legged, comfortably flexible as we in the West are not.

Silk shawls with kantha embroidery, common to Bengal, Bangladesh and Bihar. Every area, in every part of India, produces something unique, something beautiful

The iconic Indian Ambassador taxi, based on the British Morris Oxford, now sadly becoming redundant

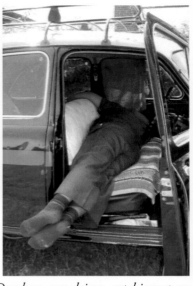

Darshan, our driver, catching up on sleep in his 'hotel room 5351' while we work with Sheila on our clothing range in her premises nearby

The Sikh Golden Temple in Amritsar, at night; putting The Book to bed in a palanquin under a velvety quilt, sprayed with rosewater; Val stirring a vast vat of vegetables

A wiring jungle in Old Delhi. Similar wiring entanglements can be found all over India

In Jaipur, Sue selecting block prints and colours for bedding and nightwear ranges

In south Delhi, Sheila working on our patterns and samples, a young assistant looking on

The school Sheila set up for the children of her workers, to reinforce and expand the tuition received in their government schools

Val helping to hand out a morning snack. Sheila, with co-founder Poonam, at rear

An animated audience at a home for disadvantaged and abandoned girls in south Delhi, learning about menstrual hygiene via the charity, Uboontu, co-founded by our young driver

Our driver with a class of schoolgirls after an educational session delivered at a local school. The charity also provides immunisations, nutritious meals, computer skills, even guitar lessons for girls in poor areas who normally never get such opportunities

Sisters Cara and Val visiting a restored haveli in Old Delhi

Buying a tanpura in a tiny, but famous, New Delhi musical instrument store. Two sisters, perched on a stone bench, occupied an hour before by the Sultan of Oman who was buying a grand piano!

A beautiful bride on her wedding day. A month later she was dead. A devastating tragedy.

The colour and beauty of produce displays, even in the humblest of places. The little pyramids of fresh eggs, with lime and chilli decoration, were on a cart in a back street near Alwar in Rajasthan.

Gopal and Chotu who look after guests at Thikana guest-house,
serving up a hot chapati; on the Thikana rooftop, with hosts Sheetal and Atul,
celebrating Holi, the festival of colour

The famous Chand stepwell showing some of its 3500 steps down
to the water at the bottom

*A joyous cow-filled temple hanging, a pichwai, handpainted on fabric
using natural dyes. Sue and I have enjoyed collecting these over the
years we have been visiting India*

The search for fabric often involves clambering over disorderly piles to find what we want. Hot, dusty and confusing; but occasionally we discover fabrics that suit our predilection for Melbourne black: geometric hand-block prints, with a touch of colour

A selection of annual invitations to our mailing list customers. Moti , the Hindi word for pearl, our business named in honour of my mother, Pearl

An indigo dyer at work; strips of dyed fabric laid out to dry on red dirt

Sue and Val at Hampi, an under-visited UNESCO World Heritage site, in Karnataka, southern India. It covers over 40 square kms, in hilly country dotted with huge granite boulders, and includes about 1600 monuments: temples, aqueducts, monasteries, stables. Mostly built 1336 – 1570 but occupied much earlier and mentioned as a site in the Ramayana. Mainly Hindu but also Jain and some Muslim architectural elements. All in varying states of repair and disrepair. A fascinating place. Some say it was once the world's second largest medieval city (after Beijing)

Sue and Val toasting the handover of MOTI Clothing Company to its new owners, twins Christine and Marilyn Shady

In Sheila's workroom in south Delhi briefing the new owners

Our 'small' boat; preparing to cast out dried rose petals and marigolds, with incense sticks and a dusting of Pearl and Donald's ashes, photographer perched precariously behind

Pearl and Donald, brought back to where they first met, in Bombay, in 1943

36: A New Driver: A Dowry Murder, Hard Work and Hope

Shifting our preferred accommodation to south Delhi has involved changing our driver. It is now more difficult for Darshan, who is attached to a hotel car park in central Delhi, to come and pick us up. Of course, he will do anything we ask, but we know he is paid better, and uses his time better, if he operates from there.

So we have found Surinder. A Hindu aged in his early fifties, he is slight and spritely with a radiant smile. The first time we booked at Thikana it was his good-looking son who met us at the airport and drove us to the guest house. The next day, we requested a car for the day and his father Surinder arrived to drive us. As we wound our way through the usual traffic bedlam, we chatted to Surinder and asked if he had a wife lined up for his handsome son. He replied firmly that he didn't believe in arranged marriage. We asked why not and there was a pause. In the rearview mirror, I could see tears welling in his eyes. This is the story …

Surinder and his wife arranged a marriage for their eldest daughter, as is the custom. He had to sell his house to raise money for her dowry. She went off to live with her new husband

and his family. One month later they heard that she was dead. Son Satish was called to the in-law house, to be told his beloved — and beautiful — sister had allegedly hanged herself. He cradled her still-warm body and wept.

This is how Satish wrote it for me:

I was the first person from my family who saw Manbhar dead ... she was on the floor wrapped up in cloth ... I grabbed her in my arms and cried like hell, still can feel warmth touch ... her eyes were filled with tears ... so many scratching red marks on her arms, her neck was not broken but there was round blueish mark because of rope which they used to kill her ... Only one thing I hear every time I think of that moment: Tu aaya nahi na mujhe lene. [You didn't come to get me]. I always think of that moment as I was the only hope for her, since I was the only son and brother. I loved her so much.

Satish knew that she wouldn't have hanged herself. He knew she had been murdered. They knew she had been killed because the dowry wasn't enough. Surinder had lost a beloved daughter and now the family had no house. Their hearts were broken and their economic lives ruined.

They needed an extra car to rebuild their finances as drivers but, without their house as collateral, the bank wouldn't lend. So they borrowed from a moneylender at 17 per cent interest. 'But did you tell the police about the murder and who did it?' we asked. 'It's no use, madam, we can't afford to pay the police.' The husband's family had allegedly bought the police off. And he would marry again, pulling in another dowry.

On a more recent trip, we discovered that Surinder had

arranged a marriage for his other daughter at about the same time. Four years later she has come back to live with her parents, along with her two little daughters. Her husband was being cruel, emotionally and physically, because she hadn't provided him with a son. Surinder and his wife feel stricken, as if they have failed their two daughters, fatally in one case. Now we understand why he no longer believes in arranged marriages.

So Surinder and Satish have to support three extra people. They say the remaining husband is lazy and sends no money to support his wife and daughters. In their rented two-room flat, father and son sleep head-to-toe in the bed in one room, while mother, daughter, another unmarried sister and two granddaughters sleep in the other, which doubles as a living room and kitchen. They are keen to get the little girls into a private school, as they don't think the government schools are good enough. This will require an extra 10,000 rupees a month. There is a ballot, and possibly some baksheesh, to get them in. We haven't yet heard the outcome.

There was another problem looming for poor Surinder. He had heard that his son has a girlfriend. Good news I said, because I knew he was keen for the young man (not so young by Indian standards, as he is now in his thirties) to find a love-match. But ... she is Muslim.

Although Surinder seems kind and tolerant, his reaction was extreme. He said some unpleasant things. We were shocked. He said the extended families on both sides would be unhappy about the religious difference. My daughter, Charlotte, who met Surinder when she accompanied me to India, said he confided to her that he would find it hard to trust a Muslim. Such basic prejudices would be difficult to overcome if the relationship survived these hurdles. On a subsequent visit, he told me, 'I will suicide if he marries her.' What a ghastly response and what a threat to impose on the poor son. It seemed so out of character with the gentle Surinder we thought we knew.

Satish said his father loved him and would come around. And last year (2019) Surinder did seem reconciled to the possibility. We were much relieved. Satish told us the wedding was imminent. We prepared an envelope of cash to give as a gift. But there was a mysterious delay. It didn't happen. We returned to Australia and awaited news. No word came.

A year later, on our next trip, we found that Satish and his girlfriend had married, in a civil ceremony with no parents present. This would have been a double humiliation for his father. And presumably for her parents too. Yet, even though this reads like the actions of a modern young couple in a new India, Satish's wife had given up her job and come to live with her in-laws, as tradition demands.

I realise now that one of the reasons to marry within one's religion, and even within one's caste, is that when a girl moves to her in-laws' home, she will be accustomed to the same beliefs and rituals, especially around food. While it's hard enough to leave your own family and adapt to a new one, at least certain norms and practices will be shared and understood. But when your habitual rituals have been different, it is far more difficult for everyone. We really hope this all works out.

37: Health, Safety and a Middle-Class Market

One day in Delhi, Sue had a nasty cough. Surinder opened the glove box and offered her an antibiotic. One Amoxil tablet. He is proud of the fact that he has taken this precaution, just in case he gets a cough: 'I can't afford a day off and passengers don't like it if I am coughing.' He also has another variety of antibiotic, just one tablet, in case he suddenly gets tummy trouble.

He assumed we would be impressed with his foresight. Instead, we were appalled at this misuse of antibiotics. The difficulty in India is that it's counter-intuitive to explain to someone on a very tight budget that they must take at least four days of antibiotics, a full course, even if they feel better after taking only one or two tablets. This is a major problem for India, and for the world, since antibiotic resistance has implications for us all.

In India one can buy antibiotics over the counter at pharmacies and hospital clinics where the poor queue up to buy single tablets. Some hospitals deliberately dispense them one at a time, getting people back each day to swallow their next dose. They know that if they handed over the full course all at once, the patient would probably keep the 'extras' for the next bug, or distribute them to others, rather than take them consecutively as required.

There is a lot of rather disturbing quackery in India. Sheila tells us the latest fad amongst her staff is for intravenous saline drips. These are delivered by kerbside quacks, with minimal hygiene, let alone sterilisation of equipment. And the recipients seem to judge how sick they are, or how seriously they are being taken, by the number of bags of saline the quack pumps into their veins.

We often go to Khan Market in central Delhi to stock up on travel needs, including some pharmaceuticals. Khan Market is listed as an upmarket shopping precinct in guidebooks. It consists of strips of shops in parallel U-shaped semi-circles (roughly-speaking), some single level only, and some two- or three-storey sections. On our first visit we were dismayed. In no way did this look 'upmarket'. Crumbling grubby footpaths, loose wires, rackety air-conditioners screaming Legionnaire's disease, pi-dogs sleeping across the throughways, paths in a chronic ceaseless state of ineffective renovation.

But we began to go there regularly, and we no longer notice (or at least not much) the decrepitude. When espresso coffee first came to India, it was available in chains like 'Café Coffee Day', which opened branches in places like Khan Market. A couple of delicatessens sell expensive French pâtés and cheeses and other imported goods. Resident expats crowd the counters. And there are cafés and bars with noisy Western-style music and designer food: fresh juices, bruschetta, salads, patisserie and slightly odd versions of Japanese cuisine. It's all 'very loungey,' as one of our young Indian friends described.

Many of these places are accessed by staggering up steep

staircases, after making your way across hazardous broken paving and dodging circling SUVs. The stalwart shops Fabindia and Anokhi are here, as are Ogaan and Manan, and the well-known Jaipur jeweller Amrapali. Neemrana also has a shop. There are upmarket Indian clothing labels and high-end Indian ayurvedic facial creams, one face oil allegedly containing real gold.

There are lots of trendy-looking Indian shoppers in jeans and large dark glasses. It is mainstream shopping. It is true that there are more quirky, interesting boutiques in less touristy areas. But fortunately, the really big international name brands have not invaded Khan Market. In fact, after a few years there, an unwelcome McDonald's closed. International brands, and the new-rich Indians, prefer flashy air-conditioned shopping malls, which we generally dislike. Though we do now understand the appeal of malls in a land of extreme weather: they can be havens from steaming heat or monsoonal rains.

Sue and I like Khan Market for still being eccentrically Indian while purporting to be something other. We often go there between appointments or at the end of a day. There are two very good bookshops. Bahrisons is an old one at ground level, packed to the gunnels being an understatement here. Any book you ask for can be found, sometimes after an agile staff member climbs precarious ladders. Staff are well-informed about their stock, there is a crush of people in the tiny space, and books are incredibly cheap by Australian standards. A pity about luggage weight limits.

Similar conditions apply at the tiny pharmacy we visit. It is perhaps two metres wide by four metres deep, and stocks every medicine imaginable. Again, the younger staff members are ordered by expressionless elders to climb up and retrieve whatever drug one wants. We are never sure about the storage conditions — the temperatures at ceiling height must soar in hot weather. (It's important in India when buying medicines to choose a pharmacy where the goods are not displayed in full sun and where there is some air-conditioning or refrigeration.)

Sue buys Valium for her very nervy dog that quivers in thunderstorms. They are a fraction of the price one pays in Australia, so she can afford a large sheet of them. Which they hand over with impunity. For some reason we feel obliged to explain, apologetically, that they are for a dog. The supercilious shop-owner (is he a pharmacist?), normally indifferent, looks horrified. Who would spend that money and trouble on a dog?! One year Sue bought the last of their supplies. I idly wondered if there were a lot of anxious middle-class Indians who had to go without their Valium for a while, little knowing that a dog in a place called Moorooduc in Australia was benefiting instead.[28]

We drop off our glasses for new lenses, much cheaper than at home, we enjoy the bookshops, we change money at the Money Changers nearby, we have lunch in trendy new cafes and restaurants. Some have open rooftop areas, where we sit breathing in upmarket pollution from the cars circling for parking. Sometimes one needs a change from Indian spice flavours, whatever the cost in lung function.

But there are also — and we hope they stay, though greedy landlords may change this — old-style printing businesses, a general store that sells cheap Sellotape and those canvas striped 'refugee' bags. We always need yet another to pack our stuff

---

28 On our most recent visits this has changed! No longer will they hand over such drugs without prescription. Inconvenient for us, but as it should be, and very good news.

in for the return trip home. On densely packed shelves it has luggage straps, padlocks, ribbons, plastic containers. I love this sort of store.

British writer Tarquin Hall's fictional detective, Vish Puri, in a series with titles like *The Case of the Deadly Butter Chicken*, has his office upstairs in Khan Market, and it is a joy to read these when we are back in Melbourne, as they conjure up the surrounds so vividly.

Surinder has friends at Khan Market. He likes to have a glass of milk from the dairy stall there. He has his regular parking spot with an attendant to whom he passes a few rupees to look after things.

In the main car parking area there is officially parking for 78 cars. A sign says so. We once did a rough count: there were about 350 cars squeezed in. Everyone was blocked. Some drivers had left their keys with the attendants so their cars could be moved. Most just left the handbrakes off and the attendants achieved miracles.

Cars get pushed a bit this way, a bit that, to allow someone three rows back to get out. There is no ill humour. If a car has put its handbrake on and not left keys, then several attendants, plus the odd bystander, grab the chassis above the rear wheels and shift it a bit. It only needs a few inches either way for the immensely dexterous Indian drivers to weave their way out of what looks to be an impenetrable jungle of vehicles.

Surinder and his son Satish work incredibly long hours. Despite the terrible tragedy of losing a daughter, in the 12 years we have known them, they have grown to a fleet of five cars and employ other drivers. They act as routine full- or half-day drivers for people like us, or as drivers for various large corporations in

Delhi, as well as taking private tourist trips to Agra and Jaipur. They have a website.

They don't complain about their problems. We only know about them because we have asked. After losing their house for the dowry, they gradually saved enough to buy a small parcel of land, 75 square metres, on which to build a new house. A couple of years ago this goal was achieved, the three-storey house is now built, complete with an up-to-the-minute Western-style kitchen. The two little girls (Satish's nieces) now attend a private Christian school and are doing well.

Theirs is a very Indian story: the blows, the tragedy, the resignation, the acceptance, the continuing hard work, and the hope ...

38: A Curious Musical Interlude

My sister, Cara, came with us to India one year. While there, she wanted to buy a digital *tanpura*, an instrument that creates the underlying droning sound heard in most Indian music. The real thing is beautiful: a long-necked stringed instrument made from teak, highly polished and inlaid with ivory or camel bone. Mughal miniature paintings often portray lissom figures gracefully plucking the strings of a *tanpura*. By contrast, a digital *tanpura* is a disappointing rectangular grey plastic box, about 10 inches x 5 inches x 5 inches, with white plastic switches.

Cara had done her homework online and knew these were available in a few shops in Delhi. In our travels in Rajasthan en route to Delhi, we had enquired in music shops, to no avail. So on arrival in Delhi we studied her list of possible shops. Two sounded promising and were located quite near our guest-house. But the Delhi-ites we consulted said the best bet would be a very well-known music store in Connaught Place.

Located in the centre of Delhi, Connaught Place comprises rings of white colonnaded shops constructed in British times, part of the Luytens grand plan. It houses many familiar global brands, as well as long-term, old-style respectable Indian businesses. But

Connaught Place is also known for touts and scammers who prey on tourists and is a place Sue and I usually avoid. However, we thought locals must know best, and if even the non-musical among them knew this place, then it must be okay.

We set out for the 'Hare Krishna Musicals Store', armed with the address found on their website: '9/3 L Block, meznan, Connaught Place'. Cara had rung and been assured they did have digital *tanpuras*. We expected a standard large shopfront like others all around. I guessed that 'meznan' might mean 'mezzanine' so we looked to the upper levels as well. But we could see nothing by that name in the block we were directed to: no glass shopfront, no obvious signage.

We enquired of an elderly man and he pointed us in the direction we had already passed. We retraced our steps but still couldn't see it. So, he kindly escorted us to a narrow, easy-to-miss entrance, between a garish pink cupcake shop on one side and the Delhi Darba restaurant on the other. Between these two shops was a set of crumbling stairs, dark and rather grubby. Up we went, expecting that this well-known store would bely its modest presence below. The stairs led us to a tiny space about the size of an average wardrobe. This was the Hare Krishna Musicals Store.

A young man sat in the gloom at the rear of this wardrobe and indicated we should sit on a narrow stone bench that appeared to be carved into, or out of, the wall. We were in a cave of instruments, walls festooned with rows of stringed instruments suspended from hooks, three or four deep, up to a low ceiling. There were beautiful, elegantly carved Indian instruments, looking a bit like lutes. There were ukuleles and Indian wind instruments. Behind me, on the bench, lay a shiny pure white violin. Below, on crammed shelves almost touching our knees, were many different drums. It was hot and airless.

With room for just two on the bench, Sue stood and watched as Cara and I talked to the clearly knowledgeable young proprietor. His family had owned this shop for generations. Soon his father arrived, missing a few front teeth, and we saw that the guitar 'department' was located on a few gloomy stairs leading further up.

Nothing augured well for a successful purchase. Coming to the Hare Krishna Musicals Store might have been a mistake. So imagine our surprise, given the miniscule size of this operation, to discover that before us, on this same uncomfortable bench, had perched the backside of the Sultan of Oman, on his way to a meeting with the Prime Minister of India! He had dropped in to buy an instrument. 'What instrument?' we asked, assuming it would be one of the pieces that surrounded us. 'A grand piano,' was the surprising reply. It was hard to believe this could be possible. Were they making it up? But we were shown photos of the robed Sultan sitting on the cramped bench, photos time-stamped just an hour before us. It transpired that the pianos, and many other instruments, were stored in a large go-down elsewhere. We realised this must indeed be a very well-known music store.

Irritatingly, the owner had neglected to mention on the phone that he didn't have a digital *tanpura* on the premises. Grrrh, we thought. All the trouble we've had getting here. Now they tell us they haven't actually got one. But in typically Indian clever-marketing style, they had got us into their shop. They assured us that a digital *tanpura* would be delivered to our guest house tomorrow evening (we were leaving very early the morning after). Cara naturally was anxious about this arrangement. She had to pay for it, sight unseen, and take on trust that they would deliver. And she had been hoping for some instructions on playing it.

Next evening, despite being two hours late — my sister was by then looking ashen with worry as her phone calls went unanswered — the young owner arrived with the magic box. He'd been delayed supervising delivery of a grand piano to the Oman Embassy.

Soon, from the next room, I could hear promising droning sounds.

39: Smells and Whistles

A friend of mine simply can't bear the smell of the East. She hates that first inhalation as she clambers down the plane's offloading ramps. But I relish arriving to the smell of all Asian cities: you know you have arrived somewhere really different, you can smell the heat and anticipate the exotic.

India is undoubtedly smelly. My mother wrote that: 'In the days when people travelled from Europe to India in ships it used to be said that you could smell Bombay once the ship entered the harbour and The Gateway of India came in sight.'

She developed a lifelong addiction to good perfume, which she ascribed to her mother who provided insulation from bad smells:

From the earliest time I can remember we never left home without a neatly folded handkerchief with a large drop of eau-de-cologne in the middle of it. 'Hold your handkerchief to your nose,' my mother would say, or 'Take a deep breath now and then don't breathe.' I would obediently asphyxiate!

At the age of four, I went to a small Prep School not far from where we lived. My teacher, Miss Parkhill, was English, but locally born, with masses of piled-up gingery hair which was tethered in coils over each ear. She had squashy marshmallow lips and I realise now was not at all beautiful. But to me she was beautiful because she appeared to be drenched in lavender water. When she bent over me to look at my work, her long chain of beads would dangle over my head and clouds of lavender essence seemed to come out of her mouth and envelop me.

My father had a warm and comforting smell which I'm sure could only be achieved in the East since it was a mixture of the Pinaud lotion (French) he used on his thinning hair, the strong smell of newsprint from the Times of India which he read every morning at breakfast (which is when I gave him his good morning kiss) and the beautifully-clean smell of the freshly-starched cream cotton suit he wore each day. Indian dhobis, or washermen, starched these suits to perfection, and the rice-water starch they used, plus drying in the sun, gave clothes their distinctive smell of cleanliness.

My mother smelt of Coty's face-powder which she used very sparingly and almost surreptitiously. She looked cross if one ever caught her using it! Coty's powder came in round boxes on which were printed powder puffs in orange and black. There was a choice of three colours only: 'Natural' which was geared to the English rose complexion, 'Rachel' for faded English roses, and 'Suntan' which was for English roses burnt to hot pink at Bournemouth or Brighton! None of these was suitable for our Anglo-Indian complexions. When I grew up I learnt to mix Rachel with Suntan.

Today the smell of India is so thick it's like an object one meets on arrival. A combination of heat, pollution, kerosene, food, sweat, spices, open drains, and urine. The Government has tried to stop men pissing against any convenient wall, but it seems to be a habit that dies hard. I read somewhere of groups of women patrolling their town streets and blowing whistles loudly to draw attention, and shame, to men in the act.

The police love their whistles too, and their *lathis* (iron-bound bamboo sticks). We saw a policeman chasing a jay-walker at an intersection, his expression furious as he brandished his *lathi* in the air, whistle in mouth. He dispensed a good whacking. Rough justice, no mucking around with cautions.

In Purana Qila, a beautiful park full of ancient monuments in Delhi, we witnessed an officious uniformed woman with whistle in mouth. As she approached young couples, innocently sitting close together with arms entwined (not even kissing, much less anything else) they sprang apart as a loud whistle and stern admonishments followed. Our guide in Ahmedabad, with a girlfriend he meets in secret, told of similar intrusive whistle-blowing in the spots where they try to snatch a bit of privacy and intimacy.

Purana Qila translates as Old Fort. It was built in the 16th century by the Mughal ruler Humayun, and added to by the Afghan ruler Sher Shah Suri. It is thought to be the site of Indraprastha, mentioned in the early Indian epic poem, the Mahabaratha, written around the 4th century BC.

Within these beautiful, now well-kept grounds is a library building commissioned by Humayun. I have a soft spot for Humayun. Squeezed between a famously successful father (Babur the Great) and an even more famously successful son (Akbar the Great), Humayun was never given the sobriquet 'the Great'. Like Humayun, many Mughal rulers combined a poetic sensibility with fearsome aggrandisement, committing appalling atrocities despite supposedly gentle artistic souls. But Humayun literally veered from warrior to poet, never fully pulling anything off.

Humayun died ignominiously, though perhaps appropriately: not in battle but falling down the stairs of this library building in the grounds of Purana Qila. Had his grieving widow not built a grand tomb to his memory, people might have forgotten him. But Humayun's Tomb is one of the major tourist attractions in Delhi and seen as a precursor to the Taj Mahal.

On the day we first visited Purana Qila, we decided to hunt out an old step-well nearby that we had read about. Step-wells are truly astonishing. Picture a seven-level Hindu temple, stone steps leading all the way to the top. At each level, there are carved pillars, colonnaded corridors, balconies and intricately carved walls, featuring scenes of everyday life, of deities, animals, mythological scenes.

Now picture all that inverted and carved out beneath the ground, the pinnacle being reversed — it's the water at the bottom, deep down below. This is Indian subterranean water architecture.

There are hundreds of step-wells (*baoli*) in India, a few well preserved, many derelict and abandoned. They demonstrate incredible engineering and craftsmanship, the purposes religious, social and functional. As well as beautiful. Apart from providing water, step-wells provided cool refuge for locals and for travellers, meeting places, a place for secret trysts. The 9th century Chand step-well in Rajasthan features 3500 steps that descend, in perfect Escher-like geometry, to the bottom of a very deep well.

The 15th century Adalaj step-well in Gujarat carries a poignant story. The construction was started by the local Hindu king to provide water for his subjects. Before it was finished, a war broke out with the neighbouring Muslim king. The Hindu king was killed. The victorious King then fell in love with the widow,

Rupa. She agreed to marry him on condition that he complete the work her slain husband had started. The step-well was duly completed, the floral patterns and motifs delicately carved in the stonework, providing beautiful examples of this later Islamic phase of construction. When it was finished, the widowed Queen threw herself into the well and died. She hadn't intended to marry but had only wanted to see her husband's work finished.

Darshan, our driver that day, was dubious about the excursion. He had never heard of the particular step-well we were visiting, which was unusual as taxi drivers always know everything. Or confidently say they do. But with some persistence we found the well in an inauspicious location. There were high walls and a rusty tall metal gate, bolted with ancient but serious padlocks. Passers-by saw our interest and directed Darshan to a shanty nearby, where we assumed he would get permission and a key. He returned a little sheepishly, not with a key but with a precarious-looking tall bamboo ladder.

He clearly expected that we would give up. But being a bit younger and more intrepid in those days, we were undeterred. With Darshan holding the ladder and getting an unfettered view up my skirt (why had I worn a skirt that day?!) we clambered up and dropped down over the other side. Not to be shamed, Darshan's turban appeared at the top of the ladder a few moments later and he joined us in walking around this deserted well. Multiple rows of steps led down to dark green stagnant water at the bottom, a fair bit of rubbish, and bats. Lots of bats, unused to being disturbed, zapped around us. But it was interesting, and an adventure, our first step-well.

Which brings me to Ahmedabad ... an area with several stunning step-wells.

Ahmedabad

Ahmedabad was once known as 'the Manchester of the East', due to its abundant cotton production. Wealthy cotton mill owners had their houses designed by leading European and Indian architects. The 'Mill Owners Association Building' was designed by Le Corbusier in 1954. He had been brought to India by PM Nehru to design the new capital of Punjab State in Chandigarh. The Sarabhai family, whose textile collection forms the basis of the wonderful Calico Museum in Ahmedabad, also have a house designed by le Corbusier.

Old Ahmedabad was made up of mini suburbs called pols, clusters of housing with elaborate wooden gates between, often with a tall bird-feeding tower. Each pol housed particular trades or crafts.

The buildings in the pols are characterised by intricately carved decoration in wood or stone. Ahmedabad's historic old city is India's first UNESCO World Heritage City

Elegant pillars inside the prayer room of the Ahmedabad Jama Masjid (Friday Mosque). Built in 1424 in Indo-Islamic style it is situated within the old walled city. It was once one of the largest mosques in India. There is the tomb nearby of the Sultan in whose reign it was built, Ahmed Shah

In Ahmedabad there are two important Gandhi ashrams. It became a city of protest against British rule and in 1930, the famous salt march started from here. The Sabarmati Ashram, where Ghandi lived for 12 years, lies on the banks of the Sabarmati river. The ashram now includes a Museum designed by noted Indian architect, Charles Correa

40: Acquisitive in Ahmedabad

We are being guided around the old part of Ahmedabad by a young man whose feet have six toes. He can't wear shoes. Only sandals. He can't afford to have the extra toes surgically removed because his father is dead and he supports his mother and sister. His sister is studying medicine and he knows his duty is to support her until she achieves this goal.

As we walk, Sue quietly suggests to me that perhaps this is a story he spins to tourists. Maybe he gets some kudos, some god-like status from having extra toes, she suggests. Maybe he doesn't want them removed but knows Westerners would have difficulty understanding this. I think he is sincere and that, sadly, with so much deformity in India, extra toes would not be sufficient to accrue god-points.

Westerners find it hard to grasp the idea that deformity could possibly confer god-like status. There was much publicity recently for a little girl near Bangalore who was born with extra arms and legs. Villagers made offerings to her due to the similarity with the goddess Durga who has multiple arms. Thankfully, public donations helped her family obtain surgery and gave the child some semblance of a normal life.

And always in India there is the lurking thought that our

guide may be fishing for a donation. If we handed over $100 right now, would it pay for the surgery? Would he use it for surgery? I recall reading somewhere that the famous West Indian cricketer Sir Garfield Sobers had extra fingers. He allegedly removed them himself using catgut and a sharp knife. Shudder. (I looked it up later and saw that his extras must have comprised soft tissue only. If bone had been involved, then surgical expertise would have been required to remove them properly.)

All these thoughts as we continue on our walk. 'What would you do, if you could?' we ask. Ravi replies that he'd always wanted to study history but had to leave school at 15. So his job as a tour guide satisfies this interest. He learnt English by talking to tourists and reading history books. Most other guides just reel off a spiel by rote ('by-hearting' as it's neatly called in India) and get annoyed if their word flow is interrupted by tourists' questions. But this young man really knows his city and its history and we can tell that he enjoys sharing his knowledge.

Ahmedabad is one of the main cities of Gujarat, a vegetarian (and tee-total) state of roughly 60 million people. Hindu, Jain and Muslim traditions have all flourished at various stages of its long history, resulting in an interesting architectural legacy that often fuses these varied cultural influences. Founded 'officially' in 1411 by Ahmad Shah I, then the king of Gujarat, who expanded an old Hindu town to become his capital. Ahmedabad now spreads chaotically around the Sabarmati river. The old city was originally encircled by walls with 12 gates, 139 towers and thousands of battlements. The walls have mostly disappeared but it remains fascinating to explore the *pols* in the oldest part of the city.

Pols are like mini 'suburbs' within the old city, each is self-contained and traversed by narrow lanes, with huge gateways heralding the change from *pol* to *pol*. There are two- and three-storey balconied houses, often interlinked, with wonderful carved wooden facades, intricate wooden screens and decorative wooden posts and brackets. Many *pols* have tall, beautifully carved timber bird-feeding towers near the gates. Pigeons and doves are a constant murmuring presence.

Generations of families practising particular skills or crafts lived in their own *pol*: weavers, woodworkers, jewellers, printers, each in their own mini suburb. The laneways still evoke this past, even if now the trades have largely dispersed and the crippling costs of maintaining the buildings sees them neglected and under threat of collapse or redevelopment.

As we walk we learn that our guide has a forbidden girlfriend of a lower caste than his. They can only meet in secret, her face covered. He is optimistic that the families will eventually approve, despite there being as much opposition from the lower-caste girl's family as from his own. 'People look at us with bad eyes,' says Ravi, meaning they disapprove. He tells us there is a wooded spot by the river where they meet sometimes. But the area is patrolled by 'behaviour wardens' who blow whistles loudly to discourage any intimacies! Ravi wryly, but not bitterly, adds, 'I can make shit in public, but not hold hands or kiss.'

During our tour I have been noticing people walking along holding beautiful bowls in a most lustrous bright crimson colour. I resolve to find one while we are here. Are they unique to this city? Are they old or new? They look as though they are metal of some sort, perhaps with a shiny enamelled finish? Or could it be wood with a deep red lacquer? I'm not sure. I like the shape too, a squat rounded bowl gathering in at the neck. In India, perhaps surprisingly, there can be a sameness to the artifacts and techniques one sees. The eye can get a bit jaded. One looks out for something not seen before, not seen in the tourist shops or the government-run emporia. As we continue on our tour of this city, I quietly hanker for one of these bowls.

Flying to Ahmedabad, I had noticed in the Indian Air glossy magazine, amid ads for Tissot watches, top private schools and luxury holidays, that there was a full-page advertisement for an astrologer. I ask our guide and he agrees that consulting healers and astrologers is a normal part of life. Even the educated middle and upper classes in India seem to follow advice from astrologers with little reference to evidence-based practice, the sort of evidence they would assume, even demand, from Western medicine.

A close friend of ours in Mumbai, a university-educated professional woman, was suffering continuing anguish over the death of her father. So she went back to talk it over with her astrologer in her hometown, despite it being a long distance from Mumbai. From birth to death, astrology matters. Marriages are arranged around the astrological charts of the two parties, wedding dates are set according to auspicious days in the charts.

Sudhir Kakar describes the vast number and assortment of healers in Indian society, and the Indians' overwhelming preoccupation with such therapies. The profusion of gods and goddesses (some say 30 million), plus all the ancient myths and legends, provide a vast smorgasbord of choices for life's psychological, material, emotional, physical and religious needs. Every occasion is catered for, every vicissitude, every new business venture, all have a god to be propitiated or leant upon, a legend to be referenced, a myth to provide emotional sustenance.

This pervasive intertwining of gods and myths with

personal realities seems to trump what we would think of as rational. Levels of education might temper the belief a bit, but it is rarely absent. Kakar says: 'There is a god for every psychic season. A myth for every hidden wish and a legend for every concealed anxiety.'[29]

Back in Ahmedabad's lanes, I am ruminating on the ramifications of our guide's extra toes, and the nature of belief and superstition, as we step carefully around a cow munching a chapatti. This is why India is so exhausting. Every aspect of one's self, from the physical to the spiritual, is stimulated and challenged by the minute. And occasionally, I still catch flashes of sunlight off those red bowls as figures go by with one tucked under an arm.

After our stroll through the old town, it is time to turn to Ahmedabad's famous modernist buildings, especially those designed by Le Corbusier. Ahmedabad was a centre for the cotton industry, ousting Manchester from its pre-eminence around the turn of the 19th century, much to the detriment of those northern English 'satanic mills'. In the 1950s the wealthy associations of mill owners in Ahmedabad commissioned Le Corbusier to design their private houses and their corporate HQ, presumably while he was in India to design the new Punjab capital in Chandigarh.

We also plan to visit the leading business school in India, the Ahmedabad Institute of Technology, designed by Louis Kahn, architect of the parliament building in the then new capital of Bangladesh, Dacca. So Ahmedabad hosts a wealth

---

29 Sudhir Kakar, *Shamans, Mystics and Doctors: A Psychological Inquiry into India and its Healing Traditions*, first published 1982, Unwin Paperbacks: 1984.

of architectural styles, and it is all of great interest to Sue. And fortunate for me to have her architectural knowledge on hand.

Towards the end of the day we stop at a well-known Jain monastery. It is a peaceful, large open area with beautiful Jain temples and monastic living spaces in the cloister-like walls surrounding it. Now I notice there are more people carrying red bowls. Perhaps this is where I will be able to buy one and bring it home. A nearby street market perhaps. Finally it seems time for some commercialism so I point to a bowl as it passes and ask our guide where I can buy one. 'Madam,' he replies gravely, 'these are spittoons. These are holy people fasting. Jain people. When they are fasting they neither eat nor drink. They do not even swallow their own spit.'

I am shocked and ashamed of my acquisitive urge. The contrast between this self-abnegation and my desire to own the object is awful. It seems extreme to fast so seriously as to not swallow one's own spit, but it is something to be respected. I don't want one now, for slightly squeamish reasons! And even that thought makes me feel superficial.

This example epitomises a tussle one often feels in India between the spiritual and the commercial, the sacred and the profane, cheek by jowl. But I suspect Indians don't experience it as a tussle at all. It is an Anglo-Saxon thing. Sue and I have, over time, become more used to Hindu priests pressuring us for money. In the stunning Jain temples in Ranakpur we made the mistake of thinking the barely clad handsome priest was just being friendly, until he demanded money in a slightly menacing manner!

Similarly, we have been in an oppressively hot, crowded shop in Jaipur, absorbed in bargaining a good price for some scarves, hemmed in by teetering mountains of piled-up goods, when a priest came in, blessed us individually and collectively, then demanded money before placing an (unwanted) thumbed *tikka* of turmeric on our sweating brows.

Ahmedabad is also home to the famous Calico Museum, one of the finest textile museums in the world. It is based around a collection handed over to a Foundation by the Sarabhai family, who were successful textile manufacturers, establishing a cotton mill in 1880. The Museum has a quirky system in place: two opening sessions per day, the first at 10 am, the second at 2 pm. Only 10 people allowed in at a time, first come first in. So if a tour group arrives, one can easily miss out. We get there in a tuk-tuk at 9.15 am. A few other visitors are waiting, but it looks hopeful.

We are ushered into an ante-room where we are instructed by a rather unfriendly, bossy woman that we have to watch a film of the collection before we can view the real thing. It takes about 20 minutes and is simultaneously tantalising and irritating to see on video what we came all this way to see in the flesh. Sue is a bit uncomfortable that day, having had a hip replacement not long before we arrived in India. As we do the rounds of this wonderful collection, there are numerous changes of level, small steps and large. So I have taken to warning her by saying 'step' every time we approach one.

Ironically, as we walk outside, it is me who misses my footing and I sprawl to the ground, breaking my glasses, grazing my knee quite badly, and feeling rather shocked. But there is to be no sympathy from our guide, who barely breaks her step or her spiel. Inconveniences such as a fallen tourist will not be allowed to interrupt the schedule.

As I limp along, trying to keep up, I rather tentatively ask her if I could have some disinfectant when we get back to the office. 'No,' she snaps, 'I won't be giving you any Tom, Dick or Harry antiseptic. It will be causing the puss. Wait till you get back to your hotel.' Well ... so much for that! I learn later that she is renowned for being bossy and intractable. Fortunately, the collection transcends. We go back in the afternoon (knee suitably disinfected) to see another part of the collection, only to be told that, yet again, we are obliged to watch the same 20-minute film beforehand. Lucky we love India. With bemused exasperation, we resign ourselves to the repeat viewing.

41: Discordant Notes

There was a jarring note on a subsequent visit to Ahmedabad a couple of years ago. It was the only time such a thing has happened to us in two decades of visits to India. We went to look at one of the main mosques. It was 'open-faced' in the way of mosques, on a main street and open to visitors. There were no other tourists around. We knew we should be modestly dressed (we were, anyway), arms covered, sunhats on. We soon became aware of a small child, no more than eight or nine years old, hands on hips and barring our way, angrily berating us for being there: women, foreigners, non-Muslims (we assume this is what he was saying).

These words were spat out at us in real hatred. It was chilling, delivered from a small bundle of venom, watched on (more chillingly) by a couple we assumed to be his parents. We did leave. One can't argue with a child, especially not in a language one doesn't speak. It's his country, his religion, his mosque. But it was upsetting.

We have been in other situations where non-Muslims normally may not venture. Once, near Hyderabad, we were taken — with some trepidation on the part of our Hindu guide — to see silk weavers at work. These weavers were Muslim men in an area that Hindus of the town hesitated to visit. We arrived at a warehouse, a cramped space with about 10 looms from which emerged exquisite silk shawls, delicate as colourful spiderwebs. Somehow I stumbled and trod in one of the webs. Multiple apologies ensued. The weaver was forgiving and sweet, he seemed almost as embarrassed as I was, and fortunately no damage was done. I felt terrible of course, not to mention clumsy. But our guide was anxious so, amidst more apologies and effusive thankyous, we made haste out of there.

Our Hindu and Muslim friends, acquaintances, drivers, helpers tell us they feel no animosity towards each other. They often grew up in mixed neighbourhoods, or went to schools with mixed religions, played together, honoured each other's festivals. I read a collection called *Partition Dialogues*,[30] in which a conversation between writers Intizar Husain and Alok Bhalla captures this neighbourliness. People we talk to blame extremists and politicians for stirring up trouble, using conflict and rivalry for their own political purposes. This is 'Communalism', as it is known in India, what we would refer to as 'sectarianism', sadly the opposite of living 'communally'.

It brings to mind a troubling story told to me by Meenu, one of our suppliers in Delhi. We were in the garden courtyard at The Gymkhana Club, one of Delhi's most exclusive clubs, with membership waiting lists many years long and hefty annual fees. It's a nice old colonial building, colonnaded. The outside area is green lawn in the imagination, brown and dusty in reality.

Seated on slightly inelegant plastic chairs, we sipped cool, fresh lime sodas. I recounted that in a hotel the week before, I

---

30 *Partition Dialogues: Memories of a Lost Home*, Oxford University Press, 2006.

had ordered a fresh lime soda 'but no ice, please', being cautious about the water. When the waiter brought my drink, it was cheerfully jingling with ice cubes. I pointed out that I had requested no ice. He apologised and scooped out the offending cubes with his fingers!

No such behaviour here at The Gymkhana Club, though, as I sat across from Meenu who looked elegant in a beautiful tussar silk sari. Knowing her father had been ill recently, I asked after him. She said she was worried that as he aged he was becoming increasingly angry and anti-Muslim. This was the story:

Her father came from an educated, liberal Hindu family in Lahore, Pakistan. His father was a High Court judge and her father became a leading lawyer. They lived in a mixed Hindu/Muslim area and her father's best friend at school was a Muslim boy who lived nearby. Her father regarded this boy's mother as his second mother. And his friend felt the same in reverse. Every day after school, they would be in one another's houses, sharing snacks, playing together in the garden, in the street. They truly felt like brothers.

But pre-Partition troubles were brewing dangerously. One day, when Meenu's father was about 18, he was heading towards his home when he saw a hostile mob approaching down the street towards him. He instinctively turned to find refuge in the house of his Muslim 'family', which was close by. He knocked frantically, the mother opened the door. Relief.

But, to his horror, she turned him away ...

He was lucky. Nothing bad happened and he got home to his own house safely. The whole family left Lahore a week before the conflagrations. Although they had to abandon their land, houses and possessions, their jobs, their friends and generations of connections, they had family and good contacts in Delhi and began life anew.

But at that moment of peril and panic, he had been rejected by someone he thought of as a mother. The betrayal had left deep scars, only emerging as he aged, rendering a previously tolerant and sociable man increasingly withdrawn and embittered.

The British are justifiably blamed for all this Partition horror. But it was a complex picture, as such weighty things always are. The Quit India movement had a decades-long history, Indian nationalism had become a powerful force, and Indian leaders were stridently urging the Brits to depart. However, the three great figureheads on the subcontinent at the time — Jinnah, Nehru and Gandhi — were often at loggerheads and agreement between them on boundaries, representation and much more, was elusive. The ongoing impasse was tricky for British officials in India to handle and created impatience amongst politicians at home in Britain.

Other pressures to get out of India were building. Britain had its own post-War reconstruction needs after the ravages of wartime bombing. It was very cold, food was scarce, there was rationing of essential goods (in fact, rationing continued well into the 1950s). And there were a lot of damaged people to look after. In 1942, 'The Beveridge Report' had recommended a 'new world' of social reconstruction, which would bring rewards for the nation's wartime suffering. The Labour Party won the 1945 election on a promise to implement the report's recommendations, founding the modern British welfare state.

All of this would be costly. Adding to the pressure, an anti-colonialist United States was pressuring the British to pay their hefty War debts and dismantle the Empire.

But, notwithstanding all these factors — the pressures, the realities — the manner of the British departure, its haste and arbitrariness, was disastrous for the lives of millions of Indians, both Muslim and Hindu. The personal stories I have told in this book — Shamlu's and Meenu's — happen to be stories of Hindu trauma and dislocation. It is very important to stress that there are equally horrible stories of tragedy and dislocation in Muslim families. The Partition of India came at incalculable cost in human lives and suffering.

In recent visits to India, we have been dismayed to observe a rising tide of inter-religious discord. Political parties are increasingly aligned to, or using, religious groups as 'vote banks'. We hope, as do most Indians we meet, and most Indians according to polling, that this discord can be reduced and not grow.

42: Semi-Pukka[31]

In Delhi one year we were taken to an entire city suburb constructed illegally. Building materials were brought in after dark and by next morning a new structure had been added to this thriving place in which hundreds of families lived. It housed a Kashmiri *Jamawar* scarf dealer we were there to meet. We had learnt by then that weaving and embroidery is commonly the travail of men, not women, and often highly-skilled Muslim men.

In a subsequent quest for these scarves a couple of years later, we found the entire 'town' had disappeared. This was despite the fact that it wasn't a series of shabby lean-tos. On the contrary, it had seemed quite permanent with its solid buildings, lathe and plaster walls, staircases, plumbing, electricity, televisions, decorations and so on. But it must have been declared illegal and demolished. Probably by a developer in cahoots with local politicians.

A supplier in Delhi, working from her two-storey home in a well-to-do suburb, took us up to her rooftop workroom where we were amazed to find about 24 people working in a tiny space, with rudimentary roof and walls, basic but effective lighting, all

---

31 The widely used word 'pukka' means 'very good' or 'the real deal'. So semi-pukka might be closer to another widely used word 'kutcha' that means 'makeshift' or 'make do'.

erected in half a day. Here again, we found mostly men turning out elaborate and skilful embroideries. It could not be described as a sweatshop. They all looked cheerful and they were paid fairly (so we were told), happy to have work, happy to be in a small workshop in reasonable conditions.

But there was a furore in the press at the time because these quaintly named 'semi-pukkas' were threatened with closure. The Delhi Government declared them illegal and dangerous, which they undoubtedly were, and was mandating their removal. The authorities were also keen to get commercial premises out of residential areas. A worthy plan on the face of it. But there was an outcry from all concerned, employers and employees alike. Many thousands of workers would find themselves without jobs and small artisan enterprises would close down. There were so many businesses being run from these rooftop, lean-to, semi-pukkas that the government had to back down.

The beautiful Deepa, source of much of our hand-printed fabric and handworked bedding, has a semi-pukka on top of her house in Delhi. Her family occupies the bottom two floors, extended family coming and going. A staircase with walls painted a warm yellow ochre, flanked by her artist daughter's paintings, leads up to the roof level. A deep crimson handrail helps us up to the delights awaiting.

Shelves and hanging rails are arrayed with saris, bolts of fabric, shawls and dupattas. Deepa shares her knowledge of handcrafting techniques and we have gradually learned to distinguish good handwork from just average handwork: tuning our eyes to the fine-ness of the work, the consistency, the clarity of printing, the number of blocks used to create a dense multi-layering of colour or pattern.

We discuss the process of indigo-dyeing. The indigo plant material is dried and formed into small bricks. Bits of this are added to vats of water — ranging in size from small pots to large in-ground concrete 'baths'. Fabric is dipped into the dark-looking water. But the colour change doesn't happen in the actual dipping. It is only when it is pulled out and exposed to air that oxygen activates the process. This gives indigo-dyeing its sense of magic or alchemy. The colour changes with each subsequent dipping and airing, up to seven times over, starting from a muddy yellow, through a muddy green, to light mid-blue and finally to the wonderful deep indigo blue we know and love.

Deepa mentions that the Rajasthani father and son, from whom she buys indigo fabric, have a large square pit in the ground filled with the dye. They roll up their trousers and clamber into the pit to dip and stomp the fabrics. She tells us that the father only has one arm. The mental picture all this conjures up is so vivid. Then she adds as an afterthought, 'First, they turn off their mobile phones'.

Today we are commissioning metres of fine cotton in indigo prints to use for a range of nightshirts and tops. It is astonishing to think this fabric will undergo such a complex journey: through spinning of the yarn, handweaving on looms, then up to seven indigo dippings, and then, to top it off, printing by hand. Prints may be done using intricately carved wood blocks, one for each 'layer' of the particular print motif, or using fine brass blocks, or by various 'mud resist' techniques. We are all guilty of throwing on garments made of fabric with this sort of provenance without giving a thought to the skills of the workers who produced them.

At Deepa's we also buy *taghai* bedspreads. They are red

one side, black the other, stitched all over by hand using white running stitch, in parallel rows a centimetre apart. We buy them because we like the look of them: simple and dramatic. But then we learn more. Their red colour comes from the aal or alizer tree (disconcertingly there are often differing names and/or differing spellings for things Indian). It is hand dyed to a lovely deep rusty-red. The black dye is even more exotic and here is the recipe as described by Deepa:

Horse-shoes are soaked in water with jaggery (similar to molasses). Ten kilos of jaggery is put into 200 litres of water. In summer it is soaked for 15 days, and in winter for a month and a half. Then they make a powder of tamarind seeds and knead this with the jaggery and horse-shoe paste. This is then boiled for four to five hours, and they stir the solution with aal wood as this has the property of giving a glow to the colour. The black is ready. In Hindi it's called syahi (ink).

Deepa's showroom is of basic construction and the roof regularly leaks. Her husband, an internationally-known academic, also has his study up here, the rooms opening on to a classic Indian roof terrace, a place for sitting, for watching, for drying colourful quilts, while looking into the canopy of a gorgeous silk-cotton tree which produces huge red lily-like flowers that plop noisily as they fall.

43: Slim, Sexy, No Tantrums

'Slim, sexy, no tantrums' proclaims a huge billboard advertisement for mobile phones. Somehow I think this poster could only exist in India. A country where people in uniform blow whistles to separate couples who modestly embrace in public. A country where its famous Bollywood movies are still sexually modest, yet its temple carvings and the Kama Sutra are far from chaste. People don't touch much in public and we dislike the droopy handshakes, especially if one tries a handshake with women. We gather they don't like the touching and we now desist. By contrast, young men walk about holding hands in friendship, a sight we in the West would imbue with more sexual meanings.

Some other paradoxes: India has been integral to the IT revolution and yet huge old-fashioned ledgers and laborious handwritten documents still hold up commerce in every sphere. People are usually very polite, but language usage can be curt — the instruction 'come', meaning 'would you kindly follow me', has often seemed rather rudely abrupt. 'By-hearting' and 'doing the needful' are some examples of language that succinctly serves its purpose. I like the idea of a meeting that is brought forward being 'pre-poned'. Or a highway being widened having a sign reading: 'six-laning in progress'.

In comparison, Hinglish can be deliciously florid, with old-fashioned phrases making newspaper stories about crimes sound like Enid Blyton adventures: 'Murder most foul! The thieves were nabbed and the police have cracked the case! They didn't dilly-dally.' Or this subheading in a Delhi newspaper: 'Couple attempts suicide: husband dies, wife lives to watch Test match.'

In fact I have a feeling that we may all be speaking some form of Hinglish in the decades to come. It's so infectious and the Indian diaspora is ever increasing in reach and influence.

My mother described some of the juxtapositions she observed on her 1957 trip:

Here were the contradictions: the rich man in his Cadillac; the poor man with his handcart; the silken, scented ladies and the ragged urchins; the shops selling imported luxuries cheek by jowl with the small paan shops selling that Indian habit-maker, the bright green paan leaf wrapped around betel nut and spices which the people chew constantly. Here was Cowasji Jehangir Hall in which the Bombay Symphony Orchestra practised a Beethoven symphony. Outside, the crowds watched the shooting of an Indian film … the villain grasped the heroine by the throat … the hero leaped on him from behind. A counter-drama occurred when a policeman tried to move the crowd on and was resisted by an ardent film fan.

What was changed since I was here before the War? The famous Taj Hotel loomed gloomily near the Gateway of India, sulking under the restrictions of prohibition. Empty lounges are a silent reproach to the powers-that-be who decree that only Europeans or Indians who are 'addicts' may drink. I remembered the Taj in the War days when every fresh victory against the Japanese was celebrated with a fresh round of drinks.

Now the city's rich have to be wooed to the hotels and nightclubs with exotic food, European cabaret turns to newer and better crooners. The 'Frank Sinatra of Delhi' or 'Bombay's own Rock'n Roll King'. So read the notices.

Elegant women in beautiful saris dance with immaculately dinner-jacketed men; plump Parsee dowagers samba with their business-tycoon husbands. Mixed European and Indian groups eat together in a new-found camaraderie. There are more Europeans in Bombay than before the War. Nearly every nationality of Europe is represented in business circles. Never has feeling towards them been better. They are there without special privileges and only if they contribute to the building of the new India.

With pride in India's independence has come a tremendous resurgence of interest in India's culture. Art exhibitions, Indian dance festivals, drama groups flourish in the cities. European culture is not forgotten. One may see a Molière play or a Shakespearean drama performed by an Indian cast. Famous European musicians visit the city regularly to give recitals.

Red double-decker buses, exactly like the London buses, weave a perilous path between the popular six-anna meter taxis. Pedestrians waver in an unfamiliar orderliness at the newly-installed pedestrian crossings. The buses look a lot shabbier nowadays and have taken on an alarming list to one side. But no-one minds when an extra ten passengers jump on to an already crowded bus. Accustomed to over-crowded living conditions, the average Indian has a far greater immunity to personal discomfort than the European.

Since the terrible fire in a clothing factory in Bangladesh in 2013, most people are now aware that working conditions in countries with cheap labour rates can be appalling. We were shocked in Varanasi some years ago, when visiting a clothing manufacturer. We saw row upon row of machinists, heads down in concentration, but working in reasonably good lighting (for once). The owner was proud of the new lighting and told us how well he treated his workers and how good their conditions were. Curious as to their working hours and how much time off they got, we asked: 'And how many days a week do they work?' He replied proudly, 'Three-hundred-and-sixty-five days a year, madam,' thinking that was what we wanted to hear, that we would be impressed by a factory that never has downtime. We asked, 'What if they need to see their families, attend a wedding, or funeral, or celebration?' He replied, 'Well, then they can apply for time off, they can have two weeks a year to go home. If we are not too busy.'

We visited a clothing factory in Chennai that considered its facilities and conditions to be 'very modern, madam'. The manager proudly pointed to the large red 'Fire Exit' sign on a wall, somehow failing to notice that the same wall was piled to about two metres high with wads of fabric and hessian sacks of clothing, the piles extending out into the room for several metres. The sign was just visible above all this combustible material, blocking any possibility of escape.

It is all too easy for horror stories to dominate one's perceptions of India. There is so much horror to behold: factory conditions, human deformity, poverty, hunger, deprivation. The problems are so huge that it's easy to feel helpless. And some tourists feel irritated by what they see as the Indian acceptance of fate, the acceptance of inequality, of injustice, of corruption. Sue and I do get irritated, feel despair and exasperation at times. But our overwhelming feeling is one of affection for this country — despite the little we know of it, really — and above all affection for its people and the friends we have made.

I like the narrator's comment in The Great Indian Novel,[32] who says: 'India is not ... an undeveloped country but a developed country in an advanced stage of decay.'

Or there's this from British historian, Alex von Tunzelmann[33]:

In the beginning there were two nations. One was a vast, mighty and magnificent empire, brilliantly organised and culturally unified, which dominated a massive swathe of the earth. The other was an undeveloped, semi-feudal realm, riven by religious factionalism and barely able to feed its illiterate, diseased and stinking masses. The first nation was India. The second was England ... The year was 1577 ...

32 Shashi Tharoor, *The Great Indian Novel*, Viking, 1989.
33 *Indian Summer: The Secret History of the End of an Empire*, Simon & Schuster, 2007.

44: A Heart-Breaking Revelation

While I was writing this book, my mother Pearl died at the age of 93. She lives on as the namesake of our business, Moti. And in many other ways. Her acute observations and vivid writing have kept her story alive in these pages. Her Anglo-Indian outsider status had honed her skills, but they sometimes made her over-sensitive to social nuances or perceived slights. There were several friends who were cast off having, probably inadvertently, belittled her or one of her daughters. My father, not one for psychological musings, would say to me quietly, 'Darling, I think Mum might have over-reacted a bit, but, you know, it's growing up as an Anglo-Indian.'

In Australia she supported my father in his work, though she wasn't herself musical. She tutored boys who were falling behind at school, did the make-up for school plays and operettas, scripted school revues, wrote radio scripts, newspaper and magazine articles. She painted portraits of friends as well as scenes of everyday life. She wrote witty poems, some in homage to friends' much-loved pets when they died. From that balcony in Bombay to verandahs in Melbourne and Brisbane, she never stopped people-watching. In the accompanying notes to an exhibition of her paintings in 1993, she wrote: 'I've never managed to accept that it's rude to stare. People-watching has been a compulsion for me. I'm insatiably curious about people and I ask lots of questions.'

My mother had a favourite little Sheraton chest of drawers that moved with her from their house in Winchester, then to Melbourne, to Brisbane, back to Melbourne, and finally to the aged care home in which, with my father, she spent the last two years of her life.

The chest has since moved to my spare bedroom and is looking quite at home. Inside one drawer I found a couple of her distinctive manila envelopes, labelled 'Memories of India' and 'Photos of India'. In the latter is a wonderful set of photos from our time in Panchgani, the hill-station where we stayed with my grandparents when I was 10 in 1957.

Inside another envelope, I found a small, squashed cardboard box, only about six inches square and an inch deep. Inside the box were some interesting small bits and pieces. One was Pearl's Indian post-War ration book, issued in Mussoorie where they were stationed after they married. I found an English post-War ration book issued in my own name, then a one-year-old in Cambridge. I found the questions for her final year English Literature exam in 1937 at St Mary's, Poona. Set and marked by examiners in Cambridge, I could see ticks beside those she answered: '"Uneasy lies the head that wears the crown." Do you think this represents Shakespeare's feelings about kingship?' And 'In Chaucer "The apparel proclaims the man." Comment on this, referring to two or more characters from the Prologue.'

She chose to analyse a Ben Jonson poem, which starts: 'Still to be neat, still to be drest/As you were going to a feast;/Still to be powder'd, still perfumed;' and so on. I was struck by echoes of these lines in my mother's subsequent life: her work, her words, her people-watching, her attention to faces, to appearances, her interest in dress, in perfume. Also, her admonitions to us girls about being groomed as you would wish to be seen: not caught in your dressing gown, or without your lippy. (Actually, my sister and I rarely wear lipstick so that admonition failed.) But most of her married life was spent in school houses, within a campus, where students and other staff were constantly around, hence always 'looking presentable' mattered. She believed dress or make-up should be artless in effect, not overdone; that one could look interesting without spending a lot of money. She was an expert at that. And maybe it is too neat, and too pop-psychological, to see stirrings of her later life in her choice to answer a particular exam question at the age of sixteen. Anyway, it's an intriguing find.

But then — a heart-stopper — I found a very small brownish envelope addressed to Mrs D Britton in Landour, Mussoorie. Inside was a three-page neatly handwritten letter on crackly semi-transparent paper. It took my breath away:

Rangoon
c/o Gen Hospital
12/9/45

My dearest Pearl, I am free now, more or less. I flew from Bangkok in one of these old Dakotas. I always did want to see the back of Thailand from the tail end of a plane. I feel a little strange yet and hesitate to be free; I feel strange too writing to you again after three and a half long years. Perhaps you can understand. I lost my closest friend on the eve of the Jap surrender. He died from overwork and the long trek we had to do a few days earlier. I felt that the war was about to end soon so I told him he would not die but I think he knew. We went through everything together so I feel his loss a bit more than is normal.

I don't know when I'm coming back to India. The GI 12th Army sent for me yesterday. I may have to fly back to Thailand again and go upriver to one of the jungle camps to retrieve certain documents I buried there. With those documents I also buried a long letter (about two hundred thousand words) which I wrote you. It starts before the war and goes on up to this time last year when it became too risky to carry it about with me. I would like you to get it but on the other hand I don't want to go back.

Rangoon is very different now. The docks and Ry. Station & factories & many private houses have been blown off the map. I went to see the house I lived in when I was a boy but there is only the burnt out shell standing. I couldn't find the cemetery where my father was buried but I will have to tell my mother that I visited it and put flowers on the grave.

You may not have got the cable I sent you. They said they couldn't guarantee it. I am sending this letter by plane with a friend. He will post it in Calcutta. Your last letter was over a year old when I got it but I suppose you are at the same address. As I write news has come that another plane, the fourth, carrying POWs home has crashed, this time with the loss of all lives. On it was another good friend, a man called Emerson who was literary editor of The Statesman. I was going to bring him to see you. You would have liked him because in many ways he was like you. We had the same political views and he and I organised a political discussion group when things had slackened off last year. I am sorry he is dead but it doesn't make any difference does it? Two months ago he and I were talking about just this very subject but he did not agree with me. I said I did not mind if I had to die (the Japs were thinking of bumping us off) because after death there is no consciousness of a previous life so that nothing that has ever happened, no pain or happiness or disappointment, corruption, perfection, matters. They might just as well have never happened because after death there is nothing, there is no consciousness of anything. But Emerson could not agree. He said he wanted to live. He wanted to see his wife again, to sleep in a soft bed and to eat good food and to do all the small things that he always wanted to do.

I suppose you can see that all this is just padding and that I don't know how to write to you after all this time. For three and a half years I've planned my first letter to you but now that the time has come I am lost.

Let this be a general letter please and give me time to become normal again. My address is c/o Imperial Bank, Agra.

Love to everyone. God bless you all. Woody

I don't know if there was an added PS, because the paper was torn beneath his name. This was the man to whom a very young Pearl had become engaged as the War started. He had gone off to War and disappeared. Despite letters, and searches via Red Cross, she heard nothing for several years. Was he dead? Was he a prisoner? Or had he lost interest in her? Imponderable questions for a young woman in her late teens to early twenties. And then, after three years of silence and speculation, she met my father at that fateful dinner party in Bombay.

I don't know if she had called off her engagement to Woody

by mail, or cable, nor do I know if he ever received this news. We do know that she had visited his parents to tell them. One would guess from his letter that he didn't get this crucial bit of information. He clearly didn't know that Pearl had married at the end of August 1945, only two weeks before he penned this letter in September. The envelope was addressed to 'Mrs D Britton', so I suspect the letter was re-addressed and posted on from her home address in Bombay. I think the envelope is addressed in her father's handwriting.

I tried to imagine how she must have felt when she read it. Imagine receiving a letter like this at anytime. Imagine receiving it just two weeks after marrying someone else. And the letter was all the more painful for its restraint, its constraint. It was so understandable that a young woman might give up after getting no response for years. All that fun going on in Bombay: parties, dances, work opportunities. It was understandable but not exemplary behaviour: she had only once mentioned a previous fiancé to me. My sister didn't know about it at all. So breaking the engagement surely wasn't something to talk about.

It wasn't a secret from my father. In their romance-by-letter, my father several times mentioned Woody. He was anguished for Pearl as she undertook the terrible task of visiting Woody's parents to tell them of her change of heart. She mentioned to me that she and Dad had bumped into Woody once after the War, in Bombay perhaps. I don't know how the meeting went. She didn't say. I was in my twenties, I think, and didn't have the gumption to ask. My aunt also told me that Woody had called in to their house after the War when she was at home by herself. Twelve years younger than my mother, she was aged only twelve herself at the time. She didn't know what to say to him.

But leaving aside the personal details, the letter was simply gut-wrenching for the suffering it carries within it. The unspeakable POW experiences. The deaths of his close friends, tragically so close to War's end. The thought of that long letter written to her over several years, two hundred thousand words, buried somewhere in Thailand. Was it ever retrieved? Did he go back, as he said in the letter, and pick it up? It would be an agonisingly touching read. He was a good writer.

And now I have worked out who he is. My aunt, now in her mid-eighties in London, recalls his full name and thinks Mum might have met him at work in Bombay. Reading back over her writings, I see his surname amongst the men she worked with in the advertising agency while still a student at art school.

In describing 'the bohemian life', Pearl painted quite detailed pictures of the other men she worked with in the agency. But there is no description of the man who was to become her fiancé and then disappear. Only to turn up too late. I understand why she didn't mention more than just his name. She must always have felt bad: the poignancy and sadness were almost unbearable ...

45: Neither Here Nor There

I still wonder about that day in Mumbai when we arrived at Willingdon House, my mother's home for many years. I remember hovering on the threshold, then dashing away. I recall seeing a TV program about young Somalis, now Australian residents, who had fled their homeland and were taken back years later to the small shanty-town where their parents had lived. One young woman stood in front of the entrance to the tiny shack she had grown up in — and, very bravely I thought, refused to enter. Even though a TV crew was filming, and had presumably funded the expedition, she couldn't go in, couldn't cross that threshold.

This is not to draw any comparison with a refugee story. In mine there is no anguish, nothing resembling what returning refugees would experience. My sister similarly went back to Winchester a few years ago and couldn't press the doorbell of the place she knew was literally her birthplace, a home-birth in that very house. Like me, she came away feeling disappointed in herself. ('Aha,' my husband would say, a family trait — not pushy enough!)

For me, India is still overwhelming, despite two decades of regular trips. The more I go there, the less I feel I know, in every sense of knowing. And on that first visit, I certainly felt that threshold was a step too far. Like many children, I realise I missed the chance to follow up all my mother's stories. I probably haven't always got the facts right, though I have tried belatedly to authenticate them.

Anyway, a lot of the so-called 'fact' in family history is subjective, filtered, even fanciful. But it's nevertheless part of the family fabric, dare I say, the warp and weft — though I have tried to avoid the obvious clichés connecting my family story and my subsequent venture into textiles.

'*The Uses of Childhood*', an article by the late Graham Little, close friend and research colleague, resonates. He pointed out that it is not 'the facts' of a childhood that matter. What matters is the use to which each child puts those facts. Each child in a family may have — probably will have — a different version of those facts and then puts them to different uses. Were he still alive, I have no doubt Graham might be critical of my lack of self-introspection. But I think he would understand my lack of bravery on that physical threshold.

Edmund de Waal, author of *The Hare with Amber Eyes*,[34] admitted he baulked sometimes, felt afraid, left leads untaken. He recalled listening to his uncle's stories and wrote: 'I should probably record what he said … sit at his elbow with a notebook. I never did. It seemed formal and inappropriate. It also seemed greedy: that's a good rich story, I'll have that.'

Perhaps I too should have gone about it with a clipboard and checklist. Or at least a tape recorder. After all, I've been a social researcher for most of my professional life, winkling out other

---

34 Farrer, Straus & Giroux, 2010.

peoples' underlying attitudes and feelings. But instead, I leapt upon de Waal's passage as echoing how I felt. Sometimes the obvious questions have to be asked. I know this as a researcher. But when it comes to one's own family, and one's own feelings, the obvious can seem — well, too obvious. It needs someone else to do it.

So there are many i's undotted. One such emerged on a side-trip to Lucknow, where we visited the marvellous Indo-Saracenic-Gothic boys' private school, La Martinière, founded in 1845. In an article, aptly titled '*East of Eton*', William Dalrymple described it as:

> A mix of part Enlightenment mansion, part Nawabi fantasy, and part Gothic colonial barracks. Its façade mixes Georgian colonnades with the loopholes and turrets of a medieval castle: above, Palladian arcades rise to Mughal copulas.

You get the picture ...

It was the country home of 18th century French polymath, Claude Martin. Of humble birth in Lyon, he travelled to India, served in the army of the French East India Company, but later became a Major-General in the British East India Company army. Self-made, self-taught, he designed buildings, was chief adviser to the Nawab of Lucknow, made fortunes from banking, indigo, gunpowder. An amateur surgeon, he even operated on his own bladder stones. Also an active philanthropist, his legacy includes 10 major schools in Lucknow, Calcutta and Lyon in France.

In the crypt of La Martinière school in Lucknow is his tomb, to which we were dutifully escorted by a staff member. In between dodging Exocet bats, I noticed an honour board for senior pupils who had been killed while helping defend the

British Residency in the siege of Lucknow in 1857. Earlier in the day, we had visited the site of this garrison, getting a very real sense of the horrific carnage of the siege, and its futility.

As the siege continued and countless lives were lost, the British resorted to drafting schoolboys to help. On the engraved marble honour roll in the crypt at La Martinière school, there were about 60 names of these boys, who must have been only about 16 or 17. To my surprise, two were Creeds. I had never heard anything about these two young lads who died helping to defend the British Residency. I couldn't find them on my copy of the family tree. My aunt later told me there was another family of Creeds in Bombay. So perhaps they are not relatives.

A recent visit to the East India Company Archives in the British Library has not added to the bits and pieces of family story I have already gleaned. The Creed family tree can be traced back further than I have described in this book, thanks to Jacques Heugel, my mother's cousin, who initiated the process some decades ago. He also funded the publication — *The Gordon Creeds in Afghanistan*. Jacques descended from another of the 10 children of Colonel Henry Gordon Creed and Cecilia Aurelia de Bourbel de Montpincon, my great great-grandparents, whose son Louis married my Indian great granny and lies buried in the Bangalore cemetery.

Handwritten family trees in spidery ink seem far more exotic and enticing to me than do computer-generated ones. These days family-tree tracing has become something of an internet-assisted pandemic. Like us, so many people can trace themselves back to William the Conqueror that it has become less interesting. Elusiveness has a lot going for it. Family mysteries can persist and be embellished by each person to suit. Or simply fester in a shoebox. Or a blue vinyl suitcase.

And the British in India? The cause of all the poverty in India, as many Indians allege? I feel I want to defend their legacy a bit, however unpopular that may make me with my Indian friends and acquaintances. My husband is reading out snippets from a biography of Wellington in which it details some of the astonishing brutality of Rajputs against Rajputs, of Mughals against Rajputs, and of both against the Brits. Albeit I do realise that India was not the Brits to take.

The poverty and deprivation of the common man in India, especially in contrast with the massive wealth of rulers, the conspicuous displays of that wealth, yet the disdain for their welfare, all are breathtaking. And certainly preceded the British presence. These contrasts continue now. The wealthy Mumbai-based Ambani family has built a new family home in Mumbai, a 27-storey skyscraper, on some of the most expensive real-estate per square metre in the world. Twenty-seven storeys thrusting into the sky just for this family. You can't get more conspicuous consumption than that.

Anglo-Indian author, Alan Sealy, wrote a big family saga in the 1980s called *The Trotter-Nama*. A story of seven generations of an Anglo-Indian family. At one point he described Anglo-Indians as 'neither here nor there'. It's a phrase I also heard from the newspaperman I met up with at the Press Club in Delhi a few years ago. At the time I thought it was just a way of saying Anglo-Indians occupied a nether world, neither fully Indian nor fully British. Neither 'fish nor flesh', as the great Anglo-Indian soldier, Colonel James Skinner of Skinner's Horse fame, put it. Not belonging. Not 'of the soil' of either.

But ruminating on language, I am struck by the fact that these days when we say something is 'neither here nor there' we colloquially mean that it is unimportant. Is this actually how Anglo-Indians are regarded? Dismissively? To be ignored? Or should I accept that the issue that has occupied my mind is not all that important or relevant in a world of cross-cultural mixing?

46: Ashes at the Gateway: Not Quite to Plan

The father I knew when growing up was a rather stiff Englishman, a bit awkward socially, uncomfortable with explicit emotions. He presented an aloof, serious exterior and got on best with those who teased him out of his shyness. He enjoyed dreadful slapstick comedy and could act the fool himself, as long as it was acting. As a classical pianist, his fingers expressed his emotions and he favoured the Romantic composers. In the music and theatre worlds, from which my parents counted many of their best friends, there was abundant extroverted emotion that jollied him out of his natural reticence.

One can see why India would so entrance him with its un-Britishness, its chaos, its emotionalism. And after a dour upbringing, one can also see why he was attracted to an Anglo-Indian woman who came from a family who teased and joked a lot. He had loved his time in India and stayed on as long as he could after the War ended. Apart from the recent revelation of his letters to Pearl when they first met, I would have described him as sentimental rather than romantic. But we now know that Bombay was where he fell headlong in love. And where they married, and had their wedding reception in the Taj Hotel, right near the Gateway of India.

It was actually chilblains that propelled Donald across the world to Australia in 1954. The post-War British winters were particularly cold and bleak and chilblains on toes and fingers were especially nasty for a pianist and organist. In his first post at Winchester College, teaching Spanish and music, he conducted choirs both in the school and in the community, and played the organ in the famous cathedral. He could have had a successful career as a concert pianist in Britain. (Later the Australian Broadcasting Commission, ABC, rated him level with all the visiting international concert pianists). But he had loved the heat of the East and the War experience had opened up the world for him. A job in Melbourne beckoned.

Donald had always favoured bow ties, which, along with his long-ish hair, was rather dashing in '50s Melbourne, an era of short back and sides. So when he arrived at Melbourne Grammar, an all-boy private school, he encountered some resistance in what was a fairly macho environment. But it was not long before boys (and staff) realised that this tall, slim man had a steely strength, both physical and mental. His was a contained but powerful presence, plus a 'look' from deep icy-blue eyes that commanded respect (a look his two daughters were well aware of, especially in their teen years!) It was said that he was the only master who could hold a whole-of-school assembly without any other staff present.

Meanwhile, the young Pearl, with two daughters aged three and six, also had to adjust. Our first house was in an inner-city working class area. There was a small park behind the house where Cara and I were allowed to play. Two polite little English girls were confronted with Aussie kids who wielded penknives and got belted by their parents. Several fathers were in jail. They mocked our posh accents and sent me home in tears when one called me an 'educated goose'. A very tame insult by any standards. But I was mortified.

More serious was the fact that the next door house was a brothel and 'sly grog' shop and we regularly awoke to find drunks sleeping it off on our front lawn. There were occasional bricks through the window when mother turned away a 'client' who had mistaken the address. It was quite a brutal introduction to Australia. But we acclimatised and lived there happily for about four years before moving to a beautiful house the school bought for the Director of Music. Part of this was used as the Music School and, later, a purpose-built music school was added on the land at the rear.

Donald rarely talked about the War, but there's no doubt some unspoken power derived from knowledge of his wartime experience in the Chindits. His unusual combination of muscle and musicianship (with a dash of perfectionism, attention to detail and efficient administrative skills) was extremely effective: from almost nothing, he built up and administered a department of about 45 teachers; he was Lieutenant Colonel in charge of the Cadet Corps; he brought the school orchestra to such a level that under his baton it performed the first televised performance in Australia of Hayden's Nelson Mass; he directed annual school operettas and sell-out concerts; as well as introducing, in the 1950s, the very successful inter-house choir competitions — in which every boy took part.[35]

A decade after his arrival at the school, he felt he had reached a high point when the captain of the school's top football team was also the lead violinist in the orchestra. Assorted wind and

---

35 For further details: Weston Bate, Helen Penrose, *Challenging Traditions: A History of Melbourne Grammar*, Arcadia Publishing, 2002

string instrument cases scattered near the goal posts during footy practice were emblematic of change. Outside the school, he conducted university choirs, gave piano recitals, composed works for school ensembles, as well as anthems and choral works, and was the pianist in The Melbourne Trio that gave concert and TV performances.

But after 20 years, seeking even warmer climes and new challenges — and still only in their early fifties — my parents moved to Brisbane where Donald took over administration of the music programs in the state's schools. As well as conducting choirs and orchestras and inspiring young musicians and young music educators.

Letters we received on his death attested to the depth and spread of his influence, even from people he didn't teach directly. He was also Chief Examiner for the Australian Music Examination Board, duties that took him to all corners of the very large state of Queensland, as well as to Papua New Guinea, a place he loved. Usefully, he was one of only a few people in Australia who could examine all instruments. He was awarded an OAM for services to music education and was one of the first to receive the honorary Fellowship of Music, Australia.

When, aged in their eighties, they returned to Melbourne there was a wonderful scene when the removalists who had transported their household contents, including the grand piano, on a very hot day, requested a recital — one of them (unexpectedly) was a Mozart aficionado. Burly, sweaty, tired men in navy blue Chesty Bond singlets, arranged themselves on the floor of his study while a, presumably exhausted, Donald obliged. Intrigued to find the old-fashioned door chime on the front door of the new house played the two notes D and B, his initials, he composed a piece for door chime and piano that involved a long-suffering Pearl standing patiently pressing the doorbell while Dad worked out the details.

When he mentioned having his ashes scattered at the Gateway of India, I saw my mother send him a look that I interpreted as: 'What do you mean? It's my country, not yours, and I wouldn't put the girls to all that trouble.' She thought he was being inappropriately sentimental and demanding.

My father died about two years after my mother. They had each suggested a place in Victoria for their ashes to be scattered. My sister and I did that for them: one under a huge oak tree in a park near where they had lived; the other in the sea at a bayside beach where they had enjoyed many holidays. But, remembering Dad's other wish, we retained some of both of their ashes to take to India. We planned a trip that would start in Mumbai. We booked into a guest-house that was within easy walking distance of the Gateway.

Before leaving Australia, I contacted the Indian Consulate in Melbourne to ask about taking ashes to India. I was told that a lot of paperwork was required. No surprise there! Their death and cremation certificates had to be presented, after having been endorsed, not merely by a JP but by a Notary. Similarly, their expired passports or other ID. Also our passports and flight tickets. Then we should make an appointment with the Department of Foreign Affairs to have each page of every document adorned with an Apostille stamp, all at a significant cost per page. Then back to the consulate to obtain a letter of authorisation.

It was only a week until we left. Would there be time for all this? After making some phone calls, we knew there was not. We had stupidly left it too late. Friends said: 'Just take the ashes.'

But now we were aware of the regulations, it seemed too fraught. Sitting on a plane with ashes in our cabin bags, wondering if we would have to hand them over on departure from Australia or on arrival in India. Too much anxiety. Too ignominious an end for our parents if we had to hand over the ashes or abandon them in a pot plant at Mumbai airport. We also decided that our parents really wouldn't want us to have worry or hassle. Over the preceding year, I had been drying petals from mother's favourite rose. They were collected in a large silk organza bag to take with us. So I sprinkled a tiny amount of the ashes into the bag of petals.

The Gateway of India is what one first sees on approaching Mumbai by sea. It is a classic triumphal arch, completed in 1924, to commemorate the visit of George V to India in 1911. These days it is a chaotic area, a large concrete forecourt packed with families, tourists, commuters, balloon-sellers, postcard-sellers, snack-sellers and thousands of pigeons. The waters of the Arabian Sea lap against a retaining wall and the grand Taj Mahal Hotel sits on the landside. Obviously, one can't scatter ashes on concrete and there is no sandy shore, not to mention no privacy. So we had decided we would scatter the petals in the water just off-shore from the Gateway. We needed to hire a boat. We pictured something small.

There is a ticket office near a giant banyan tree on one edge of the forecourt. It sells tickets for the commuter ferries that ply the coast as well as tickets for tourists to the Elephanta caves on an island across the water. After disembarking from our flight and dropping our cases at the guest-house, we fronted up to the ticket office and joined a long queue. The booth had a wire mesh grille set at convenient height for the seated ticket-sellers, but at an awkward height for those standing, waiting to buy tickets. Daunting. When it was our turn, we had to lean down awkwardly to speak through the grille. Not much English spoken. Four men inside the booth behind the grille, noisy machines printing out tickets, an impatient queue behind us, pressing forward.

'We would like to hire a boat please.' Gruff response: 'Do you want a 45-seater or a 90-seater?' I replied, 'No, there are just two of us.' We could tell that he wasn't going to be helpful. He had already turned to the next person.

Luckily, I remembered a key word. 'We want to perform a puja for our parents.' His manner immediately changed, face softened. A puja. Now all the faces in the ticket booth looked engaged and interested. But his next sentence took us aback: 'Then you don't want one of these Muslim boats,' he said, 'you need a nice, clean Hindu one.' We gasped. Easy to think this was an unpleasant anti-Muslim comment. But it was well meant, just a statement of fact and belief: to a good vegetarian Hindu, it was necessary for this important ceremony not to be sullied by meat-eating. A normal boatload of passengers would have included meat-eaters. We apparently needed some other boat that they would arrange for us.

So we booked and paid for a boat to come at eight o'clock on Monday morning, for half an hour. Monday was a good choice as The Elephanta Caves are closed on that day, making both land and sea less crowded. There was a weekend to prepare. We went to the Spice Markets where a nice young woman told us what we would need for a puja of this sort. Fresh marigolds, a certain sort of incense, little terracotta diyas, tiny bowls in which one soaked a length of wick in ghee overnight, ready to light and float on the water. She urged us to buy bowls made of banana leaves in which to place the petals.

Monday morning we were up early and made our way to the ticket office. A lot of hand-waving indicated that we should follow someone to the boat. He rushed off. Everything was being done at high speed for some reason. We struggled after him, bearing all our offerings. We pictured our nice small clean boat. We couldn't see one. But there was a big ferry waiting. Definitely a 45-seater. Four young men on board, one for the engine, one for the steering and two with no apparent function. None of them spoke any English.

Once on board, they headed out to the open sea. 'No, no,' we said, as we gestured, 'we want to stay close to shore.' They saw us preparing our flowers, petals and incense and realised what we were doing. We gesticulated to go back, closer to The Gateway, and to slow as we leaned out through a narrow opening in the boat's railings. As there were no passengers to ballast the boat down closer to the waterline, we were quite high above the water. And we risked being pitched in by the wake of other passing boats. All young men know how to operate mobile phones, so we handed our phones to the two supernumeraries and they happily performed the role of official photographers.

We lit the incense and the diyas. We leaned out, wondering how we could achieve our purpose gently and elegantly, with suitable reverence, without falling in ourselves. Rather unceremoniously we counted to three and simultaneously dropped the two banana-leaf bowls, containing fresh marigolds and (slightly) ashy petals down into the water. They disappeared under the boat. It was not quite the delicate 'casting out' we had envisaged, though some leftover petals from the organza bag did scatter gracefully across the water.

The whole exercise seemed typically Indian: a bit *kutcha*, not quite to plan. We found it challenging but amusing and we thought our parents would share the amusement. It was not until we were back on shore and I watched our 'little' boat chugging away that I burst into tears. Two years of build-up to a hasty and slightly botched ceremony! Mum and Dad wouldn't have seen it that way.

But they would have been upset that we were turned away from the Taj Hotel Sea Lounge where we had planned to have a good coffee and a nice breakfast. A well-groomed staff member at the door told us it was only for resident guests until 11 am. It was 9 am and we were desperate for our much-anticipated coffee. We tried telling our story — but we've come all the way from Australia and our parents had their wedding reception right here in this lounge and we've just farewelled them — but the implacable young lady turned us away. So we went elsewhere.

On the way we saw a white government car with flags fluttering, spearheaded by a noisy motorcycle escort, making its way to The Gateway. We had wondered why there was an enormous cherry-picker parked on the forecourt. It transpired that this was Shivaji Day, in honour of a great Maharashtrian hero. There is a large bronze statue of Shivaji on horseback on one side of the Gateway forecourt. A politician was coming to place a wreath of marigolds around Shivaji's neck. But, unable to climb a ladder to reach said neck, a cherry-picker capable of reaching the uppermost windows of a Trumpian skyscraper, had been hired to lift this politician 12 feet off the ground.

And so we had returned our parents to the place where one

had been born and reared, where they had fallen in love and where they had married. They would never have met had Britain not built an Empire that included India. Would I have felt such an affinity for India if it were not a little in my blood stream already? And were it not lodged in my imagination via mother's stories and writings?

My own experiences in India represent only a minute fraction of the marvellous edifice that is modern India, simultaneously crumbling, stumbling and renewing. It is a most complex geographic, cultural, religious, social, economic *tamasha* of a place. A jigsaw of over a billion pieces that never quite fit smoothly. A source of endless fascination and frustration to outsiders.

I still relish regular annual trips to India with Sue. Every visit, for over 20 years now, we experience that 'tremendous rush of excitement' my mother described. We were friends before we started the business and remain friends through all of its challenges and delights. India continues to perplex and intrigue us. Often we think we have understood, we think we've got a full story, only later to discover things are not quite what they seemed. Things slip out of our grasp. Nothing can be neatly wrapped up. Loose ends abound. We ask a lot of questions. We try to comprehend the answers. We must often seem brash. But India remains elusive. Perhaps it's this constant search to understand — to comprehend the bigger issues in this vast country as well as the small details of everyday lives — that keeps us addicted to India.

Along the way I have gained a deeper understanding of my mother, of her life growing into a young woman at the tail end of Empire. I feel I have touched her, as well as touched my own small bit of Indianness. I have understood more of the insecurities that lie at the heart of being an outsider, always trying but not quite succeeding, to be part of the mainstream.

And my sister and I found a new father. Rather we found an aspect of him that had been unknown to us. I knew from photos of him pushing my pram in Cambridge, or proudly carrying Cara at her baptism in Winchester, that he always liked babies and young children. He was happy with his grandchildren when they were small, when he could pull faces and play childish games. It was amusing to catch a naturally upright, dignified, army-trained Englishman on all fours for his grandchildren. But I think he found teen years difficult and reverted to school-teacherly sternness as his default attitude. Or so it seemed at the time. But, via his courtship letters, I'm happy to have glimpsed his passionate side, his joy in their relationship. I'm sorry I didn't experience it myself but relieved to know it did exist.

Our mother, Pearl, led a fully engaged life and was a watchful, perceptive observer. Her charm, her capacity for friendship, her ability to draw pictures in words as well as in paint, have left a legacy informing the outlines of the journey I have taken decades later. I hope the journey continues for me, my sister, our children and our grandchildren. All of us proud, but gradually diluting, Chutney Marys.

Postscript: Note to Mabel

I'm sorry I didn't get to know you better. I regret I didn't manage to find any more about you, any more than a few stories. Mabel Money, my Indian great-grandmother. And I'm sorry you were named Mabel! If your adoptive parents, the Money family, wanted a bit of alliteration, why not Mary or Margaret? Good solid Anglo names and prettier than Mabel.

It's a curious coincidence that in 1999, the year of my first adult trip to India when I began exploring your life, my first book was published. It was called *The Secret Life of Money* and was based on my doctoral research into attitudes to money. You too have remained a secret and your life even more so. I could have called this current book *The Secret Life of Mabel Money*.

I wish I knew if you always felt yourself an outsider, perhaps even an outcast. First, you were taken in as a child by a British family on a tea estate. Did your adoptive family treat you warmly, as a daughter, or as a poor unfortunate they had graciously rescued? Later you married a young man next door, my white great-grandfather. Were you treated with disdain by his family? His relatives and friends? And how did his servants feel about you? Did they treat you with respect?

I think from the little I have seen in letters, that your husband was kind to you. I can tell from those letters that he loved the four children you had together. But society viewed the relationship as shameful and his social life suffered. It was definitely a transgression. Your children, who looked more Indian than English, clearly loved you. I don't think they were ashamed to have an Indian mother. I certainly hope not. But did you have any friends of your own?

I'll think of you as Shakuntala, an Indian girl's name I liked even as a child. As for your surname, who knows what it once was. But you have supplied my touch of Indian blood, my one-eighth. It has been an important eighth. A tangible eighth. I have always been pleased to have it. Belatedly it led me to India. And then to starting a business, something I had never imagined doing.

And I have to acknowledge a new discovery: my sister has had a DNA test. Although the DNA of siblings may vary slightly, mine will be similar. The result suggests she has 19 per cent Indian blood, more than an eighth, almost one-fifth, and a figure ironically closer to the guestimate of one-sixth, made by Australian officials in London back in 1954!

We called our business Moti, the Hindi word for 'pearl', my mother's name, and it activated an ongoing connection to India. In the last few years, both Pearl and Donald have died, each in their nineties. And we have sold the business, after 16 years. We were sad to let it go. But it was time. The new owners have changed it to their own style. Like us, they love India and things Indian. Our Moti name now lives on in a well-to-do hamlet on the Surf Coast of Victoria, Australia. And, as it happens, it also lives on, engraved on a brass plaque on a toilet incinerator in a home for abandoned girls in Delhi.

Mabel — I am relieved to know that you died in my grandparents' apartment, in their care. It is the place where I first stood, bewildered on the footpath, at the start of my Indian journey.

Acknowledgements

I thank my sister, Cara Britton, who supported this public airing of our parents' private lives. Her vivid childhood memories, as well as her more recent India experiences, were woven into the tapestry.

With Sue McFall, I shared two decades of adventures in India, exploring as much as we could of this fascinating country, as well as the risky project of launching and running a business. We started as friends and we remain friends, no small achievement. Her companionship, her reflections, her skills and insights have been invaluable.

I thank readers of early drafts, especially Barbara Kane who endured its tribulations on our daily morning walks, and made many useful suggestions. Our weekly walking group – Barbara, Anne Hewett, Lynne Frid and Gwen Schwarz – contributed the good cheer (and good coffee) that helped keep the project going.

Other readers, including Kerstin McKay, Oliver Wilson, Sue McFall, Joan Grant, Amanda Sinclair, Helen Elliott, Bill McKay all offered constructive criticisms and generous encouragement. For assistance with extra photos, I'm grateful to Gwen Schwarz, Christine and Marilyn Shady, Susanne and Warwick Forge, Oliver Wilson, Sue McFall and Charlotte Wilson.

In India, the hospitality, friendship and insights gleaned from many people in the past 20 years have enriched this book in ways they probably don't realise. I apologise if I have hijacked their stories and experiences, sometimes without express permission. I am especially grateful to Sheila Desai who has fielded endless questions and provided ever-perceptive commentary. My thanks to Shamlu Dudeja, Amrita Chowdhury, Deepa Sharma, Swati Verma, Madhavi Ganeriwalla, Atul and Sheetal Bhalla, Daljit Singh and Deepa Sethi.

Particular gratitude to John Timlin, my agent, who was an early enthusiast and never wavered in his efforts. And Jacinta Markoutsas has contributed necessary marketing and social media flair.

Warwick and Susanne Forge adopted the book under their imprint, Bloomings Books, even though it was a bit left-field for their list of beautiful horticultural publications. Their enthusiasm for India, and the garden tours they lead, made for a receptive duo. Warwick offered thoughtful suggestions and has guided me on the twisting path to publication.

My husband, John Wilson, encouraged the writing through the several years of its gestation, even when I faltered midway. Our children Oliver, Edward and Charlotte Wilson have each visited India at various times and provided material and feedback for stories. And grandchildren Sophie, Adela and Axel could always be relied upon to raise the spirits.

Along the way I was fortunate to encounter masterful editor Dr Euan Mitchell, and designer Luke Harris. The proof of their skills is in your hands.